Old Italian Neighborhood Values

By

Stephen L. DeFelice, M.D.

ISBN: 1-4033-6272-6 (e-book)
ISBN: 1-4033-6273-4 (Paperback)
ISBN: 1-4033-6274-2 (Dustjacket)

Library of Congress Control Number: 2002093801

This book is printed on acid free paper.

Printed in the United States of America
Bloomington, IN

1stBooks – rev. 9/27/02

La Dedica

To my family, friends, neighbors and other folks in the old Italian neighborhood—wherever you are! Many thanks for the memories and the gained wisdom that came along with them.

Acknowledgements

To Jane Cavolina, for both her professional editing effort and helpful comments on the story itself.

Also, many thanks to Dan Flynn, whose tireless help on the technical aspects of the book proved invaluable.

Table of Contents

Introduction

Though I am sure that small enclaves of bona fide old Italian neighborhoods still exist, they are either shrinking or vanishing. A glance at Little Italy in downtown Manhattan dramatically spells out the national pattern. It is difficult to find an Italian American of this generation who speaks even a little Italian, let alone knows in what *paese* of Italy their grandparents and great-grandparents were born.

I am told that there is a movement among modern Italian-Americans to learn about the old culture. I hope that it continues, for that culture is rich and its wisdom great.

The men in this book were reared in the old Italian neighborhood. Their core values were established in that environment and largely shaped their adult values and opinions.

For these reasons, it's important to have some idea of what the neighborhood was like in order to better understand the issues and opinions voiced around the dinner table in this book.

Many Americans are now somewhat familiar with the Italian concept of *la famiglia*. It has been described in many forms, in books like *The Godfather* and in films like *Moonstruck*.

Some of the major characteristics of *la famiglia* were as follows:

- Tight relationships with a kind of love that is always there: Even when a very distant relative visited, he was warmly welcomed and treated as royalty even if he was a horse's ass.

- Love of food, wine, and open communication around the dinner table. The family dinner scene in Dom DeLuise's video on Italian cooking vividly tells the story.

- Italian music heard throughout the day. It ranged from Caruso singing Verdi arias to Carlo Buti singing *Napolitani* songs. It was mostly the Philco radio that delivered the music, but once in awhile it was the beloved Victrola.

- An abundance of laughter, *abbracci* and warm touch. Except for funerals and in Don Corleone's home, I can't remember many nights when these things were absent.

- The dignity of work. Laziness was despised; if you didn't have a job and didn't try hard to get one, you were considered as *merda*, and virtually ostracized.

- Great gusto for the privilege of life exemplified by highly expressive language. The people often spoke with booming voices, based on the belief that the louder the voice, the more sincere and truthful was the message behind it.

- The scarcity and importance of money. Very little money was spent on optional things. When extra money was available, it was deposited in the bank for future basic family needs. If a woman bought a fancy dress or a man a fancy car, it was considered an act of *vergona* or a *brutta figura*.

- Self-reliance and guts. Survival was primarily up to the individual. Unlike the Italian Italians, the Italian Americans were Victorian. There was no tolerance for men who complained about their problems. The man was the only money-earning member of the family and had total responsibility for their financial security. The women in almost all households, however, controlled how the money was spent.

- The necessity of helping others. Any time—and I mean any time—a family member had problems, particularly economic ones, *la famiglia* got together and the problem was invariably solved. Neighbors were helped, too, but not as much. It was usually not obligatory. The Italians strongly believed that "Blood is thicker than water."

- Belief in the greatness of America. Everyone was extremely pro-American. The sons of these immigrants were indoctrinated with the message that America is the "Land of Opportunity," and that one could be whatever one wanted to be. All the sons accepted this belief. Optimism and hope abounded. Cynicism, a negative characteristic of modern American men, was almost entirely absent, and when expressed, was quickly suppressed.

The women were not as patriotic as the men. During World War II, they disliked having their sons going to war against their own and frequently cried when they saw photos in the newspapers showing how American bombs had destroyed the cities in Italy where their family and friends still lived.

- The ability to smile at tragedy. This, to me, is one of the great Italian virtues that is very difficult to explain. When something goes wrong in life—either small or big—Italians find something in the misfortune to smile about. This something lightens the burden of the pain. Why? *Chi lo sa?*

There are other characteristics, like shouting, insulting and cursing at family members during a disagreement. After twenty-four hours, however, incidents like these were almost always forgotten. It was an excellent way to blow off emotional steam. No psychiatrists were needed. If these outbursts occurred in an Anglo-Saxon family, bad blood would run through the family for years, if not forever.

I remember when the delicious odors coming from the kitchen would awaken me for Sunday *pranzo*. As I descended the stairs, I was greeted by a robust, *"Buon giorno!"* There was a grouch in every family, however. In my family, it was my grandfather. He rarely said *"Buon giorno"* at home, and rarely smiled. But when he was out of our home, in the presence of others, he underwent a personality change and became a smiling guy who had no problem saying, *"Buon giorno."* The primary reason for this transformation was so he could avoid having the image of the *brutta figura*. In the old neighborhood, image was everything.

But there was a good and dependable side about him. He immigrated to the United States during World War II, along with his wife and six children. He had twenty-five dollars in his pocket and couldn't afford housing. The Italian families in the old neighborhood took the family in until he got a job and earned enough money to buy a home. The guy had *coglioni*, like the rest of the immigrant men and women.

We always ate at home. No one went out to eat, because they couldn't afford it. It was considered a waste of hard-earned money. Even the women who did the cooking and arduous dishwashing by hand thought it was a waste. There were no restaurants in the old neighborhood because there was no market for them. One had to find them elsewhere and few families had cars. Though there were pizza, hoagie, and steak sandwich places, these foods seldom replaced home-cooked dinners.

Jerry Della Femina, the brilliant advertising marketer, never dined at a restaurant until he was fourteen. I, Lorenzo Baccalà, experienced my first restaurant meal at age seventeen. Compare this to the kids today, who, at age five while eating at high scale steakhouses, complain that the filet mignon is too rare or the lobster overdone.

Superstition was quite common, particularly among the women. My grandmother believed in the existence of witches and werewolves, among other creatures. She claimed she had met a few in the mountains of Abruzzi. When I had one of my rare but severe headaches, she would lead me to the sofa with mysterious rituals, which eventually got me to a supine position with two pillows beneath my head. She then proceeded with the pagan incantations, at the same time making repeated Signs of the Cross on my forehead with her left thumb. Invariably, my headache disappeared quickly. Catholicism and paganism are often harmonious.

Yes, these people also had certain bad characteristics. Being a hardhead or *testadura* was a hallmark of Italian American masculinity. Once an opinion was formed, it was extremely difficult to alter or change it. This characteristic caused many problems but, paradoxically, it was sometimes essential in those difficult times. The quality of flexibility came to later generations of Italian Americans who had become more Americanized.

Another characteristic had both a good and bad side—revenge. When someone caused actual or perceived harm to someone else, revenge was mandatory to correct the transgression. There was no attempt to psychologically understand and forgive the transgressor. One couldn't blame it on the childhood experiences with their parents. Revenge was absolute and delivered absolutely, without remorse.

The old Italian neighborhood and, particularly, *la famiglia* provided all the experiences that were necessary to venture forth into life, either within or outside of the neighborhood. There is a modern misconception that one must travel away from the family to mature. That may be helpful, if one first learns about life within the family and neighborhood structures.

G.K. Chesterton agreed. The brilliant British philosopher and author frequently and emphatically emphasized that being reared in a close family is the best way to prepare for the trials and tribulations of the world. Important basic experiences and learning occur in this complex setting of personalities and situations.

I hope this brief overview of how things were in the old Italian neighborhood will render the temperament, intellect, emotions, and opinions of the men and the woman in this book more understandable to the reader.

The Boys & the Madam

This is a story about some guys who grew up together in the old neighborhood—and a lady—who all met for dinner one night at La Strega restaurant in New York City to discuss what's going on in the world in the year 2001. The boys had been getting together for dinner once a year for the past forty years. The lady was a newcomer, and this was her first night.

The old Italian neighborhood, in south Philadelphia, was a tough one where few made it to college. Yet, tough as it was, it was devoid of crime. Crime simply was not permitted. All gang fights and other unsavory events occurred outside the neighborhood.

There were three ghettos in this neighborhood in the fifties and sixties: Italian, Irish and Jewish. And though our neighborhood was only about a quarter-mile by a quarter-mile in size, it was not common for any of the ethnic groups to cross over, by crossing a single street, into the other's territory. There was little animosity; it was just the way it was and no one questioned it. All the boys at dinner were from the Italian section; we're still not sure of the neighborhood origins of the lady.

When they were teenagers, something powerful brought them together. It was strong enough to hold them together for over forty years. A combination of good food, drink, and sincere and open conversation about life and what it means played a part, but it was the love of opera that was the main catalyst for this long range and

1

continuing friendship. The era of the fifties and early sixties was a golden one for the sheer beauty of the operatic voice. In those days, opera reviews dealt primarily with the performance of the voices. Today, the reviews deal with the sets and production—issues that, with certain exceptions, are not considered important by the boys. The boys were openly and knowingly biased—they loved the tenors. Unlike today, where there are perhaps two tenors with impressive voices, there were many to hear and enjoy in those days. Del Monaco, DiStefano, Bjoerling, Tucker, Corelli, Vickers, Vinay, Bergonzi and Tagliavini, among others, filled the opera houses with their thrilling voices. Mediocre performances were rare.

The boys preferred Italian opera. Some non-Italian works, like *Salome*, *Carmen*, *Pearl Fishers*, and *Das Rheingold* were certainly equally appreciated, but the number was limited.

They frequently met at Victor's café, an Italian restaurant in South Philadelphia, where, in those days, the largest 78rpm opera record collection was housed. The genial proprietor, Armand, would stand by his Victrola for the entire evening playing one record after another until closing time. The uplifting sounds of Galli-Curci, Gigli, Volpe, Tebaldi, Flagstad, DiStefano, and the rest flowed continually.

One night, a well-known tenor showed up and belted out some very big Verdi arias. Most of us felt that our eardrums would burst because of the tremendous decibel level projected from his thorax and throat. We had heard him sing in the opera house; his voice was of medium size. That was the night that we first appreciated that a voice of average size in a large opera house is of thunderous size in a small restaurant. We tried to imagine what it would be like to hear a voice that is big in an opera house belting out the same Verdi arias in this small restaurant. It was tough to imagine how it could get any louder, but we knew it could.

Other personalities added to the beauty of being at Victor's, people like Umberto, the most passionate opera fan perhaps of all time. He claims to have seen close to a thousand operas including some during the early part of the twentieth century. He was a wiry and very intense man.

One night, when the boys were in a Caruso mood, Armand played 78 after 78 of the tenor's greatest arias and duets. We were on a real operatic high that night. Everything clicked. But we noticed that something was bothering Umberto. I asked him if anything was wrong, and he proceeded to give us an opera lesson.

"You boys think that Caruso has the biggest voice of all time, *vero*? Well, let me tell you a story."

One of the guys kicked my leg under the table and whispered, "I have to make a *pisciata* pretty badly. I can't hold it in. Tell him to wait until I get back."

I knew this simply could not be done because we would lose the magic of a great moment if we interrupted Umberto and he lost his flow. He would, in addition, consider it an insult.

I replied, "I can't do it. Hold it in!"

Umberto began, "My father took me to the Metropolitan Opera House to hear Caruso sing in *Aida*. As he was singing the big aria, "Celeste Aida," my father cupped his hand behind his ear and told me he could just about hear him. 'What do you mean?' I said to him. He smiled and said to me, 'Son, I heard the great tenor, Tamagno, sing this opera last century. His voice was twice as big as Caruso's.'"

To be sure, we were all aware of the legendary power of Tamagno's voice. But he sang in the nineteenth century before the phonograph was invented, or so we thought.

Umberto continued, "And do you know why he had the biggest voice of all time?"

He waited for our reply, which we gave him in unison—"Why?"

He smiled and, almost shouting to make sure we heard him, answered, "Because he had the biggest *coglioni* of all time." *Coglioni* is the Italian word for testicles, and everyone knew that word in the old Italian neighborhood.

One of the boys was a medical student so I asked him if he'd ever heard about this medical phenomenon.

He smiled and replied, "Regarding the record of body organ sizes, I know of only one example, that of the famous British philosopher, John Stuart Mill. He had the largest brain, as judged by weight, of all time; I doubt whether there's any information on the weight of anyone's balls."

I was about to ask Umberto where he got his information about the size of Tamagno's testicles but decided not to ruin this wonderful moment by being rational. "Reason is a whore," Martin Luther said. What he meant is that the use of reason often distorts things. Victor's genial proprietor closely observed the ongoing dialogue and had the look on his face people have when they want you to know they know something you don't know.

"Hey, you guys, listen to this!" he shouted.

"Listen to what?" I replied.

"Listen to one of Tamagno's rare recordings, the 'Esultate' of Verdi's *Otello*." *Otello* is one of the most difficult tenor roles in all of opera. It takes a big voice with a lot of staying power to sing this role. Few tenors can do it. The 'Esultate' is the very first singing part of the tenor role where Otello comes out to center stage, without having warmed up, and hits very high and stentorian notes.

Armand then told the story of the recording. Tamagno was very sick and bedridden, plagued by severe congestive heart failure. Devices to record the voice had just been invented. As he was dying, his friends implored him to make a mighty effort to get out of bed (with their help, of course) and sing his swan song to the talking machine for posterity. And so he did.

We listened carefully and were a little disappointed. We foolishly expected more from a weak dying man singing into the first primitive recording machine. Such is the fickleness of man. But we must give ourselves some credit. We were all taught in the old neighborhood to respect our elders. Imbued with this moral categorical imperative, we all applauded mightily and shouted, "*Coglioni, coglioni, coglioni!*"

Umberto smiled, nodded his head in approval and walked away from our table. He spoke no more that evening and listened to 78 after 78 with the same smile fixed on his face.

In addition to the world of opera, we always addressed other issues while we ate and drank, and all of us loved to eat and drink. In the beginning we paid the most attention to foreign policy, political and theological issues. For example, we had heated debates on who was more qualified to handle the Soviet Union, Nixon or Kennedy, or whether one could go to heaven without being baptized.

It seemed perfectly logical to me that Nixon was the better man. He was smart, tough and experienced. Though I liked Kennedy, I thought he was too inexperienced to handle a guy like Nikita Khruschev. A few of the boys heatedly disagreed, believing that Kennedy would take us to greater heights. Though I couldn't agree with their reasoning, I appreciated their enthusiasm for the dynamic Kennedy personality. History robbed us of the privilege of finding out which one of us was right. It was in this period of my life when it was beginning to dawn on me that people do not live and make decisions based on reason. The way people behave and make decisions in various walks of life and in various situations became, with the passing of the years, the major theme of our conversation.

An example of a heated religious debate involved the subject of contraception. One of the Catholic Church's main arguments against contraception is based on the Old Testament story of Onan. Onan's brother died and, afterwards, he made love to his brother's wife. But just before ejaculation he withdrew his penis from her vagina and spilled his seed on the ground, or, as we use to say in the old neighborhood, "pulled out." Because of that, God punished Onan.

The Church interpreted this as punishment for not completing, and therefore violating, the act of sex, whose primary function is to produce children. But there could be another interpretation. Under ancient Jewish law, it was obligatory to marry your brother's widow and sire her children. So because Onan "pulled out" and "spilled his seed," he violated the law and was punished by God. There's nothing in the Old or the New Testament that states that "pulling out" is, itself, a sin to be punished. Believe it or not, we used to spend hours vigorously debating this and other religious issues.

The boys also loved to quote writers, philosophers, and politicians, and particularly loved the wisdom of the common folks in the old neighborhood who, by suffering and dealing with the responsibility of supporting and nurturing their families, developed wisdom by actually fighting life's battles instead of intellectualizing them.

As time passed, I sensed that the dinners together at Victor's and other places were, like all good things in life, coming to an end. The boys were getting ready to go forward in their vocations, wherever they may take them. This was about the time that our society was beginning to become mobile and kids left home to live in distant places. Knowing that our moments together were a once-in-a-lifetime gift of God and fearing that our gatherings would soon become relics of the past, I decided to take action. So I planned to make a proposal at our next dinner. I planned to do so before we had our drinks, when our minds were sober. The good will that follows martinis, wine and *grappa* leads to exaggerated sentimentalities and unrealizable and forgotten commitments.

I said to them, "Guys, I have a proposition to make. Think about it for five minutes and then let's make a decision. We have something rare and beautiful going on here. Over the years, all of us have enriched our lives and become closer and closer friends at these unusual gatherings. It's not getting worse, in fact, it's getting better. I really have to tell you guys that I not only enjoy myself at our meetings, but I learn a lot. Let me tell you the most important lesson I've learned. It is not to be absolutely sure of anything and never to be absolutely flexible. Straight out, I am proposing that, wherever life takes us, we get together once a year for dinner at a mutually convenient place where we all feel at home, and continue our dialogue on what life is all about, until we run out of gas.

"I know a guy called Mario, in the Big Apple. He owns La Strega restaurant, near the Holland Tunnel. The folks who go there are the old neighborhood types, with one exception—they generally have money. Mario is *un vero Italiano* and is a superb host, plus, the food is good, really good. Though opera is not routinely played there, he promised about one hour of opera when we're there. He said that more than that would drive even his Italian customers crazy.

"I told Mario that we would like to come there once a year, and sit at a table far enough away from the madding crowd for us to converse comfortably but close enough to feel the energy of the other diners. After I told Mario what happens at our dinners, his eyes lit up. He told me he loves life and its upper moments. He embraced me and said, 'I will give you the right table, the best food and the best service along with your opera under one condition—that I can join you for awhile. Too many people think with their *coglioni* and not their brains. I need to hear people who try to understand what's going on in today's world where things are changing so quickly.' That's the proposal, guys. Almost five minutes have passed already, so let's order a drink and by the time it comes and we feel the impact, it will actually have been ten minutes."

I forgot to mention that this was one of the rare times that we got together for lunch. The boys didn't like to drink in the afternoon. They believed that it destroyed one's capacity to fully absorb the experiences of life for the rest of the day. There was, however, one outstanding exception. It's called a "lupper." A "lupper" is a contraction of the words "lunch" and "supper." The term was coined by one of the guys many years ago. "Lupper" usually begins about two in the afternoon, and involves four phases—good food, bountiful wine, brief but high-intensity sex, followed by a delicious, restful nap. The boys all agreed that, with the right woman, a "lupper" is the closest thing to heaven that one can find on earth. After you awakened and returned to earth, you'd be refreshed and able to fully experience the rest of the day instead of wallowing in a depressive, post-alcohol torpor.

As we were waiting for the waitress to bring us our drinks, one of the locals that we knew walked over to us without hesitation and said, "President Kennedy was just shot. They put a bullet through his head."

What followed at our table was something to behold: total silence, and I mean total silence. The man waited to hear what we had to say. We said nothing. He waited a little longer and then walked away. The silence continued for about two minutes, which is a very long time at the dinner table. The boys were meditating—heavily.

The martinis arrived and I, along with the others, raised our glasses, without saying a word, and gulped down at least half of the stuff. At appropriate festive moments, we sometimes did this with wine, but this was the first time it happened with martinis. I thought of what Freud once said: "In life, we all need our palliatives." I broke the silence. "St. Aquinas once said that the contemplation of death teaches us what's important in life." I felt, after I quoted it, that it was a dumb and trite thing to say. No one said a word. Then came the big and pleasant surprise. The boys agreed to get together once a year at La Strega. The death of a charismatic personality made it happen. And we have been doing it for forty years!

It was the year 2001, and we were to meet at La Strega. We left it to Mario to select the items from the menu or to cook some different things. We had a theoretical right to veto anything he chose but the boys never did for fear of offending him. Instead, they'd order an additional dish or two over and above his choices. This worked out very well and although it cost us a few extra bucks, Mario was never offended and that made us enjoy dinner more. It was an altruistic and selfish act combined, which was a major way of conducting life's business in the old neighborhood. There's nothing wrong with a well-placed lie that makes life easier for everybody. Taking it a step further, the philosopher Wittgenstein said something like, "What's wrong if you tell a lie—big or small—that helps you personally in life and that you get away with?" We would all agree with him in the old neighborhood, if no one was hurt or someone was helped.

La Strega is similar to the restaurant seen in *Moonstruck*. There is a cozy elegance about it. You feel very much at home and at the same time have the feeling of being in a classy place. It was noisy enough to create an atmosphere of excitement but quiet enough to hear everyone's voice clearly at our table, without fear of being heard at the next.

Mario always seated us at the center table of the restaurant where no one faced a wall. We thought he would put us at a corner table. We never ask him why he selected this table and not one in a corner, but we guessed, and probably correctly so, that he wanted all of us to be able to see the other people dining and talking together which served as additional cerebral and emotional fuel for our own lively and creative moments. Who knows? But we were always happy.

Mario also did other small things to add to the beauty of the evening. He loves to create mystery. He announces just before each course his choice of the antipasto, the pasta, the main course or *pietanza* and the dessert. After he makes the announcement, he waits about five minutes to deliver the dishes to the table. And he always has Vinnie serve our table. Vinnie is one of those top-of-the-line waiters that you meet once in a while who is affable but not intrusive. He knows when to talk and when not to. He has a sense of rhythm regarding the pace of the meal. He knows when to pour the wine and when to signal Mario it's time for the next dish. There's nothing like a pro, in any walk of life.

In a nutshell, our evenings at La Strega are the closest thing to the Aristotelian golden mean—plenty of good, solid moments and nothing excessively negative to ruin them. Of course, there are always exceptions to the rule. There were and always will be moments of heated exchange. But these were never strong enough to spoil the evening. In fact, they truly added to the experience of the evenings as long as no one went bananas. I believe it's important to lose your temper now and then in order to purge the mind of mental constipation. It's a much-needed stimulant to feel the broad pulse of life. Italians do it all the time.

I remember as a kid the volatility of many members of *la famiglia*. Curse words and even curses were hurled at each other ranging from "You're a *puttana* and no Goddamn good" to "May you burn in hell, forever—and I mean it!" But what was and remains uniquely Italian is that, more often than not, these insults were quickly forgotten, as if nothing had happened. The anger and outrage is brief and dissipates rapidly—on both the giving and receiving side.

It is the world's best catharsis to vent pent-up emotions, which all of us have more often than we would like, in a way that everyone understands. I believe that this is one of the great traits, among many others, that hold Italians together. For whatever reasons, Italians know that the mind is a very complex thing and needs to be periodically relieved from its emotional baggage. What better way to unload than with family and friends who understand you? Yet if an Italian would say to an Anglo-Saxon, "You're no fucking good. You're a liar and a fake and may you perish in the flames of hell," it would be considered an almost unforgivable act that could destroy a friendship, not only for years but perhaps forever. In my opinion, if this Italian custom of effective catharsis were adopted by our culture, there would be a dramatic reduction of visits to psychiatrists.

Back at La Strega, we always have two average-sized martinis before Mario tells us what's for dinner. He makes sure there are plates on the table with butter, olive oil, bread and small quantities of fried zucchini. He does this to slow down the absorption of alcohol, as well as to stimulate our appetites by hitting the palate with tasty tidbits. Drunkenness is forbidden at our table but we certainly enjoy being a little bit high. The latter is essential at moments like these. Is it possible to enjoy a good dinner without two drinks?

Before the dinner begins, you should know something about the guests. It is important to remember that in the old Italian neighborhood, some of us still cling to certain Victorian as well as Italian traditional customs.

One of them was "ladies first." So we will begin with a description of Genella. Genella, as far as the guys were concerned, had no other name. Rocco never told us, and we never asked. Rocco is one of the gang that used to come to dinner, but he died six months ago. Before he died, he asked me if Genella could take his place, at least for the year 2001. Though I didn't like the idea of a new person, particularly a woman, coming to our dinner, how the hell does one refuse a dying friend? I told him it was okay.

As I mentioned before, Genella isn't Italian. She's Irish. In fact, Genella isn't her real name. None of us knows her real name. She was Rocco's *amante*, or girlfriend. What we didn't know at the time was that Genella was and remains a big-time madam dealing with big-time clients on the fancy side of Manhattan. A couple of weeks later, I learned about her profession from one of Rocco's friends.

Rocco rarely spoke about her, and that was fine with us. In the old neighborhood, secrets were honored—not always, but most of the time.

We invited her in 2001 as a posthumous gesture of respect for Rocco. I subsequently learned about and told all the boys about Genella's occupation before we got together for dinner. No one was comfortable with this knowledge. Little did we realize she would contribute mightily to the heated give and take at La Strega that night.

Next to Genella is Emilio Serio or "The Pig," a state-paid social worker and dropout from a Catholic Dominican seminary. Very few males in the old neighborhood were called by their Christian names. All were, somewhere along the line, given nicknames. Why and how this cultural phenomenon occurred, nobody knows. There is usually a meaning behind each name, a characteristic, be it physical, occupational, something unique in the personality or even a lack of these things. A really impressive nickname could elevate someone to a higher social status than others with ordinary nicknames. I knew

Dewey Q, Nemo, Tangerine, Rotten Eggs, Nooner, Nails, Hairs, Tootsie, Demented, Barbells, Meatball, Noble Head, Sniz, Goldberg, Toonerville, Yangy, Dago Benny, No Gas, Bulldog, Froggy, Freddy Um Pa Pa, Joe Fats, Mud Balls Nino Mo, Zipper Lip, Domo the Dip, Funzi, Yin Yat, Charlie Lump Lump and Joe Communist.

The Pig was almost constantly obsessed with the great questions of life and the hereafter. Most of the guys and gals in the old neighborhood considered him an outright bore, and they were right. Yet there was something puzzling about his behavior that contradicted this image: he loved to play the trumpet, and he loved jazz. Apart from his trumpet, I cannot recall a single event in which a spurt of adrenaline was apparent. We all thought he was perfectly suited to become a contemplative monk like Thomas Merton. Something happened in that monastery that caused him to leave. We still don't know what it was.

He claims to be happy in his job as a social worker rather than being a priest, but none of us believes it: To us, it's like comparing Clinton and Paula Jones to Kennedy and Marilyn Monroe. It ain't the same thing!

We do know something about the Pig that is kind of sad, but in a sense, beautiful. It's his very first social case. We heard it from one of his local union leaders.

A little kid, about eight or nine years old, was being physically and mentally abused by his parents. One night the neighbors called the police because they heard the kid crying a lot. They reported that he had lost lots of weight and was skinny as a rail. The Pig went to

15

visit the house to check the situation out and, to make a long story short, the Pig fell for the kid. He viewed him as the son he never had. He started to buy him clothes and gave the parents his own money to buy food. Now the parents were bona fide manipulators and con artists, real sociopaths. They milked his soft heart. They began to raise the ante on the food and other weekly costs for the Pig to have the right to see the kid. He was going broke and did not have a strong enough will to back out of the situation.

His boss got wind of the matter and immediately transferred him to another district. He was told never to have any contact with the boy and never to have a relationship like this in the future. When the boss was asked how the Pig reacted, he said, "Relieved, very relieved."

On to Mo, or Carlo Carluzzi, the owner of a large construction company. He was one of the few really physically big—and I mean big—guys in the old neighborhood. It wasn't his style to play the role of the bully, but once in a while he used his hugeness to get his way or to help someone. He is a genuinely kind but very tough person mentally.

There was a pretty boy called Gino in the old neighborhood. He didn't play at sports or hang on the street corners with the boys. He wore a jacket and tie at the Catholic Church dance. He was the only one who dressed that way. His hair was groomed with the aid of a hair dryer. This was not only frowned upon by the males in the old neighborhood, it was forbidden. There were no home hair dryers then, no hair dryers in barbershops either in those days, which meant that he had to go to a lady hairdresser shop to get his hot air. What made the situation more unacceptable was his prettiness; it exemplified weakness. He was a little bit too feminine looking. One night, he was dancing with one of the most coveted sensual girls in the neighborhood. I remember it well. One of the old neighborhood bullies was the Goat. He was respected and feared for his ability to level an opponent with either a left hook or a right cross, and he frequently did so. He used the surprise, or cold-cocking, technique. In other words, his opponent never saw his fist coming. While Gino was dancing with the pretty girl, the Goat walked over, pushed him away, and slapped him in the face. The Goat wanted the girl for himself. Total silence fell upon the dance hall.

Mo walked over and admonished him. "Hey Goat, why did you slap Gino in the face? What did he do to you? It's not very nice, you know. I think you should apologize."

The silence now became more silent. The Goat did not apologize. You just didn't apologize in the old neighborhood. If you did, you lost your claim to masculinity—for life. The Goat walked away to the other side of the dance floor.

In the old neighborhood, that meant Mo won the battle.

Next is Spinuzzi, or John Esposito, a physician who specializes in clinical research with new medicines. He was unique in the old neighborhood because he had high visibility but no enemies. His immigrant father was a self-educated man who gave his son weekly instruction in everything from history to vocabulary. Spinuzzi always maintained that the greatest lesson he learned from all his father's lessons was Aristotle's advice to "Observe, observe, and observe." And so he did. One of his interesting observations dealt with lipstick. Lipstick was just beginning to come into vogue in the old neighborhood and Spinuzzi didn't like it. He observed that lipstick worn by women while they were eating disappeared from their lips and was carried by the food into their digestive system. He told us that if the trend continued, massive lipstick poisoning of women would soon occur. To this day, no one has looked into this possibility.

Spinuzzi remained aloof from controversy but on rare occasions changed his colors and became a full-blown participant. It first happened when he was about twelve years old at the Saturday matinee. The movie theater was the only place in the old neighbor where the boys could get physically close to the girls. Most of the girls were entering puberty and were beginning to blossom, wearing tight sweaters to show off nature's wonders (though not as tight as today, I might add). Spinuzzi, along with the other guys, needed no lesson about girls from Aristotle. They observed and observed and observed. Some boys, perhaps two or three out of two hundred, were fortunate enough to have the gals sit on their laps during most of the movie, then they could then fantasize about a real sexual experience while they jerked off. Every one else had to manufacture their fantasies from scratch.

This particular afternoon, he arrived a little late for the matinee. He usually sought the end seat because he had a slight touch of sitting-in-the-middle-of-the-row phobia. But all the aisle seats were taken, and he had no choice but to sit in mid-row. To compound the problem, he sat next to the Snake.

Though Spinuzzi had no great respect for the Snake, he was well aware that he was the leader of the "Snake Gang." Though it only ranked about fourth or fifth in power and prestige, it was still a force to be reckoned with. Next to the Snake sat a truly attractive young lass, the type that would send Keats into poetic ecstasy. She was, however, not the type of innocent gal portrayed in "The Eve of St. Agnes." Her innocent face belied the fact that all her clothes were intentionally very tight, a rare sight in those days, maximizing her credentials.

The Snake never read Aristotle. Instead of observing her and enjoying her beauty, he grabbed her like Attila the Hun and tried to seduce her—more or less because the real thing was almost impossible in the old neighborhood—midway through a Roy Rogers film.

As he was trying to hump her, she made imploring eye contact and shouted, "Spinuzzi, Spinuzzi, help me!"

Observing no more, Spinuzzi spun the Snake around and cold-cocked him with a firm left hook, right on the center of the Snake's nose. Rivers of blood began to flow from both nostrils. Observing this, and observing that the members of the Snake Gang were also observing, he left the movie on the run.

He waited for at least a month in anxious anticipation of revenge from the Snake Gang. It didn't happen. He subsequently learned that the girl was a first class tease and wasn't worth saving. A teaser was rated much lower than a whore by our code. According to old neighborhood values, therefore, the Snake was right and Spinuzzi was wrong.

So on to Pignachi, or Dante Marrone: He was one of the first to move out of the neighborhood. He was also one of the few that didn't go to Catholic school. His father never told him why he sent him to public school. Paradoxically, he was nominated by the guys as the most Catholic person in the neighborhood.

Pignachi was selfless and went out of his way to help people. He rarely spoke of himself. Some of the guys believed he never even thought of himself, which, I knew, was impossible. Sometimes his even temper and gentle smile really annoyed the boys. He seemed to be a phony and, in the old neighborhood, phonies were treated with disdain. What really puzzled the boys was his lack of interest in girls. Some thought he was a *finocchio,* a Roman term for a homosexual male.

After he left the neighborhood, something unexpected happened. We know this to be true because Pignachi's mother told Spinuzzi's mother the whole story. After he graduated from high school, he went to a secular college where he met and fell in love with a sensuous Jewish female student. In the beginning they were both happy and enjoyed the classic chaste relationship, which was common in the days before the advent of oral contraceptives. There were, however, certain problems, which were big in those days. Her parents wanted her to marry a Jew. His parents were a little bit more flexible and would not stand in the way. Frankly speaking, Pignachi's mother told Spinuzzi's mother that they'd been afraid he would never marry and were tickled pink that he finally found a woman. In those days, Jews, according to old Jewish neighborhood values, were not permitted to date, let alone marry Gentiles. *Goyim* were often not even permitted in the house. For that reason, she asked Pignachi to change his name to Dante Goldberg before he met her parents. And so he did. They both worked hard to create a Jewish history for Pignachi in order to fool her parents and make things work more smoothly. Surprisingly enough, things went well until their biologic heaters started to accelerate.

She was extremely hot-natured and a teaser, and he was beginning to learn what real sexual heat meant. They would spend passionate hours alone and talk about some of their heretofore hidden sexual propensities and other secrets. In those days Jewish people, particularly women, rarely drank much. She was an exception. She loved the stuff and taught him to love it, too. And with this change came the breakdown of barriers to passionate expression.

They were fast approaching the moment of sexual consummation. He wanted to wait until they were married. He had made a decision, like the Mayans once did, to masturbate a lot to relieve the sexual pressure until they were married. The Mayans also encouraged premarital male homosexuality to relieve the sexual pressure of male youths until they married, and to maintain the virginity of the female, which was highly valued.

Dante wanted to suggest that she also masturbate until they were married but, for some reason, he was afraid to ask. It was not the thing to do in the old neighborhood. It bordered on masculine heresy. On the other hand, a gal like this, in my opinion, needed no advice on masturbation. She probably was way ahead of Pignachi.

Disturbed by his behavior, she decided to take matters into her own hands. She rented a room at a cheap hotel (there were no motels in those days) and planned to get him drunk. Cocaine, marijuana, Quaaludes and Ecstasy were not available in those days. He did get drunk, however, and she did entice him to the hotel room. They both undressed and then passionately embraced. And then it happened! He suddenly leaped out of bed and stood before her with his erection in place. He whispered, "I'm leaving. It simply won't work. Only if we marry can I do it. You probably don't understand this, but that is the way I am. Will you marry me?"

She hesitated and then forthrightly said, "No, our worlds are too far apart." By the way she said what she said, he knew that this was her final decision. There's nothing, at least there wasn't in those days, as powerful as tradition.

He put on his clothes and softly said goodbye. They never dated again.

He went on to become a parish priest.

Miserabile, or Francesco Cicco, is next, and was, without doubt, the most unpleasant member of the group. He rarely complimented anyone and his smile was frequently a cynical one. He was a very talented athlete and became a fairly good basketball player but lost his job early in his career when the more talented black players took over the sport. We all believe that something went out of him because of this. His fire had left him. But he was the most generous of us all. When someone was in trouble, he was always there to give a helping hand.

Miserabile was the first one in the old neighborhood, male or female, to get divorced. He married "the Prize," the most attractive and sought-after woman in the old neighborhood. I vividly remember when his father called all the boys together in an effort to get them to join his fight to prevent the marriage.

He told us, "Though we can all be jealous, Francesco is an extremely jealous lad. Jealous or not so jealous, it is not wise to marry a beautiful woman who is also sensuous. There can rarely be peace of mind when most other men desire and some seek to have your wife, be it for a moment or forever."

Miserabile's old man continued this beautiful monologue for at least another five minutes. It was powerful and convincing. I don't know about the others, but he convinced me never to marry a Rita Hayworth type. He did, however, convince all of us to try to stop this marriage. We tried and we failed.

History proved his father right. "The Prize" was fair game in the old neighborhood and Miserabile couldn't handle it. Heated domestic battles ensued and shortly after the wedding, they divorced. Out of curiosity, we sent out "feelers" in the neighborhood to find out who had been messing around with her while they were married. You must appreciate that, in those days, it was virtually impossible to keep anything a secret in the neighborhood, particularly anything sexual. We came up with nothing. We sadly concluded that she had been a faithful wife, and Miserabile's jealousies were unfounded.

After his divorce, Miserabile disappeared for a few years. Though most of the boys were tight-lipped about their personal problems—it was a sign of weakness to talk and lament about them—he had a reputation for having the tightest lips of all. He never told us where he disappeared to or what he did, and we didn't ask. What we do know is that he returned with a deep, deep tan.

He went to work as a trucker and went to law school at night. He became a successful politician and was eventually elected to the House of Representatives. He is a pragmatist without a fixed ideology. I personally don't understand men like him. Something is missing.

Last is Pussey Rapper, or Joe Ravelli, the publisher of a very successful local newspaper. As a youngster his theme was "Wine, women and song." He had a way about him that none of us could truly understand. For example, within an hour or two of meeting a woman for the first time, he would say something like, "I don't know how to say this, but I think I'm falling in love with you." For reasons we could not fathom, the gals frequently fell for his line. Perhaps he really did feel that he was falling in love, and his sincerity was sensed and accepted by the ladies. The mind is a fuckin' funny thing, and women love sincerity. Whatever the case, it worked.

I'll never forget the time when all the boys were together discussing the miracle technique of Pussey Rapper. One of the boys, Set-a-Hare, decided to use the Rapper technique at a nightclub. The bars in Philadelphia closed about midnight in those days, so we all decided to cross the Ben Franklin bridge and go to a fancy spot in New Jersey. At the bar sat a few unaccompanied ladies, each waiting for a man, but also ready to reject him unless they didn't want to. It's like they're sending out a message that says, "Here I am, but you can't have me, but I may be interested in meeting you," all at the same time. Set-a-Hare decided to go for the best-looking one.

I advised him to approach one of the less attractive ones where the probability of success would be much higher than with the most sought-after one. This ersatz Pussey Rapper took my advice and approached a pretty but not sensual gal. We all observed that the initial approach went well. She smiled and seemed to relax. Set-a-Hare, being an impatient guy, delivered the "I love you" line about fifteen minutes after the conversation began. She smiled and they held hands. He ordered a drink for both of them and then they danced. After the dance they left the club. And the rest is history.

Then Pussey Rapper went to New York City for a week to visit his cousin. When he came back he was a changed guy. I'm no Sigmund Freud, but I observed that something had snapped in his mind. Like Saul of Tarsus on the road to Damascus, he became a more serious and moral man. Though he always professed to be a Democrat, he never had the fire in his belly to change things. Now he passionately embraced the spirit of Lyndon Johnson's Great Society and even wanted to enlarge the distribution of wealth to the poor over and above what had been radically proposed by Johnson. What the Rapper didn't know was that I had a close friend who was a close friend of his accountant. He told my friend that Pussey Rapper told him to do everything he could to help him avoid paying taxes. In other words, he wanted others to pay for the distribution of wealth that he advocated. Such was the nature of an old Italian neighborhood liberal.

The boys' annual dinner was set for a Friday night. After all, who can fully let loose on the night before a working day? There are three ground rules that govern the annual evenings. First, everyone must arrive on time, at 6 PM, come hell or high water. We call this "Pignachi's rule."

Many years ago, before we had our very first dinner at La Strega, Pignachi recommended we establish fixed rules for our dinners. He believed that, since we only met once a year, there must be an established rhythm that all of us must honor to make it easier for the gang to get into the flow of the evening. He believed that it was critical for everyone to arrive at just about the same time. We all agreed. None of us was or is a night owl. We are all in bed well before midnight, and up early in the morning. As it worked out, everyone was almost always there on time. In fact, they were usually a little bit early, but waited outside the restaurant until the others came. This simple act elevated the importance of the evening. It made it a special event. It is an example of the power of the ritual. Milton, the poet, once said something about how the mind creates its own destiny—it can make a heaven out of hell, or a hell out of heaven. All the boys preferred heaven.

The second ground rule (I forget who brought it up), is that we must answer the questions asked of us unless there is a very good reason not to. In order to remove undue pressure, the person to whom the question is asked has the right to decide whether to respond or not. He need not explain the reason for refusing. The rule worked well. I would estimate that, over the years, about ninety percent of the questions asked were answered.

The third ground rule is that an executive summary of the dinner's discussions and conclusions must be written within seven days after the dinner and immediately mailed to all the boys. Some of the boys are into e-mail but the summary has to be sent by regular registered mail to everyone. These guys are suspicious of modern technology when it comes to something confidential and close to their hearts. They don't feel there is privacy in personal messages sent through e-mail. If young kids can enter the computers of the Pentagon, anyone could surely intercept one's personal correspondence. For dinner in the year 2001, the assignment to write the executive summary was given to Mo and Pussey Rapper.

History pleasantly repeated itself this night. Everyone showed up on time, including the newcomer, Genella. As she walked through the door and moved toward us, we almost shit our pants. We expected to see a worn-out lady in mourning with a sad look upon her face, but what we saw was a just-right fleshy, well-shaped sensuous women in her late fifties or early sixties. What I noticed, and I am absolutely sure that the boys noticed too, was the rarity of her type of rear end, or *culo,* as we used to say in the old neighborhood. It formed about a twenty degree angle with the base of her lumbar spinal column. In other words, it jutted out perfectly. She had the perfect *culo* by the sexual standards of the old neighborhood. The net effect was extremely sensual. As we used to say and still do when observing a woman with the right credentials, "She's got it baby, she's got it."

I know the other guys noticed her rear end because at dinner the previous year we discussed the rear ends and the nature of the sensuality of four famous women: Betty Grable, Marilyn Monroe, Ava Gardner, and Rita Hayworth. The guys felt that Grable and Monroe would never have turned on the men in the way that they did if it wasn't for those sensuous derrières. It was a matter of basic biological geometry.

We also compared the figures of Gardner and Hayworth to the other two. There is no comparison. They were beat out by a mile. But there was another quality about Gardner and Hayworth that turned us on: the way they looked at you and the way they held themselves. It was more a psychological hormone hit than a physical one. These types of women are the true "man-izers"—the female version of the womanizer—and love to play the mental sex game.

Guys go bananas over them, but these chicks are, without a doubt, the ones to stay away from. When a poor guy fell victim in the old neighborhood we used to say he'd been head-fucked. ("Head fuck" now means oral sex, but not in the old neighborhood.) Though there are very high sexual moments, the bottom line is: there's usually nothing but pain in these relationships. We concluded that there are many men who love to suffer, and that's part of their sexual makeup. It's like Don Jose in the opera, *Carmen*. Who the fuck needs it?

We probably will talk about man-izers tonight because Genella's rear end has brought the subject to the attention of the boys.

La Strega was very much alive, that night, the way we like it. Conversation and laughter flowed from the tables. The waiters and busboys were in constant motion and most of the diners were happily smiling, listening to the person doing the talking at their respective tables. La Strega was what we used to call an "Upper restaurant." We once estimated that one out of ten restaurants falls in this category.

Most of the restaurants in this category are managed by owners, not paid managers, who are almost always on the premises. They are there to greet you when you enter and make you feel at home. There's nothing like that personal touch. It adds to the joy of eating in a big way, which is very important in life. The art of eating is discussed at practically all of our dinners, and I am sure it will be discussed tonight.

Mario took us to our table. By the time we sat down the infectious enthusiasm of the crowd had had its effect. We were on the road to an intense and stimulating evening.

Cocktails

Mo said to Mario, "Before you go away, bring us our usual unusual martinis. Do you remember? Tanqueray on the rocks with a wedge, not a twist, of lemon and two tablespoons of tonic, but no dry vermouth."

Mario smiled. "I have not forgotten your, may I say, weird martini formula, my friends. You are the only guys that have ever ordered this drink."

As he was about to turn away to order the drinks, he paused and said to Genella, "*Signora*, would you like to experience this most unusual drink or would you prefer something else?"

Without hesitation, Genella replied, "I'll join the boys. Bring me the weird martini!"

The boys saw for themselves that this was no ordinary lady; she knew how to make men feel at ease. I'm sure they were all thinking about what when on with Rocco and this babe.

Turning to the third ground rule, I said to Mo and Pussey Rapper, "Don't forget, you guys: it's your responsibility to write the summary of tonight's conversations. You're getting old, my friends, and I want to make sure that you remember everything that has been said tonight. Your aging minds plus the booze will rob you somewhat of your ability to remember. I, therefore, brought along two note pads and pens so that you guys can write the important things down. There's an old Chinese proverb, you know: 'The palest ink is far superior to the greatest of memories.'"

Mo, a little bit pissed-off, said, "*Affanculo a te e tutti i quanti!*"

Pussey Rapper added, "I agree with Mo. Stick the pads and pens up you-know-where!"

Everybody laughed a relaxed laugh, for they enjoyed the fact that the boys were pissed-off. Humor is the best foundation for an enjoyable evening. How the hell can you enjoy the beauty of life without a sense of humor?

The gang was just about to settle down and begin serious conversation, when it happened!

The loud, shrill voice of a child abruptly reached our table. The conversation then stopped, and all heads turned to the shrieking kid.

"I told you mommy, I don't like this, and I want something else to eat."

"Johnny, we're not at home. We're at a restaurant, and the food is very expensive. You have to eat it," pleaded the mother.

"I don't care," responded Johnny, "I just can't eat it."

The mother, appearing tired and resigned, turned to the husband with imploring eyes that lacked any hope and asked, "John, would you tell Johnny to behave himself and eat his dinner?" The husband sensed that we, as well as others in the restaurant, were observing this unpleasant, disruptive scene. Because of this, he was ill at ease. He was on center stage, and we were all watching him.

The boys sensed the man's nervousness and the reason behind it. That was a tip-off to the boys. He knew he couldn't control the kid, and we, as well as the others in the restaurant, would soon discover this weakness. But he also knew he had no choice but to try to have the kid eat his meal in an attempt to save face. Hope springs eternal! He couldn't refuse his wife's request under these circumstances. Even weakness has its limitations.

"Johnny, listen to your mother. Eat your meal. You can't have another one and, as mommy said, it costs a lot of money."

A palpable silence settled over the restaurant. There was tension in the air. All eyes were riveted on that kid's fuckin' jellyfish father. I have never experienced anything like it.

Mo leaned forward and quietly remarked, "I'll bet all you guys ten bucks that the little fucker tells the old man to shove it up his ass, and gets away with it."

"Daddy, daddy, you don't understand. I don't like the food. I really don't like the food, and I want something else. Please, can I have something else?" And then the little brat began to cry. Every one of the boys, including me, wanted to walk over and kick the brat in the ass and throw him and his father out of the restaurant. Regarding the mother, the boys always respected mothers and believed that the fault of the child's behavior was usually the father's, and not the mother's. Right or wrong, that was a firm conviction in the old neighborhood. I knew the boys couldn't handle the scenario much longer, so I called to my *consigliere* friend, Mario, for advice.

As he approached the table, I kind of knew that Mario already knew what I had in mind. And I also knew that he agreed. "Mario, get rid of those people before something happens. They're giving us too much *agita*, okay?" Mario answered, "*Si. Non c'e` un problema. I'll take care of it.*"

Mario walked over to these miserable modern misfits and managed to treat them as decent human beings. He offered them a beautiful Italian-style excuse for a gracious exit.

In his smoothest Italian accent, Mario said, "I could not help but hear some of the conversation at your table. It is not wrong that people are sometimes unhappy with restaurant food. This happens even in the best of restaurants—even at La Strega. For this reason I apologize, and the meal is on the house tonight. I will have it prepared to take home with you, if you like. *Va bene?*"

Before they could respond, Mario walked quickly away from the table toward the kitchen doors, in order not to make it necessary for them to make an embarrassing response. Mario never mentioned the real problem caused by their ugly table manners.

The parents quickly understood what was going on, accepted the offer of the expensive doggie bags and left the restaurant in a hurry, looking neither to the left or the right and not quite sure whether they should feel like shits or not.

Mo let out a big sigh and blurted, "They're gone. Those goddamn idiots are gone. Didn't I tell you the kid wouldn't eat anything? The fuckin' kid won!"

Everyone laughed heartily. We were relieved. We knew that a solitary child had the potential of ruining our annual get-together. We grabbed our martini glasses with joy, shouted, "*Salute!*" and drank.

I turned to Genella and asked, "What do you think about what happened at that table tonight? You're the only woman at our table. I'm sure you know that all of us blamed the father for the brat's behavior. There were very few brats—you know, I don't remember any—in the old neighborhood. Brat behavior simply was not permitted." I sensed that Genella was waiting for questions about whether she had kids, but they were never asked. The boys knew better that to put a lady on the spot. Though we didn't know it then, she did have a daughter out of wedlock when she was very young, and managed to stay close to her. Few, including Rocco, knew of her existence.

Genella paused, then raised her glass and, with the smile on her face, said, "Let's have another toast, you Italian machos. Here's to kindness."

The boys weren't sure what she meant by this, but there was undoubtedly an important message behind the toast. They finished the rest of their martinis, the waiter promptly arriving to fill them anew. I tried to stop him, but it was too late. I realized that we would be drinking more than our usual quota tonight, and I'm sure that everyone else realized it too. This was now the established drinking rhythm of the evening. No objections were made.

"I've never had a child," Genella said, "so I can't say from personal experience what it's like on the real battlefield. My experience is based solely on my personal observations of many, and I mean many, similar events."

She suddenly began to speak at a higher-pitch level, with almost lawyer-like language. The boys looked puzzled.

"It first struck me about twenty-five years ago when my very close girlfriend, Alice, used to invite me to her home for dinner with her husband and two children, about once or twice a month. Her husband was a nice, soft guy who worked hard to support his family. But he wasn't good at earning enough money to support her lifestyle. She wasn't happy with that so she decided to go to work. Then I noticed a change in her behavior. She lost much of her energy. Before, she was a really bubbly and warm gal devoted to taking care of the family. In fact, she really ran the family show like a true business manager and enjoyed it.

"She used to prepare separate meals for her husband and her children. She did this because the kids, almost daily, used to complain to Alice and her husband that they didn't like what she prepared for the entire family. Because of her high energy level, she decided she could handle cooking separate meals for her children in order to maintain the peace. I remember she told me that she really didn't want to do it and asked her husband to straighten them out and tell them to eat what's on the table or don't eat at all until the next morning. She told him that she couldn't stand the nightly battles and that she was becoming a nervous wreck. He, like that *schmuck* tonight, tried to control the kids, but they wouldn't listen to him.

"Now I know what you guys are thinking: the kids are brats and the husband is to blame and is a horse's ass. Right?"

"What do you think, Genella?" asked Pignachi. "You told us that you've seen lots of examples of situations like this. You must have drawn a general conclusion or at least have some ideas about what the hell is going on in today's culture."

"I'll tell you what I think, but first, let me finish the story." I couldn't figure out whether Genella was trying to avoid making an honest judgment or just trying to finish the story in order to get off the hook about her personal life.

Genella continued, "She continued to cook separate meals even after she started to work, because the kids wouldn't let up and because the husband still couldn't get the kids to eat what was on the table. It was a nightmare with no cure in sight. Now that I think of it, you're right, guys. He and the punk that just left the restaurant are horses' asses—in spades.

"Though Alice isn't Italian, she, like the Italians, believes that the family that eats together—particularly when the food is good—stays together. She knew that if the only daily get-together where the family can talk about things was terminated, the family would begin to fall apart. To what degree, she didn't know. But she was so goddamn tired, almost every moment of the day, that she had no choice but to surrender to reality. She began to order take-out food for the kids, which the kids ate at about six o'clock. In order to avoid the *agita*, she almost always gave them what they wanted. She often ordered take-out food for her husband and herself from another restaurant, which was delivered to their home at about 7:15. There was no time for her and her husband to spare for enjoyable moments.

Everything was on a time schedule, including sex. How the hell do people live like this?

"They all ate their meals directly out of the restaurant food containers so she wouldn't have to do the dishes. She did, by the way, cook home made meals on Saturdays and Sundays. They were simple, though, because she was constantly tired and had so many things to do around the house, including paying attention to the kids. Though she loved to cook, there simply wasn't time for more elaborate dinners.

"During the weekdays, after they finished eating, Alice and her husband had to help their kids with their homework. She told me that the new kind of homework is very difficult to understand and drives both her and her husband crazy. It takes them close to an hour on many nights. I don't know about you guys, but when I was in elementary school, our mothers and fathers rarely helped us with our homework. We never even thought to ask them. What the hell is going on?

"Anyway, this is the kind of life these kids have today. It's a hell of a lot different than the lives we lead. It's crazy, I tell you. It's just crazy."

The boys noticed that her eyes were watery, and she was struggling to hold back her tears. I knew they were thinking what I was thinking. I could never understand why many of the boys and gals in the old neighborhood have a keen capacity to read most situations. Whether it is an Italian trait or something else, I don't know. The Jews that we knew in the old neighborhood had this sixth-sense quality, too, but they handled it somewhat differently than we did.

Getting back to Genella—the boys knew that a woman doesn't become this upset when talking about the kids of other women. We all looked at each other and the eye contact message was that Genella probably had a child, somewhere, with some kind of problem. But, of course, as I said before, the boys would never ask the question, as modern men would love to do. To repeat, you didn't ask women such personal questions in the old neighborhood. It was her move to talk about her problem.

Pussy Rapper agreed with Genella and added his thoughts to the conversation. "Only a goddamn idiot would not admit that kids today cannot be held to yesterday's standards of behavior. I just read a few articles about how the schools are manipulating and trying to control kids' behavior without even involving the parents, particularly around sex and violence. In Atlanta, an eleven-year-old kid was suspended from school because she came to school with a very thin ten-inch chain that connected her keys with her purse. The school justified its action based on its policy of zero tolerance for weapons. How the hell a ten-inch thin chain represents a weapon beats the shit out of me. I would think that her shoelaces represented a more dangerous weapon than a thin chain. It would be easier to strangle yourself or someone else with your shoelaces than with a thin cheap chain.

"And then there's the story in New Jersey of four kindergarteners who got three-day suspensions for shooting at each other with their fingers. They didn't shoot with toy pistols, but with their fuckin' fingers! I even heard about a kid who was suspended for carrying a potential lethal weapon—a nail clipper!"

Mo interrupted, "Pussey Rapper, you are a liberal, which is the way most of you media guys are. You guys are big on individual rights, privacy and other things like that. Believe it or not, I agree with you. You can bet your ass they are extremely important. Why don't you write about and tell you readers and media friends about this legalization of the manipulation of our children's minds, seemingly without restraints? Where, by the way, are the chicken-shit parents? Do they agree with this shit?"

Pussy Rapper paused and took a deep breath, which meant that the issue troubled him. "First of all, the parents have been intimidated by the numerous shootings, bombings and whatever else that has been going on. Frankly, they are confused and don't know what to do. Those parents who object to this mental manipulation of their kids know that if they objected in a public forum, the powerful forces of the misguided do-gooders would come against them and label them as irresponsible moms and dads. There is yet no leader out there to stop these mass national mental experimentations on children. Kids in many schools can't even touch other kids without being punished, and I mean touch ever so gently.

"But you're right, Mo, I should write about this but now is not the moment. Nobody will listen. If you kick your kid in the ass, on the street, for being a brat, someone will call the police, or some child abuse group. On the other hand—I'm thinking out loud now—if someone doesn't start the dialogue and promote it, nothing will happen. I remember very well that my father told me that unless you do something, be it looking for a new job or pursuing the woman that you love, nothing will happen. Let me think about it, Mo. Goose me on it in a couple of weeks."

Then the Pig joined in. "Since we're trying to cover the goddamn waterfront on this kid mess, let's not forget the big one that is infecting our kids every day. It's the all-powerful mind influencer, the computer. Now I know that the computer gives us some great stuff and can be used to propagate the good. I think, in fact, I know, that it can be a very destructive thing. I don't want to get into a general discussion of the good and the bad of computers—it's difficult to quantify—but let's talk about some of the bad that it's doing to our children.

"My neighbor just recently told me a story about her personal experiences as well as that of many of her lady friends regarding some of what happens with their kids and computers. Before I forget, this gal and her friends are all well educated, but they still cannot handle the problem she told me about.

"The problem is trying to block the kids from having access to the porno and other undesirable websites. She told me that her husband is a computer expert and knows how to place restrictions or blocks in the computer to prevent the kids from having access to these websites. If I remember correctly, there are different categories of restriction to website access under such headings as 'mature' or 'teen.' These programmed categories are somehow used to block the kids from seeing a blowjob or sodomy or whatever is dirty on the computer.

Now don't forget that her husband is an expert in making these computer-access blocks to the kids. Guess what? Her kids can figure out ways to get around these blocks and watch all the porno they want.

"They frequently get advice on how to do this from the older kids. Just try to imagine what the older kids are doing and what impact it's having on their minds. It all boils down to sex and violence, which every age group simply loves. It's the eternal marketplace, and it won't go away.

"One day, her four-year-old asked her if he could access a website called something like 'animal site,' or whatever. She thought that was a good idea to learn about animals and said, 'Sure.' When she told her husband about it, he managed to find the same website. And do you know what he saw? He saw men and women making all kinds of love to animals, ranging from cunnilingus to sodomy. I mean, all kinds! Can you imagine the impact of this on a four-year-old kid? I really don't think we can, nor can anyone else guess correctly. What we can say is that it is best that kids don't have the ability to look at this and other types of unsettling shit. I think it can be safely said that sex and violence do not happiness make."

Mo asked, "Did she talk about the computer chat rooms? God knows what's going on in this private, free-flowing world of talking about everything under the sun including animal screwing. One night, one of the guys that works for me told me, after a few drinks, of course, that he has a conversation with a gal on the chat box or whatever the hell you call it, where they both jerk off at the same time while chatting about their fantasies. Would you believe it? He said he had his biggest orgasms ever doing it this way. Something big is going on in these chat rooms, my friends, and it ain't just dumping a load."

Pussy Rapper said, "She didn't talk to me about chat rooms, but I agree with what you're saying. The chat rooms will have a much greater negative effect on our kids than the porno sites. Both together are frightening to think about. No one has yet devised a way to measure the impact of the computer on the mental health of our kids let alone adults. It's almost impossible to do, which presents another huge problem. You can't measure it. In a funny kind of way, I don't think the parents want to know about how big the problem is. It's scary and they don't understand nor have the time to learn what the hell is going on, let alone how to solve it. Many are playing ostrich hoping someone else will solve the problem for them. It's a classic case of denial. There's no doubt that this problem will surface on the national radar screen very soon, and the people will force the government to do something about it. Then we'll have a great battle on the First Amendment, and God only knows what the outcome will be."

Spinuzzi commented, "And don't forget that lots of kids who have medically-diagnosed mental conditions are on drugs—I mean the legitimate as well as the bad kinds, like Ritalin and Prozac for hyperactivity syndromes, depression, compulsive behavior and other so-called mental disturbances. No one knows what the hell is causing these problems. Before I forget, I'm not so sure what percentage of these problems are really problems, or are simply the creation of incompetent people who try to justify their existence and occupations by creating new diseases. This is a big thing today. Everybody has their own cause, trying to create, justify and expand their markets. There is no doubt, however, that there are big mental problems out there. The potential cause of the problems range from pollution and junk food to too much information and too much performance pressure for the kids to handle."

Pignachi observed, "I think we left out a big part of the problem. We all remember the old neighborhood. Traveling a half a mile from its center was a major journey. The entire family lived within a very small radius, and every neighbor knew every neighbor. Kids had no geographic and mental freedom compared to today. They couldn't hide.

"If you did things that were wrong like pick on a little kid or answer back to an adult, there was invariably someone, be it family or neighbor, who saw you and reprimanded you for doing it. There were constant checks and balances on the way kids behaved. Now, who the hell knows what they're doing in their bedrooms or during their overnights at someone's home with their computers and videos? And even if they are supervised, it is done by nannies or babysitters or whatever you want to call them who aren't family or close neighbors and whose level of love, obligation and concern are not even close to those you grew up with. And the parents, more often than not, really don't know what these part-time parents do with, or what impact they have on their kids."

Pussy Rapper added, "I remember reading a survey a few years ago. I don't remember the exact details, but I was immensely struck by its findings. It scared the shit out of me. The survey asked questions about what institutions in the U.S. have the greatest influence on the moral value of our youngsters.

"About a decade or so before the current survey, the family, church, schools and media and entertainment industries in that order were the main factors in establishing the basis of moral values. But the current survey had the media and entertainment industries first on the list followed by the family. The church was off the list of the top four! Pignachi, where the hell are the churches, and what the hell are they doing?"

Before Pignachi could answer, the Pig said, "Though I'm not a media guy, I do support the First Amendment. Even the media cynics who view media as primarily a business industry, which it is, support freedom of expression. But when we have rappers who talk about the glorification of murder and rape, when we have sex and violence on TV shows, and magazines filled with photos of bare breasts and provocative bare asses, you have to begin to wonder about the limits of freedom of expression.

"We seem to have forgotten that sex is an extremely powerful thing. It is not simply a pleasure like eating a great meal. It is a potentially-disruptive driving force that, I believe, affects most behavior, good and bad."

I then said, "Lady and gentlemen, if the lady doesn't object, the next subject to discuss is the issue of modern sex and what it is doing to us all. To hell with the kids. Let's talk about adults and their quest for orgasms, be they accomplished by flesh-to-flesh contact or by the imagination."

Everyone laughed. It broke the ice of pessimism that was clouding the dinner table.

Mo raised his glass and barked, "Hear, hear!" And everyone drank.

Then Mo said, "Before we talk about sex, I want to say what I have to say. The modern deluge of stimulants fed to our kids doesn't change anything that much. They are still brats, and you or I don't know the reasons why. They still cause a lot of unhappiness, and we all have to accept this uncontestable fact. Why can't parents just say 'no' to bad behavior and kids respect that command? Why do kids continue to manhandle merchandise in stores, even when their parents tell them to stop? Why do they keep whining at the dinner table, ruining everyone's dinner, and refuse to obey the parents' command to shut up?

"I think it was Arnold Schwarzenegger who said that his father would not permit him to talk at the dinner table. Now I'm not an advocate of total silence but that is a thousand times better than whining spoiled brats giving me indigestion. The situation today leads to tension between husband and wife followed by argument after argument. In fact, I believe that the failure of parents to reduce kid-induced tension is a major cause of divorce. Who the fuck needs it?"

Just as I was about to open my mouth, I was cut short by the ebullient voice of Mario. He was at our table with Vinnie at his side, and another waiter standing next to the cart that held our first course. The entire scene was perfect theater and everyone's spirits responded to its positive message of excitement and pleasure. After all, what is life all about?

Antipasto

Mario began, "And now, *i miei amici*, I have prepared for you one of the most tasty and beautiful dishes that you will ever find in New York City or anywhere else in this great country of ours. It is a *contadino* dish, a dish for peasants that is also fit for kings. The ingredients are simple but they are good. Too often we cook according to good recipes but the final product *puzza*. It stinks, because the ingredients aren't fresh or of the best quality. It is made with peppers, olive oil and garlic—nothing else. What makes it different it is the way I make it.

"Yesterday afternoon I cut green peppers into slices, not too thick and not too thin. I don't use red or yellow peppers for this dish. You certainly can use them, if you want to, but the 'hit' on the palate is not the same. To me the green peppers are better. And don't forget: Don't take the skin off the pepper, like these ignorant modern chefs do. It's plain *merda di toro*. Signora Genella—that, in Italian, means bullshit. The skin gives the pepper a physical quality that goes well with the bread, which I'll talk about in a minute.

"I put the peppers in the pan with garlic and oil, and I cooked them together under a medium flame for about half an hour. Then I put them in a flat dish, so that the oil covered them all. You can put them in a bowl, but I wouldn't recommend it. I sat them on the kitchen counter, where they cooled off at room temperature. Before I closed the restaurant that night, I put the peppers in the refrigerator. It was the 'ice box' in the old neighborhood, do you gentlemen remember? When I came back this morning, I took them out of the refrigerator and put them back on the kitchen counter, where they returned to room temperature, and where they have marinated until now. I guarantee that they are now *perfetto*, and damn tasty.

"But you need good bread to complete the taste. What I mean by good bread is good Italian or French bread, with a firm crust. You dip the bread in the juices, put the bread and the peppers in your mouth at the same time, and then chew slowly. The more you chew, the more flavors will come to your palate.

"This dish does not necessarily need a drink to go along with it, but I like a gulp of a lively, heavy red wine after I swallow. *Capito?* In this way, you will get the full flavor and satisfaction of the two together. Good, old-fashioned Chianti is good enough. Chiantis, in case you didn't know, are much better than they used to be. *Grazie a Dio!*"

I carefully observed Mario's delivery, and what can I say except to say that everyone was salivating!

As Mario walked away, Genella, with a burst of enthusiasm, said, "Okay, now let's talk about sex. This is my specialty."

There followed a brief moment of surprised silence followed by cautious laughter from all the boys.

Mo refused to surrender to Genella's request. He continued, "Even when I was a kid, I didn't like kids. What used to bother the shit out of me was when I heard in sermons in church about what Jesus said about kids. Do you guys remember? Jesus said something like, 'If you don't become like one of these little kids, you can't enter the kingdom of heaven.' When I was young and first heard this, it sounded truly beautiful to me; innocent children, you know. Who doesn't initially react in a good way to the message? Then I got a little older, and began to take notice of the real world of children. I suddenly woke up! It's all bullshit, this child worship! I was brainwashed! I noticed that kids only think of themselves, and when they don't get the things they want, they go ape shit. They don't give a damn about you or anyone else. They're the most selfish group of all.

"Getting back to the point, the New Testament was written at least half a century after the death of Christ. Though it says that Jesus said something like you must become like little children to enter the kingdom of heaven, I don't believe he said it. My theory is that someone must have gotten it wrong by word of mouth, which was the way much of history was recorded in those days. Jesus probably said something like, 'You truly can enter the kingdom of heaven as long as you don't really behave like children.' You know guys, heaven ain't for selfish people who make life miserable for others."

"Hey, Mo," Genella abruptly interrupted, "You certainly are anti-kids tonight. What the hell happened in your childhood?" Everyone liked that zinger and everyone laughed, even Mo. Genella had gotten a humdinger in there.

Genella continued, "I know what you are talking about, but the picture is more complicated than that. I believe the kids today have it much, much tougher than we had it. I know we didn't have the money. Except for maybe once or twice a week to buy a soda or an ice cream cone, we never went out to eat at restaurants; and yes, these kids are spoiled rotten. They have a thousand toys that they don't appreciate when we had only a couple that we really loved. But that ain't the point. They didn't ask to be brought up that way, and I think they are confused regarding what's real and what's not real. They ain't so dumb, you know."

Almost unnoticed, Mario arrived at the table with a third round of martinis and took the empty glasses away.

"*Tutto va bene?*" he asked.

I replied, "*Si.*" I decided we would wait a while for the pasta and main course. The conversation was going too well. By the way, we never had martinis after we began to eat. It was always wine. Tonight was the exception, but once more, no one objected.

"Sure, they ain't what they used to be," continued Genella. "But their moms and dads are almost always tense and tired. Working and commuting both ways to work five days a week is a killer, Mo."

The Pig then jumped in and said, "Hey, Mo, Genella is right. And do you know who's to blame?"

Mo hesitated to answer simply because he hadn't the slightest idea what the Pig was thinking. But according to the rules of the annual gatherings, he was obligated to respond to a question. He paused and then said, "Who?"

"Miserabile!" the Pig retorted. Now everyone at the table, including the Pig, knew that Miserabile was not personally responsible for the modern problems of children and their parents.

But they knew that the Pig is a very smart guy and probably had something of value to say. They knew that Miserabile stood for something in the Pig's mind.

"Okay, Pig, tell me what you're thinking. Why am I the responsible one? How the hell did I create this horrible mess? And, more importantly, what can I do about it?"

"It's Congress that's to blame," he answered.

Feeling the big martini hit, I said to the Pig, "Let's continue with Congress after we taste something good and gulp some wine. With the basic Italian meal we're going to have tonight, it would be out of order only to sip the wine."

As Mario left for the kitchen, Miserabile leaned forward and said coldly, "Okay, Pig. How did the fuckin' Congress and I create these problems?" Miserabile, the supreme pragmatist, believed that his style of pragmatism helped people, not hurt them. Remember, he's a guy with a kind heart. The Pig knew he was a little pissed-off, but he knew that eventually everyone would get pissed-off that night because that's the way it always was, and that's the way it should be.

"Look, Miserabile, I am not one of those people who view the Congress cynically. It's tough to be a congressman and have enough time to thoroughly think through and analyze the total impact of every law this great institution passes. For example, Congress passes new laws that provide billions and billions of dollars to construct new highways, which permit people to travel great distances at high velocity. As a result, corporations build their headquarters where people can drive to work from great distances. The large neighborhood corporation is virtually nonexistent, unlike the time when we were kids.

"Moms and dads have to get their asses up early in the morning, drive twenty or more miles in heavy traffic to get to work at 9 AM, or even earlier. Not infrequently, it takes an hour or more. Even if public transportation is available, the commute is still arduous and long. Before they leave for work they somehow have to take care of the kids. They frequently require outside help. Then they leave work and arrive at home somewhere between 6 and 7, tired and tense. And guess what? The kids are waiting for them, expecting to receive lots of attention. And that's what normal kids should expect, *vero*?

"Then, the mother and father have to make the effort to be a normal mother and father on a part time basis, while they hide their guilt feelings. Many times they would prefer to be alone, and put up their feet and have a cocktail or a large glass of wine. They would…"

"Wait a minute, my friend the Pig. What does this have to do with how Congress can solve the problem?" interrupted Mo.

"That's a good point, Mo," added Miserabile. "What can the Congress do?" The martini effect was now in full bloom and the adrenaline was beginning to flow in everyone, including Pignachi, the priest.

Genella, the wise battle-scarred but sensitive woman, rushed to the support of the Pig. "Let him finish, you guys. Give him time to make his point. He may be on to something."

All of us looked at Genella with Italian warmth in our eyes. It is a kind of understanding that is independent of words. Genella is *una vera donna*, a real woman who instinctively protected men under fire. They all liked and respected her more for that quality, among many others they observed that night. Now they would also respect her opinions on almost the same level as the other guys. She seemed to have made it into the old neighborhood club and probably would become a full member of the annual get-together unless she said something real crazy later on.

The Pig continued, "Where was I? Yes, the parents really wanting a drink after work, and wanting to be alone together, but let me add that they are afraid to admit this, even to themselves.

"By the time the evening comes to an end, they are dead tired. I mean dead tired, not in a positive way, when one has been mentally or physically busy in as good kind of way. Their exhaustion is tension-laden, not the stuff that makes for beautiful marital moments. They aren't even able to enjoy a long and intimate embrace as well as make love. Though I'm not married and lack the personal experience of being a husband and a father, I've seen what makes marriage work and it's hard to find in many households. Modern lifestyles kill many sex lives, you can bet on that."

"*Affanculo*, Pig. I'm somewhat confused," interrupted Miserabile. "And I'm becoming a little impatient with your repeating what has been said before. What the hell does this have to do with Congress? Evidently you're saying that the building of highways has created this mess, *vero*? Are you now saying that Congress should stop funding highway construction in the United States in order to save the family and the sanity of the kids?"

The Pig, with obvious rising enthusiasm, responded, "Not at all! Even if Congress wanted to do it, it couldn't. Too much of our economy depends on this source of funding. The voters would throw them out of office. I say keep the spending at its present level but do something different with the highways."

"And what is that?" asked Miserabile.

"I want Congress to spend the money to eliminate half of the highways that currently exist. This would reduce the ability to commute long distances, forcing companies to relocate into community settings. People then would not be forced to spend a substantial part of their time traveling to work but could be with the family instead."

There was silence at the table. No one said a word because they were attracted to the Pig's intriguing proposal. I know the boys. They like creative ideas, but I knew that they would conclude that it probably would work, if implemented, but would never happen unless a king or an emperor with absolute power enacted such a law.

There was indeed an emperor with absolute power who built roads. He was Caesar Augustus. In order to increase the mobility of the Roman troops, to extend the power of Rome and to further protect it from its enemies, he ordered a vast program to build roads to the outer limits of the Roman Empire. This certainly played a major role in bringing about the Pax Romana, but it also destroyed Pagan Rome. Why? It made it possible for the proselytizers of Christianity to travel, preach and convert the pagans. Within a few centuries,

Christianity had become the state religion of Rome, in large part because of the roads.

Pignachi was now visibly upset, and decided to do something about it. "Listen you guys, one can go on and on about the kids. One can talk about other sad things such as parents constantly talking to their kids as if they were adults. Yes, our parents were always really 'there' when we were kids, and they're not really 'there' today. But what's going on with parents today is due to larger forces beyond their control. Let's drop the subject for now and come back to it later on when we have talked about other things that are going on today. Let's change the subject to something else. Hey, Spinuzzi, I almost forgot. What's about this theory of yours on calcium supplementation and divorce?"

Miserabile agreed and said, "Pignachi, *una ottima idea.* Now and then during Congressional hearings, I get the same feeling I have now. It's time to change the subject. Spinuzzi, I agree with Pignachi—let's hear it."

Spinuzzi sipped a little wine and answered, "It's the bowels, my friend, the goddamn bowels."

Miserabile, with a glint in his eyes, asked, "The bowels?"

Spinuzzi answered, "Yes, the bowels."

I then said, "Spinuzzi, you've always been the master when it comes to lightening up life's heavy moments. Are you now offering up some type of comic relief?"

"No," Spinuzzi insisted. "I'm dead serious. There is little doubt in my mind that calcium supplementation has had a major impact on the bowel movements of millions of Americans, which has played a major role in our increasing divorce rate. This hypothesis is based on sound scientific and medical reasoning."

Spinuzzi now turned to Genella and asked, "Genella, do you take calcium supplements?"

"Yes," she replied.

"For how long?"

"For a few years; I will say about fifteen."

"Are you constipated?"

Genella paused, sat back in her chair with a playful look in her eyes and answered, "Now Spinuzzi, a gentleman never asks a lady about her bowel movements. But since you are a doctor that makes it less difficult and even proper. And also, since the rules of these gatherings, as I understand them, obligate me to answer a question unless I really don't want to, I will. Because, frankly speaking and pardon the pun, I don't give a shit."

"*Brava*," said Miserabile.

"*Tu sei in gamba*, you're really okay," said the Pig.

"May God bless you," said Pignachi.

The boys again looked at Genella with admiration. They loved the *chutzpah* of this chick. What the hell did she ever see in that boring guy, Rocco? Love is indeed blind—or is it?

Genella then leaned forward and looked directly into the eyes of Spinuzzi and said, "You asked me whether I am constipated. The answer is 'yes,' big-time. And this is the last time I'm going to talk about my bowel movements. What I want to know is why you want to know."

Spinuzzi, with his usual charming smile, smoothly responded, "Because, my love, you are taking calcium supplements for your osteoporosis, and you are paying the 'bowel' price."

Mo then interrupted, "Stop speaking like you're some goddamn Delphic Oracle, and tell us what the hell your hypothesis is."

Spinuzzi continued. "Now, my friends—listen closely. Traditionally people do not speak about their bowels in polite company, right? It is *verboten*. They are comfortable talking to others about their arthritis, migraine headaches or recent heart attack. To speak about their fatigue and even their cancer is certainly acceptable. But who talks about their constipation? One simply is uncomfortable talking about their shitting problems in public. *Vero*?

"Now if one doesn't talk about things, they remain unnoticed, even in our current information revolution. Shitting patterns simply are not on the national radar screen. If there were a computer website on shitting, the censors would ban it. This avoidance behavior seems to be concentrated in the genital and anal areas. One feels free to speak about his viral pneumonia but remains silent about the viral herpes infection on his penis. Women don't speak about their problems having orgasms and men won't mention the fact that they have a hard time getting a hard-on."

Vinnie arrived with more of the peppers. He portioned out only small amounts, in order to leave room for the other courses that would be coming. They were truly a gustatory knockout. Everybody wanted more, but they understood what Vinnie was up to.

Vinnie then said, "I brought a different type of bread to dunk in the juice. The bread doesn't have as strong a flavor, so you can still taste the peppers. I know I don't have to remind you, but just in case: don't forget, after you dunk the bread in the juice, to put both the bread and the peppers in your mouth at the same time and chew slowly. Then you will taste different tastes until you are ready to swallow. *Va bene?*"

"Why no red or yellow peppers? Mario didn't give us the reasons why!" commented Mo.

"Mario doesn't like to serve these peppers at night. He says they're too light for nighttime eating and are better for breakfast and lunch. He also doesn't like to mix them together with sausages, like almost all other Italian chefs do. In the morning he sometimes mixes the peppers with eggs, and he eats them with bread and butter and drinks a hot cup of coffee. He doesn't understand why many people don't drink their coffee very hot. At lunch he does eat them with sausages on the side, along with lots of Italian bread without butter and at least a couple glasses of heavy red wine. Then he takes a brief nap."

No one said a word, and Vinnie walked away. They suddenly realized that they were still hungry plus they again realized they were way ahead of their normal drinking pace, and had to slow down. The latter is tough to do on occasions such as this.

"I love these peppers," said the Pig. "I remember when my mother used to serve them right out of the frying pan at dinner. They were usually green peppers with the skin on. Sometimes she cooked them with sausages. But I agree with Mario. They taste much better without the sausages. After dinner she put them on the kitchen counter and not in the icebox. We didn't have a refrigerator until I went to high school.

"When I came home from school the next day for lunch, I couldn't wait to eat them with lots of bread. I rate this dish among the ten finest I've ever had. Yet you never see it on any Italian restaurant menu. These modern chefs have forgotten about simple tastes, and they're trying to be too fancy in their cooking."

Mo then said, "Hey Pig, you didn't tell us what effect these peppers had on your bowels. I don't know about you, but they make me go. Maybe we should tell all the gals on calcium supplements to eat the peppers in order to avoid divorce. Peppers make lots of folks boom-boom, you know?"

No one laughed, for it seemed like a serious, creative idea. If Spinuzzi's hypothesis were correct, this might not be a bad idea.

"Spinuzzi, keep going with your hypothesis," Mo said. "My sister has been on high-dose calcium for a long time. She doesn't do anything in moderation, and periodically busts my brother-in-law's chops in a big way. He blames it on the monthly curse. What the hell did we call it in the old neighborhood?"

The Pig answered, "Being 'on the rag,' or something like that."

Pussey Rapper laughed and said, "Speaking of the 'rag,' do you know where the term Ragtime came from? I recently read about this somewhere, but I can't remember where. *La memoria*, my friends, ain't what it used to be.

"Anyway, it was first coined in New Orleans bordellos. When the ladies of the night were 'on the rag,' or had their periods, and were out of commission, they would take on another role with the piano players in the bordello. While the customers were waiting to be serviced, the gals would help entertain them and sometimes sing. The piano players would be in crazy types of moods and become very creative, thanks to working together with the gals. The new music that they created would come to be known as Ragtime. Put this in your memory bank of trivia."

Mo, growing somewhat impatient, said, "Pussey Rapper, would you please let Spinuzzi go on with his story?"

While they were all dunking their bread in the juices and eating their bread and peppers together in single mouthfuls, Spinuzzi continued, "I don't know about you guys, but I'm very regular; every day I do my boom-boom. If I miss a day, I go bananas and become very irritable. I don't know what it is, but it's a real phenomenon. It has only happened to me about a dozen times in my life, and, my friends, that is far too many.

"Now, my theory: though there are few published studies in the medical literature on this subject, physicians have commonly observed that women are not as regular as men. Quite a few women only go twice a week even while taking various types of remedies.

Calcium is a great constipator. It shuts down the bowels, big-time. Since the federal government recommended calcium supplementation for the prevention of post-menopausal osteoporosis almost twenty years ago, millions of women have been taking the stuff, many on a daily basis. In my mind, there is little doubt that millions of women have become constipated or more constipated because of this. And doctors know that increased emotional irritability is associated with constipation, be it in men or women. My hypothesis is that the divorce rate in our country has increased because of calcium. This increased female irritability has put a strain, along with other stress factors in our country, on the stability of the institution of marriage. I haven't made any precise calculations, and it would be difficult to do because of the lack of pertinent information, but there is little doubt that there is some type of correlation between the increased consumption of calcium, increased constipation, and our increased divorce rate."

Everybody was listening. They had finished eating the antipasto and were now more receptive to food for thought. Genella broke the silence and said, "The gals that used to work for me talked a lot about their bowel movements. It was almost always about constipation. Though I only take the stuff once in awhile and not for purposes of doing you-know-what, they told me that all it took was a couple of sniffs of cocaine and off they went to the john to do boom-boom. Hey, you guys have me using that boom-boom language. I like it. It tells it as it is.

"So why don't women know about this? I've been around and never heard about it. Why don't the doctors and the health reporters tell us about this?"

"I don't have the answer to this," Spinuzzi replied, "but it's probably due to the fact that few women talk about their bowel patterns and the companies that sell calcium products are reluctant to mention it for fear of losing their customers. But they might not even know about it. It is one of the best kept secrets in American health."

"Don't men get osteoporosis?" Genella asked. "Don't they get constipated and irritable too, when they take calcium?"

Spinuzzi answered, "About twenty percent of people that get osteoporosis are men. But I haven't seen any reports on whether they take calcium. The corporations and the media have focused entirely on women because it is the larger market and because women are more concerned about their health than men. Also, they read a lot more than men do on issues regarding their bodies and minds. About eighty percent of all of the health books published are purchased by women. I'm not sure whether men even know they can get osteoporosis. I don't personally know of any man that takes calcium. Maybe they're less irritable and better off because of this. How's that for a unique medical point of view?"

Suddenly Genella said, "Are you guys ready to talk about sex, or are you macho Italians too embarrassed to talk about the thing that makes the world go around in the presence of a woman?"

No one answered. The guys were at a loss for words. A story about macho men, told by the singer Vic Damone flashed though my mind. He was being interviewed on television, I think on the Larry King show, about his friendship with Frank Sinatra. Sinatra had just died and lots of his pals were on the talk shows. Damone said that he, Dean Martin, Don Rickles and, I believe, Joey Bishop, used to take steam baths in Las Vegas after show time. One day, Damone hired one of the sultry chorus girls to enter the steam bath totally naked while the gang was sopping up the steam. The surprised macho boys were greatly embarrassed, wrapped their towels around their pubic zones and ran out of the room. Only one guy, Martin, didn't make a move. He just sat there on the bench, looked at the naked beauty and said, "Beautiful, just beautiful." I believe that the boys here tonight, with the exception of Mo, are the type that would have run.

Genella continued, "Or is it because we are in the presence of a priest, and to talk about sex openly would offend him?"

Pignachi, the priest, knew it was his responsibility to break the ice. He knew the boys would not speak for him.

"Genella, my dear lady friend, I thank you for your diplomatic openness and concern. But don't let my presence stop you. We priests, you'd be surprised to know, are almost in the same ballpark as you ladies of the night when it comes to the sins of the flesh. You ladies manage the sexual act itself. We hear about it in the confessional and try to repair the damage."

"Well spoken," said Pussey Rapper. "You should have been a philosopher." Everyone giggled a bit.

Spinuzzi added, "Genella, you have to understand the mentality of the guys in the old neighborhood. There were no oral contraceptives and not enough good antibiotics to prevent or treat venereal disease. Abortion was anathema. Girls were not allowed to go out at night. And when they walked down the street during the daytime, their dresses were so long that if we saw a bare knee, which didn't happen that often, we would go bananas. Most of the time the gals were in the house doing their chores. If they left the house, they avoided aggressive male flirting.

"Only a very few of the boys got laid—and I mean very few, and when they did, it was almost always with someone outside the neighborhood. I don't remember ever having seen an unmarried pregnant woman in the old neighborhood. I'm sure it must have happened, but no one ever knew about it. But the boys almost constantly talked about sex. When they got older and finally got laid they stopped talking about it, particularly if they were married. Sexual relations with your wife were strictly confidential and not to be discussed with anyone. In general, matters involving the family were not to be discussed with outsiders, kind of like the Sicilian Mafia's *Omertà* or 'oath of silence.' It's not like today, where lots of these weakling guys talk about their problems openly, including sexual ones. Personally speaking, I think lots of these fuckin' modern guys must sit down to pee.

"I think that all the guys sitting around this table used to jerk off a lot. Now I hear that about fifty percent of the gals that graduated from high school have lost their virginity. I also hear that lots of ten-year-old gals are screwing." He looked around the table. "Hey guys, we really missed the boat!"

The boys smiled thoughtfully and remained silent. It was true. They had difficulty discussing sex in front of a woman, particularly an expert one. They knew that she knew more than they knew about the physical and mental aspects of man's eternal search for the big orgasm.

Spinuzzi decided to try to get it going by talking about some of his experiences with women. "When I was in college and medical school it was still very difficult to take a woman to bed. There was the fear of pregnancy. Abortion was not readily available and, even if available, somewhat dangerous. But there's something much more profound that these modern day guys and gals, particularly the gals, don't seem to understand. I don't give a shit what the experts say, the act of sex is something far more than eating a good meal, particularly to a woman. Yes, there are some animals out there whose only goal is to dump a load, but I'm talking about most people. They have been sold a bill of goods about the nature and meaning of sex. It ain't like eating great apple pie, my friends, not at all!"

Mo jumped in. "Spinuzzi, how many times did you get laid in medical school?"

All ears at the table perked up. "You know Mo, it's none of your fuckin' business. But I can tell you this: I often wonder whether I could ever have made it through medical school with today's moral values and environment. When it comes to sex and sexual exploration, I'm a very weak guy. When it comes to pleasure—of any kind—I'm a very weak guy. I love pleasure. I worked my way through college and medical school and had very little time for hanky-panky. I had very little money to spare. The free time that I had was either spent studying or sitting on barstools at night in local taverns drinking beer, watching, and listening to what the customers were talking about. Needless to say, I had many bartender friends. I liked those guys and learned a lot, I mean a hell of a lot, from them, as well as from the customers, about human nature. There were very few ladies in taverns in those days. Unlike today, it was a man's domain.

"I probably would not have made it to medical school in today's scene. Who wants to study physics or anatomy when you've got a car, money to buy coke, smoke and booze, and tons of gals willing to spread their legs?

"Let me tell you, lots of guys were naïve about sex—and I really mean naïve. I was in first year medical school. There were these really distinguished professors who loved to teach. But they were tough, to say the least. Occasionally, they would assemble the students in an historic amphitheater that was affectionately known as the 'pit.' One day, the oldest and best professor had a female and a male corpse, each on a different stretcher, in the center of the pit. A few students were asked, one by one, to come down into the pit to perform physical examinations on the cadavers. Fortunately, I wasn't called. The professor was in a particularly tough mood that day.

"About ninety percent of the first year medical students were about twenty-one years of age. There was one student in his early thirties. Why he was admitted to medical school was a mystery to us.

But my colleagues were in general agreement that he was a kind person and would be the type of doctor everyone wants. He would be truly concerned about his patients and would take time to listen to them. By the way, ours was the last all-male class in the U.S. We didn't have to worry about this politically correct shit—and it *is* shit.

"Well, the professor asked him to perform a pelvic examination on the female corpse. He gave the student a pair of surgical gloves, and instructed him to introduce his fore and index fingers into the vagina.

"After he had done so, the professor asked him, 'Herbert, have you reached the cervix?'

"He replied, 'Yes, sir.'

"'Herbert, can you feel the cervix?'

"He answered, 'Yes, sir.'

"The professor continued, 'Herbert, describe in detail the physical characteristics of the cervix.' And, much to our amazement he did a beautiful job describing the consistency of the cervix and even the size of the cervical aperture and the thickness of the uterine wall.

"When he was through, the professor asked, 'Herbert, are you married?'

"Herbert said, 'Yes.'

"'Do you have any children?'

"Herbert answered, 'No.'

"The professor, in grand style, stepped back, looked Herbert straight in the eye and said, 'No wonder you don't have any children. Your fingers were in the rectum, not the vagina. Now that you've learned this, perhaps you'll have more success in having a baby in the future.'

"The students didn't know how to react. Then we saw a sparkle in the professor's eyes, which was all we needed to relax and let loose with some mighty belly laughs. Herbert, needless to say, did not join in."

Genella decided to offer her opinion. "We were all naïve about these things in those days, but not that naïve. I'm sure poor Herbert knew which hole was which, even though the anal and vaginal canals are very close together, separated by a thin wall of skin and muscle."

"This brings to mind one of my favorite people, St. Thomas More," said Mo.

"*Mamma mia*," sighed Pignachi. "A classic example of Freudian free flow association. I can't wait to hear it."

Mo continued, "I really like the great saint's style. He was a real fuckin' man. He believed that the joy and beauty of life were more to be found with the common folks than with people of wealth and power. I agree with him. My father told me the same thing when I was a kid. He said that something happens to them and they become phonier and less free in spirit. I know that this sounds like a religious platitude but, in my experience, I've found it to be true.

"Getting back to my friend, Tommy More; his buddy, Erasmus, wrote that it was common to hear laughter around his dinner table almost every night. He was either nuts, or a guy that knew something we don't know.

"He also didn't mind borrowing money from the rich, and he didn't feel obligated to pay them back. He reasoned that he spent the money on worthy things, which he did, and his rich benefactors pissed it away. I must confess, however, that there was another practical reason—he didn't have the money to pay them back. He spent it all.

"What I really admire most about him is that he stuck to his Catholic guns and refused to grant Henry VIII a divorce. He lost his head because of it. Erasmus knew this was coming and advised him not to be so 'Catholic' in this matter. Tommy must have had big balls to stick it out and go all the way to his execution."

Pignachi said, "It wasn't his testicles, my dear friend, it was what we call faith, which means that he placed God before his and his family's welfare."

Mo continued, "He wasn't like these chicken-shits that are around today who will do anything to save their asses or get ahead. Even in the Mafia they're starting to squeal. In the old neighborhood, a squealer was considered one of the lowest forms of life and was treated that way. It's like that Pussy guy on *The Sopranos* who became an informer for the Feds to save his own ass. When the Soprano gang found out about it, they put him away. I don't remember if any squealers were put away in our time, but we certainly made their lives miserable—and I mean miserable."

Genella then said, "Mo, what does this have to do with the anal and vaginal canals?"

Everyone smiled. They really liked Genella and were becoming more convinced that she would become the first lady in this all-male club.

"*Gesu Cristo*, I almost forgot," answered Mo. "I do get carried away sometimes, particularly after a few.

"It is now accepted that More was serious both about his pleasures and his God. One day he wondered why God had placed the two canals, which carry two different types of processed material, and both of which carry different kinds of pleasures during the discharge period, so close together, less than an inch apart. Though he rated the sexual act as a pleasurable one, he believed it was overrated. He believed that a good boom-boom can be equally as pleasurable and the act itself should be cultivated as we do with sex. By the way, Casanova, the great Italian lover, made the same observations."

The Pig jumped in and said, "As President Reagan said, 'There you go again.' We're back to the friggin' bowels, again. *Mamma mia*, I think that one major discovery that we all agree upon tonight is that the bowels are more important than we have ever imagined, and have had a major impact not only on the quality of life of individuals, but also on history. I think it was Plato who said that the political state is a macrocosm of the microcosm of the mind. In other words, regular and irregular boom-booms affect the minds and therefore, the actions of the people and their leaders. Maybe Henry VIII and Attila the Hun were constipated, and Caesar Augustus and Queen Elizabeth, regular. Maybe one of us should write a book called, 'The Personal and Political Mysteries of Doing Boom-Boom.' I'll bet you it will be a best-seller for a long time."

Everyone laughed and surprisingly seemed to agree that the issue is a real one and to be considered seriously. Indeed, the bowels are important and have been ignored to the detriment of the people; and also, may I add, of history.

Spinuzzi couldn't resist getting in one of his bits of historical trivia that perhaps a dozen people in the world knows about. "Maybe Henry was constipated, but that wasn't the reason he became a cruel son-of-a-bitch. He was very trim and athletic as a young man but then began to eat himself into obesity. In those days, it was a sign of wealth and prestige to be obese. Almost everyone else was skinny. After he became obese, Henry developed diabetes and then diabetic ulcers on his legs that were so putrid and foul-smelling that women didn't want to sleep with him because he stank so much. So he understandably became a very bitter and nasty man and got rid of his women and other folks, including More. Someone should write a book on the impact of disease—as well as constipation—on history."

La Pasta

Mario, sensing what was transpiring at the table, decided that now was the time for the pasta. He was concerned that the drinking had gotten too far ahead of the eating. He arrived at the table with Vinnie at his side, which was an Italian way to indicate that we were more important than usual. You either understand this act or you don't.

Mario, leaning forward in a way that indicates that "I am in charge but, of course, I am here to serve your culinary interest and not mine," announced, "Tonight, *I miei amici*, I offer you two pasta selections. They are spaghetti *aglio olio* without *pepperoncino* and small rigatoni with a unique red sauce that is served only at La Strega.

"Before you ask questions, let me tell you why I chose these pastas *stasera*—*Signora* Genella, *stasera* means 'tonight'—and how they are prepared. I do not like *pepperoncino* or hot peppers on my pasta with garlic and oil. I know that almost all Italian restaurants prepare this dish with hot peppers, but it is a mistake. I like it the way my *mamma* made it. It is a peasant dish and I am a peasant, and you should be able to taste the garlic and oil and not ruin this flavor with hot peppers. If you like hot peppers on this dish, then do it. But try it without them and you will be surprised. Now another heresy: I cook the garlic in the olive oil until it becomes a little brown and a little crispy. If it becomes too crispy, then it becomes *un po amaro,* or bitter. After you mix the spaghetti in the cooked olive oil and garlic, you add a mixture, not too much, of *pecorino*, the cheese from sheep, and *parmigiano*, the cheese from cows. Then you add *prezzemolo*, the Italian parsley, and toss the dish with your hands as my mother used to do. I believe that tossing with the hands is better than tossing with spoons and all the other things that people use. Things mix better that way.

"The second pasta dish is pasta *al Stefano*. To repeat, you cannot find it anywhere else, not even in the best Italian restaurants. It is simple to make and *veramente* tasty as hell."

Pignachi then said, "I appreciate what you're saying about your rendition of *aglio olio* because, except for the mixing of the two cheeses, that's the way I ate it as a child. But where the hell did you come up with this small rigatoni *al Stefano*? I never heard of it, and I've been around."

"*Buona domanda*," said Mario. "It's a good question. There is a doctor who comes here alone every week to drink a half a bottle of wine, eat some pasta and drink a little *grappa* after. He likes red gravy. Nowadays, they call the gravy 'sauce.' But he insists that the red sauce be very tasty. If it is not, then he eats a little, pays the bill and leaves. He never sends the food back. He's really a strange person, but I like him. He never complains but he knows that I know when he's unhappy with the food. One night he ordered *bucatini amatriciana*, a Roman dish with red sauce, *pancetta* and onions. It's tough to screw up this dish, but chefs do it all the time. He had one taste and pushed his dish aside.

"I went to his table and before I could speak he said, 'Mario, let's not talk about the pasta. *Agita* ruins the meal. It is stupid for me to get upset over the fact that your chef hasn't the slightest idea how to make a good red gravy.' What he said is true of almost every, and I mean every, Italian restaurant that I've been to in New York. You wonder if the owners of the restaurants ever taste the dishes that their chefs prepare. You gentlemen must be wondering how I know these things. Well, I make it a point to go out once a week, religiously, to another restaurant, both to enjoy myself and to see what's going on. Most but not all of the time, I go to other Italian restaurants.

"The doctor said, 'Now listen, Mario. Tonight I need a hit. I need a tasty pasta, and I am willing to wait for it. Here's a recipe that I would like your chef to prepare for me.'

"Then he went on to explain the ingredients and how to prepare them. It's a mixture of lots of shallots, a little garlic, sweet butter, beef stock and whole canned tomatoes. He insisted that the tomatoes be freshly crushed for he believes it makes a big difference in the taste. Tomatoes that are crushed before they are canned, he said, lose some flavor. I made it for him. After he finished the pasta, the doctor let out a sigh that almost everyone in the restaurant heard. He then smiled and ordered a double *grappa* with *ruta* in the bottle—a specialty of Patsy's restaurant—and a cup of boiling *espresso*. *Ruta* is not always available so, for the doctor, I place yellow raisins in the *grappa* bottle for about a week, and serve him that instead."

Everyone was a bit confused because they were presented with a choice, and options create anxiety. They all loved *agli olio* with spaghetti, including Genella, which was unusual for a lady. They didn't care if it didn't have hot peppers as long as it tasted good. But this new dish, "pasta *al Stefano*," was unusual and sounded like it could be very tasty, particularly since Mario vouched for it. Silent culinary indecision reigned at the table and Mario observed this. His role in the restaurant was to be a problem solver and make people happy. He had a simple solution.

"I'll tell you what. I will bring enough of the two pastas for everyone. I'll put them in the middle of the table and you can choose what you want. You can even chose both pastas but, though everybody has their own tastes, I think that eating two different pastas at the same dinner takes the taste away from both of them. I'll give you a minute, and will come back and suggest some good wine."

Mario walked away, and as soon as he was out of earshot Mo said, "He's full of shit. In Italy, one night, I had five pastas and it was a wonderful gustatory evening. *Ciascuno al suo gusto*, my friends. Go along with your own tastes."

Genella stood up and announced, "Guys, I have to go and make some golden rain. After I do pee-pee, I have to make a quick call to a friend. And believe it or not, you evil-minded guys, it has nothing to do with sex or anything else. I'm committed to stay here until closing time."

The guys looked at her as she was walking to the john. Incredible as it may seem, all the boys at the table caught something in her words.

Spinuzzi remarked, "She's a wise woman, that one. She just sent us a message that she's enjoying herself tonight, and has decided to stay to the end, even though she has other options. Normally, if anyone said that to me in simple condescending English, I would tell him to go fuck himself and get the hell out of here. It's not what you say, said some philosopher, it's how you say it. How true."

I decided to take a bold step, for now I was sure what was on Genella's mind, and I knew that the boys, if not prepared, couldn't handle what she was almost sure to do.

"Gentlemen," I asked, "do you know what 'golden rain' is?" Only the Pig nodded his head in the affirmative.

"Pig, tell the boys what it means," I said.

"'Golden rain' is when someone pisses on someone to get him sexually turned on, culminating in an orgasm. It was in vogue a couple of decades ago, but I don't know where it is today."

Pignachi murmured, "Now, I remember a guy confessing to this but I didn't know how to handle it. It was a gray zone type of sin, in my opinion, and I decided to ignore it and let it ride."

Mo said, "How the hell do you get a hard-on and an orgasm if someone pisses on you? It would kill my pecker. It's a perversion, I tell you, a perversion. But I must confess that my father told me that everyone has his own perversion, that it is more often than not a normal condition of life, and it is best to overlook them unless they cause you or your loved ones big personal trouble."

"Now listen to me, you guys," I said. "I believe Genella is high and in a naughty and playful mood. She wants to talk and play with you guys about the issue of sex, including perversions. She's going to ask you direct questions about your opinions on sex, and even about what turns us on. She may have to pee-pee and call a friend, but I tell you what I think she's up to. I think she takes cocaine. My vibrations tell me that she is now sitting on the toilet seat sniffing a significant amount of coke to bolster her courage to get on with the sex quiz.

"Now I have a plan. We have a rare opportunity to find out what goes on in the bordello from one of the world's experts. I don't know about you guys, but I'm curious as hell. If I tell you it's for intellectual reasons, you won't believe me—and maybe you're right. But that's not important. What is important is that this is a rare opportunity.

"Here's what I have in mind. All of us should now write down two questions that we would like to ask her about her profession. Let's give them to Pussey Rapper, and then he'll ask her some or all of them. It depends how things flow. Pussey, make sure she doesn't see the papers with the questions on them or it will fuck up the entire psychology of the scene."

"Why me?" asked Pussey Rapper.

"Because you're a reporter and journalist, and you know how to ask questions. That's your profession. Besides, you're a liberal and liberals are more interested in certain sexual practices than conservatives and normal folks."

"What the hell do you mean by that?" asked Pussey Rapper.

"Forget it," I said. "Guys, just write down your questions before she arrives. And mark my word—she'll come back all coked up, and will show the characteristic pressure speech and she won't eat anything. Coke suppresses the appetite in most people. Who knows, maybe she's an exception."

The boys wrote down the questions and gave them to Pussey Rapper. Genella soon returned with a broad smile on her face. Pussey Rapper took a quick look at the questions before she sat down. There were ten of them.

"Too many," he whispered to himself. But he knew that he had to try, because the rules of the annual dinners required that he do so. In one sense, he was apprehensive, and yet, as a reporter, he was looking forward to a real and rare journalistic coup. He was already wondering, if the interview were successful, what the hell he would do with it? No one, as far as he could remember, had ever published a detailed scientific interview with a real bona fide madam regarding what happens in a bordello. "What an opportunity," he said to himself. He decided not to tell the boys of his intent to publish the findings of this interview because he knew they would not permit it. According to the rules, whatever was deemed confidential at these gatherings was to remain confidential, forever. But the person doing the talking must say that the subject matter is confidential. So far, Genella hadn't brought up the issue.

Genella returned, sat down and immediately asked, "Where the hell is the pasta? I'm starving." She continued to smile and appeared to be quite calm.

The boys quickly glanced at me, transmitting the silent message, "You got it wrong. She's not on coke, and stop being so goddamn clinical." I read the message from the boys and agreed that she did not show signs of a coke high. But I was convinced that she went to the john to take something to bolster her courage and make her relax.

I made the diagnosis that she probably took a dose of Ecstasy. In a sense, I hoped I was right, for it would make for a much more interesting evening, unless, of course, it led to some ugly moments, which I also believed was possible and hoped to avoid. I decided to pay close attention to the conversation and, if necessary, step in at the right time to abort potential unpleasant moments.

The pasta arrived and Miserabile, his mood now more relaxed, said, "I don't know about you guys, but I'm going to have both pastas." Nobody disagreed. Vinnie recommended that the pastas should be eaten separately—the *agli olio* first followed by the *al Stefano* one. Once more, no one objected.

"Vinnie, Vinnie," she said. "No white wine, please. It just doesn't go with most pastas, particularly the ones we're having tonight. I like it red, and I'm sure the boys do, too." Now I was convinced that she had taken some coke, simply because she was way out of order requesting red wine for every one at the table, without asking them their preferences. Just enough to relax herself, but not enough to obviously stimulate her. I continued to believe that she also took the Ecstasy to take over when the coke effect wore off.

The boys and I knew that the Pig loved and almost always drank white wine, even with his steak. In fact, red wine sometimes made him sick. But he said nothing.

In order to make the Pig happy, I said to Vinnie, "Vinnie, let's do like we used to do when we went out together for dinner in the old neighborhood. Bring us each two wine glasses, one for the red and one for the white. Give us two bottles of red, and two bottles of white. Then we can decide for ourselves what we want. *Capito?*"

I could see that Vinnie, the pro, was a little upset. "Do you mean you want to pour the wine yourselves?"

I sensed that he was hurt because we abruptly, and unexpectedly, rejected his ability to time when and how much wine should be poured throughout dinner. This know-how was one of the great virtues of a professional like Vinnie.

"No, *mio amico*, you do the pouring and we do the drinking. This is the way we did it in the old days and we enjoy doing it this way. *Va bene?*"

As the conversation at the table continued, I motioned to Vinnie to lean over and lend me his ear, and I told him to pour white wine for the Pig.

"*Va bene*," said Vinnie, with a smile.

I was relieved that our proud server was relieved. Can you imagine a dinner with a disgruntled waiter and bad service? It is something to be avoided at any cost! Better to stay at home. I often wonder what these guys that own restaurants are thinking when they serve up mediocre food coupled with bad service and high prices, which is not uncommon. They shouldn't be in the business. But most folks don't know what good food is. They eat the crap, pay the price, and walk away, contented. When I say crap, I really mean that a good hamburger that costs a few dollars has much more taste than a neutral-tasting dinner at thirty bucks or more. When we judge a meal, the price should always be a major factor in making a judgment. The

New York City crowd is one big sucker for bad food and high prices. That's because the vast majority have never tasted really good food. Most of the New York chicks can't even cook a good original meal.

Genella continued, "Red wine goes with all kinds of pasta. The feeling on the palate and the stomach is much more beautiful and more relaxing than white wine, and what is eating all about? To enjoy the feeling of food and drink in the presence of your friends is one of the greatest gifts of life. It is not fickled like sex."

Though the boys agreed, there was an uncomfortable feeling around the table, because of the Pig.

"I remember a story that Rocco told me. In the old neighborhood, only a few men drank on a regular basis and the women hardly at all. One of the reasons was they simply could not afford it, particularly hard liquor. His grandfather, however, insisted on drinking a glass of wine with both lunch and dinner, and one more, after dinner.

"He used to make his own homemade 'dago' red wine in the basement. Every summer, the crates of grapes were delivered to his home by a guy who had his own vineyard nearby. In those days, there were still little plots of land within the city limits where folks grew fruits and vegetables.

"His 'wine machine,' as he use to call it, was in the basement, and he spent hours manually churning the grapes and doing whatever one has to do to make the stuff. Rocco's father, unlike his grandfather, did not drink and, except on special occasions, would not permit the children to drink the *dago* red, or any other alcoholic drink. But the grandfather loved life and saw nothing wrong with drinking along with eating. He despised the few drunks in the neighborhood and called them *stronzi,* or 'shits.' He told Rocco that we all need pleasure in life, and that wine was a good crutch to lean upon.

"So when the grandfather finished making the wine in the basement, he would call Rocco to come down and have a few sips with him. He called his wine 'homemade Chianti.' God knows what it really was. He told him to learn to enjoy this type of wine.

"He said to Rocco, 'Your father fears the bad side of alcohol and wants to protect you but, if you can avoid getting drunk in life, drink this wine and enjoy it. It is a gift of life that God owes us to reduce the pain of the gift of living.' After that, Rocco almost always drank red wine."

The wine arrived and was poured for everybody; the Pig got the white wine and the rest got the red. Then they all began to devour their food and no one said a word until Genella blurted out, "Are you guys ready to talk about sex? I must warn you that I have no problems talking about sodomy but I refused to talk about shitting or anything else to do with my bowels anymore. You guys got that straight?"

Miserable said, "Genella, baby, you can rest assured that that's the farthest thing from my mind while I am eating this great pasta. By the way, this pasta *al Stefano* is one of the best I've ever had. What do you guys think?"

"This is pretty fuckin' good, I must say," said Mo. "I'm sick and tired of these chefs making this new pasta dishes with all kinds of, if you will pardon me, Genella, crap mixtures like chicken, mushrooms, vegetables and whatever. And not only are the noodles not *al dente*, they are mush. Women love the stuff but men go for the plainer, higher palate-impact sauces."

I suddenly remembered that I had invited Mario to join us sometime during the evening's conversation.

I knew that Mario loved politics, and I was saving this subject as the last item on the discussion agenda. But we were drinking more than usual, and I wasn't sure we would ever get there. Also, Mario talked too much and might dominate the conversation on any subject. The boys wanted to hear from Genella, and learn about the 'other world,' first hand.

I made a decision and called Mario over to the table, and asked him if he wanted to join us in the conversation on sex. I also told him that this was Genella's show time, and we were to listen rather than dominate the conversation.

"*State zitto*," I told him. There was a sparkle in his eyes and he looked very pleased. He pulled up a chair and, would you believe this guy, placed it right next to Genella's. I then realized that Mario would not remain silent, but would be a big player in the conversation with one of the great ladies of the night.

Mario was unaware that Pussey Rapper had the list of questions for Genella. He was a truly free spirit who, when the time is right, has no problems letting it all hang out. I sensed that, for whatever reasons, he was in the mood to let loose. And I was right.

He began, "First of all, let me thank you all for coming to my restaurant tonight, and let me say a special hello to *la bella Signora*."

(He noticed that she wore a wedding ring, which we had failed to observe, and he avoided the mistake of calling her *Signorina*. Though a modern woman, Genella would have noticed the mistake and Mario would have lost points. Mario knew this and Genella knew that Mario knew this.)

"You look very beautiful tonight, Genella. I notice things like that, you know," Mario said.

Genella changed roles and played the blushing, shy, but flirtatious woman. She smiled a disarming smile and replied, "*Grazie, tanto.* You are a generous man to pay this aging woman such a compliment."

All the boys sensed that the chemistry between the two was there, and the mental foreplay had already begun. I knew that none of us was a match for her in this scenario. There was little doubt in my mind that Mario could handle her, and that she not only knew it, but welcomed it. How would it end—who the hell knew?

Mario continued, "I regret that I cannot stay for a long period of time, for I must take care of my customers. I would like to discuss the sex issues that most interest me. You see, Genella, I think a lot about sex, but have so little time or opportunity to do anything about it."

Everyone smiled, but Genella's was the broadest. Mario, the free spirit from Salerno, had broken the sex ice. The boys would definitely be more open now, but not nearly as open as Mario. Spinuzzi is, by far, the most experienced lover of the group, but he always had a tendency to become tight-lipped when it came to his personal experiences.

"*Cara mia*," Mario said, "tell us something about your bordello. What kind is it and what goes on?"

"My business deals mostly with successful men, but not, with a couple of exceptions, the super rich. The gals that work for me range from sixteen to thirty-five. I did not and do not handle the very young girls. There's another house in town that specializes in the area of prepubescent girls. Contrary to popular belief, my girls are not homosexual, but do enjoy making love to other women once in a while, particularly in the presence of men or if the men actually participate. You know, a *ménage à trois*.

"About fifty percent of the men come in for regular sex. What I mean by that is, all that they require is a gal with a sexy outfit and decent body—she doesn't necessarily have to be naked during the encounter—and they will either have normal sex like the animals do, have oral sex, have the gals masturbate them or, only once in awhile, sodomize the girl. Very few of our gals like to be sodomized, but there are a few who love it.

"The other fifty percent come in for special treatment, which comes in many forms. The most common are going through the many phases of a transvestite, a physical sado-masochistic scene, mental or verbal domination and the many types of voyeurism."

Genella, in a playful mood, turned to Mario and asked, "What turns you on?"

Without a moment's hesitation, Mario answered, "You!"

Genella said, "What about me?"

Mario said, "All of you."

Genella said, "Is there anything in particular that you like about me?"

Mario said, "Your ass and your mind—not necessarily in that order."

Fearing things were beginning to get out control, I asked, "Does anyone have to go and make pee-pee?"

Mario said, "I do. Genella, do you?"

Genella said, without hesitation, "I do."

Mario said, "*Andiamo.*"

Genella said, "Okay, let's go!"

And off they went to the toilets, but we still weren't so sure that it was to make pee-pee. Within five minutes, they both returned together. Who knows, Genella might have convinced him to take a couple lines of coke, in order to loosen him up—as if he needed it!

We were witnessing the beginnings of a potential amorous relationship. Would Mario end up as a regular customer in Genella's brothel or at her home? This possibility entered all of our minds, I was sure of that.

Mario said, "I never paid to make love to a woman or to have a woman make love to me. I have nothing against this; it doesn't bother me at all. I'm not foolish enough to believe that these women would enjoy being with me. It's their profession, and they have to go through the motions."

Genella shook her head, "Mario, that's not the way it is. Most of the girls don't dislike men. In fact, they like them. And I'm not being a snob here, but the wealthier the men, the more the girls like them. But it's not only the money that's important, it's the way men with money behave. They are more pleasant to be with and more sensitive to the gals' moods and personalities."

Mario said, "Genella, let's talk about the money! Let's be truthful. You're all out to make money. We, at this table, are all out to make money. I'm curious. How much do you charge for your services?"

"That's a personal business question that I refuse to answer. But it depends where you're located in this country. Prices can range from a hundred to five hundred dollars and hour. A lot also depends on the quality and nature of the service. For example, some gals specialize in S and M, or sadism and masochism. For these services, they can get higher prices.

"Prices can really get ridiculous," she continued. "I just read a story in one of the newspapers about a New York City madam who made four million dollars a year. She claimed to have top models on her payroll who were available at prices ranging from one thousand to four thousand dollars an hour. If you wanted to spend the night with a top model, the starting price was twenty-five thousand dollars. One night, the police sent an attractive undercover woman to this madam to interview for a job. They told her to undress, looked her over, and told her she didn't qualify for the job. The reason? Her body could only command six hundred dollars an hour, too low for the marketplace. But these figures are kind of out of sight."

"One of my regular Greek customers used to tell me stories about Greek and Roman history," Mario said. "The Greeks were pretty moral people, but did permit, on a limited basis, selective places of sin.

"There was a famous brothel in Corinth that housed the most famous and expensive prostitute, probably of all time, Lyda.

"You guys remember the great Greek orator, Demosthenes? He's the guy that used to put pebbles in his mouth on the beaches of Greece and try to speak over the sound of the surf to help develop his speaking voice. He lived at the same time as Aristotle and Alexander the Great, and, by the way, all three died in the same year. Greece lost its greatest orator, philosopher, and leader at the same time in history. After that, it was all downhill for Greece.

"Anyway, Demosthenes had a hot nut for Lyda and wanted to spend a night with her. And do you know what the price was? It was about thirty months' pay for the average free Greek man.

"I don't remember whether my customer told me if Demosthenes paid the price or not."

Genella laughed a big one and said, "That reminds me of a story that Rocco used to tell, which was written by a guy called Boccaccio in a book where there are lots of short stories. I've forgotten the name."

Spinuzzi interjected, "The *Decameron*."

"*Grazie*, Spinuzzi," said Genella. "Anyway, there was this young, sultry, innocent virgin girl named Alibech, who was looking for the meaning of life and ways to find God.

"She decided to go to the desert, where the religious hermits lived, isolating and depriving themselves of pleasure to make it easier to communicate with God. She visited one after the other, seeking advice, and they all turned her away, afraid that they would not be able to control their sexual desires when alone with a blossoming young babe.

"Anyway, she finally ended up at the door of a vigorous young hermit called Rustico. When the young hermit bull saw her, his hormones began to flow. He decided to invite her in and teach her about religion. Evidently, she postured herself in such a way that he got a hard-on."

Mario asked, "Was her ass like yours?"

Genella smiled. "I'll leave that to your imagination."

Mario smiled too, and said, "I like you, Genella, I like you."

Genella continued, "Well, Alibech noticed his erection and asked him what it is. He answered that it was the devil, and it was his duty to put the devil into hell. She asked him where hell is. He told her that hell is where her vagina is, and it's her duty to help him put the devil into hell.

"She agreed, and, within a week, became a nymphomaniac. At first, he had a ball, but as time went on, he couldn't take it any longer. He was worn out, my friends, while she was getting stronger.

"Fortunately for Rustico, she got wind that her father had died and she left. If she had stayed, she would have killed him.

"So you see, guys, the pecker is no match for the pussy. In fact, if we want to get rid of all the wars, we should make gals like Alibech available to all our male leaders. The gals would fuck their brains out so they won't have enough energy left to make war."

Spinuzzi mused and said, "Interesting hypothesis, Genella. There's a poem written by a Roman—I've forgotten his name—at the time when the Roman Empire was turning from war to pleasure. It's called '*Nulla Puella Negat*,' or 'No Girl Says No.' The poem says that all you had to do, in those days, was ask the girl to go to bed with you, and she would do it. Perhaps all the Romans got their heads fucked out and lost their national energy, making it possible for the barbarians from the north to topple Rome." There's little doubt that Spinuzzi had the most creative mind of the group.

Mario said, "Genella, would you volunteer to be one of those girls?"

Genella said, "It depends."

Mario said, "On what?"

Genella said, "On who the man is."

Mario said, "How about if it were me?"

Genella said, "I'd have to think about it."

Mario said, "What if I tell you what I want?"

Genella said, "Go ahead. I'd love to hear it."

Pignachi said, "I have to make an important phone call. One of my parishioners has a problem that can't wait 'til tomorrow. It'll take about fifteen minutes."

After Pignachi left the table, the Pig said, "There is no problem, and there is no parishioner. Pignachi doesn't want to be around to hear where you two guys are heading."

"I don't blame him," said Genella. "This Mario is a bad boy with a big appetite for life. God knows what's in his head."

Mario picked up his glass of wine and silently signaled that Genella should pick up hers. He did not reach out with his glass to touch hers—touching glasses would have destroyed the mystery. They both drank heartily, looking into each other's eyes.

This was real theater with two exciting performers on stage. What was the line from *Hamlet*? Something like, "Life is a like a stage of actors, full of sound and fury, signifying nothing." Bullshit, I say. If Shakespeare were here, witnessing this scene, he would have added, "Signifying nothing, except when it comes to sex and people with great sensual appetites."

The boys were having a ball. There was life going on around the table, and the evening had a long way to go.

Mario said, "I'd like you to tell me something about yourself, about what you would like from a man."

Vinnie suddenly arrived at the table. "Mario, the place is filling up, and the customers are asking for you. The Mayor is a little pissed-off that someone is sitting at his table."

Mario replied, "How the hell did that happen? Move them to another table," he said to Vinnie, then turned back to us. "Please excuse me for a moment, for, as some idiot once said, 'Business before pleasure.'"

Mario left the table, and silence prevailed for at least a minute, which is a very long time at a dinner table.

I decided to bring down the hormone level as quickly as possible, and asked, "Genella, are most of your girls divorced?"

"It's a good question, and I'm thinking about it as I answer you. I would say, maybe a third are divorced. And let me tell you, the stories I hear make me wonder whether it's worth going through a divorce. The pain is out of sight.

"Rocco used to say, 'Why don't those idiot men get a mistress and stay married?' I told him that it's very expensive to keep a mistress. He said, 'So is a divorce.' What could I say to that? It's true.

"I'd like to get a story in before Pignachi comes back. One night, we were talking about a very painful divorce between two people that we knew. I must admit, as much as I hate to, that the wife was a real pain in the ass. But in her defense, I'll also add that her fuckin' husband was a weakling, and put up with a lot of her shit.

"We were having our martinis when Rocco went off on a long-winded speech about how people suffer when they don't need to. He said that in the old neighborhood, it was possible to put someone in the grave for a fee of twenty-five thousand dollars. He estimated that today's price would be about fifty to seventy-five thousand for a person who was not a big shot. He said that if he were the husband he would pay the price. The pain in the ass would be gone forever, and so would his *agita*."

Pussey Rapper asked, "Genella, would Rocco really put a hit on someone?"

Genella laughed. "No way. Rocco was a soft-hearted guy, and wouldn't hurt a fly. But he would advise someone else of the option of getting rid of the spouse. It's kind of like saying, 'Don't do as I do. Do as I say.'"

Mo then said, "Fortunately, with the exception of Miserabile, no one around this table has had to endure the fuckin' unnecessary pain of divorce."

Miserabile did not appreciate Mo's remarks at all, but he let it go.

Pussey Rapper uncharacteristically exploded, "What the hell are you talking about, Mo? I have three fuckin' kids and they're all divorced. I was stupid. Instead of minding my own goddamn business, I got heavily involved in trying to patch things up. When that didn't work, I entered the negotiations for their settlements. And to top it off, it cost me many additional stressful moments just trying to keep the bad news from my wife. You can't tell me that I haven't endured the agony of divorce. It's a long and mean process. It's loaded with venom and is one of the seven proofs of the existence of the Devil."

Pignachi had just returned to the table and heard what Pussey Rapper said. He looked puzzled and said, "I have taken a vow to defend the Catholic faith. This is the first time that I've ever heard of these seven proofs of the existence of the Devil. Where can I read about them?"

"My mother wrote them down and gave them to me before she died," answered Pussey Rapper. "A physician professor from the medical school at Salerno in Italy told her about them. It may be the oldest medical school in Western Europe. Here's a piece of information to put in your trivia bank: the famous saying, 'An apple a day keeps the doctor away' came from the Salerno medical school."

Pignachi sensed that the media-wise Pussey Rapper was trying to avoid answering his question. "Where is the paper your mother wrote them on?" he asked.

"It's in my security box at the bank. Listen, Pignachi, I don't feel like talking about my mother and the seven proofs of the existence of the Devil, tonight. Suffice it to say, they are pretty convincing. They convinced me, particularly after my experiences with the three *maledetti* divorces. Let's talk about it at another time—just you and me."

The Pig, seeing that Pussey Rapper was very uncomfortable, joined in the conversation. "Let's talk a little more about divorce. I believe that knowing about the high probability of divorce before you even get married is creating a large number of dysfunctional and insecure people in our country. Instead of people who rise to the occasion to solve their problems, what we are seeing now are, as we used to say in the old neighborhood, a bunch of crybabies. They are always complaining about their mates and just about everything else. In those days, if you were a crybaby, you were a big fuckin' zero. Nobody wanted to be around you and, even worse, nobody paid any attention to you."

Pussy Rapper then said, "Pig, well said. Pignachi, what do you think? I'd appreciate your opinion on three subjects: mobility, drinking and wealth seeking. Then I'll tell you what happened with my kids."

Pignachi replied, "You must remember, guys, that I am talking of a limited experience with middle America. But I firmly believe that you have to start somewhere to try to understand what is going on in the divorce scene. The problem is a general lack of personal strength, and something has to be done about it. My father used to say, 'If you do nothing, nothing happens.'"

Miserabile suddenly burst out in laughter. Unable to figure out why, the boys exchanged glances.

"Miserabile, you inscrutable one, what did I say to make you laugh?" asked Pignachi.

Miserabile answered, "Pignachi, my friend, it wasn't you I was laughing at, but what your father said, that doing nothing gets you nothing. I've never heard anyone express it more clearly than your dad. I'm reminded of a story I read when I was a teenager that really taught me a lesson.

"During the Peloponnesian war between Athens and Sparta in the Golden Era of ancient Greece, the great Athenian leader, Pericles, called all free Greeks to the public square to tell them of his strategy in dealing with the Spartans. Athens was a great sea power and a strongly walled city. The strength of the Spartans was its army or ground forces. They were the fiercest of fighters and spared very few of their enemies. It is legendary how a few hundred Spartans, in the battle of Thermopolyae, held off many thousands of Persians.

"Anyway, Pericles said something like this to the Athenians citizens, 'The Spartans are coming, and our army is no match for theirs. We will lose if we fight them face to face on the battlefield. We will all move into our walled city and wait them out. Our ships, which the Spartans can't touch, will bring us water and food. We'll outlast them.'"

Miserabile continued, "Then one of the Athenians asked him, 'Pericles, are you sure that this is the right strategy?' Pericles replied, 'How the hell do I know? All that I know is that we have to do something.'"

The gang all laughed. They were relaxing again.

The Pig said, "Pericles hit it on the nose. By the way, the great German philosopher, Kant, whom few people can understand, said the same thing in different words, in one of his more lucid moments."

"All right you guys, let me tell you about three factors that are associated with divorce," said Pignachi, impatiently. "I want you guys to fully appreciate that I know that there is something much more profound and fundamental going on than these three factors, but these are the most tangible observations I've made.

"Today's families are hyperkinetic; they are always on the move. Their life is rigidly scheduled with thrombosed calendars. There are very few moments when they are relaxed and can just be together, whether they have kids or not.

"Today we also have good, old-fashioned materialism. People are buying more, borrowing more, and more in debt. I read somewhere that the average individual or family saving rate in the year 1999 was virtually zero. Can you imagine the anxiety and unrest these people are feeling?

"Why are we so materialistic? It's the innate nature of mankind. It's the way it is. People want more. But no one, not even the churches, made a significant attempt to tell them that this is not the road to happiness and a stable family. The result has been lives full of anxiety and tension.

"It's no wonder they turn to alcohol for relief. They come home and pour themselves drink after drink looking for relief, to say nothing of drugs like cocaine and marijuana. Then they lose some control of their emotions and their reason. They begin to talk about their bills and what they owe. The tension continues to grow. If they have kids, the tension is further increased because, for some reason that eludes me, they can't stop spending money on their kids. Once more, I'm not playing Freud here, but these factors are not the stuff of happy marriages."

"Amen," said Miserabile.

Pignachi continued. "It is not uncommon for a working mother to come to me complaining that she wants to stop working because she's needed at home to take care of the family. She says that her absence from home is destroying her family life and, moreover, that she would enjoy staying at home. And, with only a handful of exceptions, the husband would strenuously object, the main reason being that they could not maintain their level of living if she did so. It's as if there is no turning back. No one—neither family, nor church, nor anyone else—told them that it was inevitable that this style of life was a sure formula for unhappiness. Those of us from the old neighborhood, of course, are not surprised about this mess because our tradition not only taught us the value of the woman as the foundation of a happy family, but that we should try not to live beyond our means. I love capitalism, and the way in which it creates material goods that help us to be happy, but it has gotten out of hand. The Pope has spoken out, on more than one occasion, against the dehumanizing aspect 'of capitalism where things material take precedence over things spiritual."

Genella then said, "Pignachi, I agree with you a thousand percent. But who's to blame, the husband or the wife? I'll answer my own question by saying that neither one is. The Pope is probably right. This modern way of living, this monster, is bigger than the family."

Genella continued, "I don't care what anybody says, it was much easier to live and be content in my old neighborhood. We had very few options and were happier with less. We knew what was right or wrong, which certainly takes the strain off the mind. Today it seems that it is being left to the married people themselves to determine the right or wrong of everything. I know they can't handle that. Very few, and I mean very few, people can. We lack the comforting rules of stable tradition. Remember that play, *Fiddler on the Roof,* where the guy sings about the importance of tradition?

"Let me tell you a story about how our women have been and continue to be screwed—and I'm not talking about the bedroom, guys. There is a gal who works for me, one of my regulars, that's a good-looker. She's in her early forties and went to one of those fancy and expensive girl colleges. She's divorced twice, has two children, and is all fucked up.

"One night at my house of work, there was a humongous snow storm. Business was very, very slow. Despite the fact that we lose lots of money, we do enjoy nights like this. We get to talking to each other and get to know one another. She and I had a couple of drinks that night and, in addition, she took a couple of big lines of coke, as well as a couple of puffs of smoke—not big time, but enough to make her open up and talk about herself more than she normally would. I do not permit my gals to get stoned on the premises. That's asking for big trouble. By the way, in case some of you guys don't know the language, coke means cocaine, smoke means marijuana, and stoned means when you take too much of the stuff. We use the word 'drunk' when somebody gets 'stoned' on booze.

"Anyway, that night we were talking about life and what's it's all about when suddenly she burst out in tears and shouted, 'They fucked me, those goddamn cocksuckers, they really fucked me! And now I'm paying the fucking price!'"

Genella continued, "Where the hell that outburst came from, I couldn't figure out for the life of me. I thought maybe she took a little LSD or something that escaped my attention, and that she was beginning to hallucinate. I then asked her, 'Why are you fucked up, and who did the fucking?'

"She wiped the tears from her eyes and took two more lines of coke—this time they were really big—way up the nose. 'Who fucked me, you ask? It was those fucking feminist college professors at college; those fucking cunts that needed to be sodomized and those fucking wimp men professors who loved to be dominated by women. I also think lots of those wimps were queer, but I'm not sure.

"'How did they fuck me, you ask? It was not only me, but all the girls, both at my school and all other similar type schools, across America. The women's liberation movement was in full swing, and everyone was on a high. Course after course was given on how great women are and what pricks men are.

"'We were told that we were finally free from the men and should be ourselves, think more about ourselves and not be shackled to the family. It was time for women to stop giving and begin taking. We could have a career, a husband and kids, and handle it all. Large numbers of men would accept this, and many of them would become house-husbands because they were being taught these things in school. With both husband and wife working, we could afford to live like the rich and hire help to clean the house, cook the meals and take care of the children. We could have it all! But we can't, goddamn it, we just can't.'"

Genella really felt sorry for the gal. We all thought the story was over, but we were wrong. She continued, "Would you believe this poor woman got breast cancer shortly after our talk? Though it was a small tumor, it was one of those serious types.

"My God, I just couldn't believe it. Sometimes when I feel sorry for myself, I think of that poor girl and realize how lucky I am. You'd think that in this day and age doctors would be able to destroy a small tumor. Spinuzzi, what is it with modern medicine? Why the hell can we send a man to the moon and not a tumor to hell?"

Spinuzzi was visibly moved by Genella's words. He hated disease and often lectured us on American science and medicine with

Mediterranean passion. He believed that if we mobilized, we could rapidly conquer disease. There was a reason behind his passion that we'd never uncovered. We'd just never asked. Genella would be the catalyst to bring this about, that night at La Strega.

Spinuzzi's eyes softened, and he gently responded, "Genella, I don't have the answer to why our country allows people to suffer and die needlessly when we already have the technology to do something about it. It is a worldwide tragedy, not just a national one. What is frustrating as hell is that it is not recognized!"

Spinuzzi hoped to close the discussion on this topic with his brief response, but Genella wouldn't let up. She asked, "But why is this true? Why do you think we are able to cure disease but don't do it?"

With growing intensity she continued, "I'm selfish. I've been in great health all my life. I've seen my friends and family getting sick more and more, and I don't like it. I'm getting old, and I know some big-time disease is waiting around the corner to attack me. If we can find new medical cures in a hurry, I'm all for it." She continued to look directly at Spinuzzi, and he felt the sincerity and fear in her words. "I'd like to know why you feel the way you do."

Spinuzzi loves women with chutzpah, and he felt obligated to respond to Genella's request, but his reserve was still there. He said, "Genella, Genella. *Che ti posso dire*? It's a long story and I don't want to bore you with it."

With a smile specifically cultivated to disarm a man, she answered, "I'll tell you what. If you tell me your story, I'll tell you mine. I'll tell you why I got into my profession, and I'll tell it to you as a guest for dinner at my home. *Va bene?*"

We all sipped our drinks and waited for Spinuzzi to respond. He stared at his drink as if it were a crystal ball. He seemed relaxed and, after letting out a barely audible sigh, said, "*Va bene, va bene.*"

He began, "It happened when I was nine years old, when I lived in that row home, you know, the one near the old ballpark. Though we had no television, my family was very excited about the installation of our first telephone. Remember, guys, how the telephone line was shared by two or more families? We used to call it a party line. In the beginning, I really loved to lift the receiver off the hook ever so gently, in order to hear the conversations of the other parties. All I heard were conversations about problem after problem, and after a while it was no fun anymore. It became so depressing that I gave up listening in.

"One day I noticed that my grandmother was beginning to lose her energy and becoming short of breath. She was a severe diabetic. My Uncle Jimmy, who lived three city blocks away, would come each day, even after hard days working in the sweltering heat, to give her the insulin injections. She gradually became so weak she couldn't walk and quickly passed into a coma. Whether it was diabetic coma, congestive heart failure or both, I'll never know.

"You guys must remember that dying in the old neighborhood was a little bit different than dying today. Hardly anyone went to the hospital because of the accepted odds: if you entered though those hospital doors, you had a greater than fifty percent chance of never exiting. A bed was placed in the dining room where *nonna*, my grandmother, could be watched over by all the adult family members that lived in the old neighborhood. The time was divided into twenty-four hour shifts. Aunts, cousins, uncles, nephews and even neighbors took turns in the continuous vigil. The kitchen was buzzing with a constant crowd of family and friends drinking coffee and eating coffee cakes, cinnamon buns, and tea biscuits. Once in a while we had coconut custard or apple pie. No one drank liquor. I think booze simply cost too much. They couldn't afford to develop a taste. My grandfather was the exception. He loved his wine in normal, happy, and sad times—in other words, every day.

"One night, I found myself alone in the house, a rare thing in those days, in relative silence. Everyone was outside sitting on the porch or on the stoop talking among themselves and the well-wishing neighbors. I vividly remember placing my face nose-to-nose next to my grandmother's and talking to her.

"I said, 'Look, *Nonna*, if you can hear me, smile or do something!' Nothing happened. I continued to cajole her, trying to get her to show some sign of life, but nothing happened. A period of silence and stillness followed when I just stared at her. To tell the truth, I was disturbed that even I couldn't elicit any response from her. Such is the innocence and optimism of youth.

"Then came the big bang. I felt a powerful feeling that would consume me throughout my medical career. It had two elements—the first was intense hate of disease, and the second, a strong conviction that it can be conquered. I remember thinking that if I could just put my finger through her skull into a certain part of her brain and move it a little in the right direction, she would come out of her coma.

"God only knows what logic I used, but I concluded that I could not move anything in her brain by myself and decided to go to the local Catholic church to talk to God, one on One. I remember being in the church, alone, at about ten at night. Church doors in those days were never locked at night, the way they are today. The Church has forgotten that one never knows what time of day one will need God's help. I knelt before the altar and stared at the large crucifix hanging from the ceiling. Then I began to bargain with God. I promised I would do such and such if he would permit my *Nonna* to live.

"I thought, honestly speaking, that I was quite convincing and had made a deal. I marched home to see her at about midnight. Boy, were my parents pissed-off at me for coming home so late, not knowing where I was. The small house was once more crowded with family and friends, all again in the kitchen eating pastries, drinking coffee and laughing hearty laughs. This is the Italian response to tragic moments: Try to laugh them away with healthy humor. My mother then ordered me to bed. I fell promptly to sleep, confident that my deal with God was sealed. When I awoke the next morning, my grandmother was not in the living room. I learned that she had died and was moved to the funeral parlor.

"About fifteen years later, I was a third year medical student and was covering the pediatric ward from six in the evening to eight the next morning. Lucky for me there were two experienced nurses working that night. We were discussing a case of terminal leukemia in a nine-year-old child on the ward. She was bloated from high doses of steroids and hemorrhaging in her skin and in her internal organs. As we were talking, about six or seven of the girl's family members walked by the nurses' station to the bedside of the dying girl. The mother and father knelt together by the bedside while the others gathered around them in silence. The scene of Christ and the manger jumped to my mind, the difference being that scene dealt with the giving of life and this one with taking it away. The nurses and I all felt the extraordinary power of this silence. About an hour later, I walked to the bedside and discovered that the child had died.

"The nurses, in no uncertain terms, told me it was my duty to inform the family that she was dead. I knew they were right and, with much difficulty, I managed to get the job done. It wasn't easy, my friends. I tried my mightiest not to cry and, somehow, succeeded.

"When the family decided to leave, it was shortly after midnight. The nurses were busy tending to the other children in the ward. I was alone with the corpse. That's what she had become in a brief moment of time—alive one second and gone the next. I thought, as some physicians do at moments like these, about religious issues and the incomprehensibility of the cruel death of a child. The mind is a strange thing. As I was thinking about life's imponderables and looking at the lifeless child, images of my grandmother in a coma in the living room flashed through my mind. I suddenly felt the same thing I felt then, a hatred of disease and an urgency to conquer this beast. Since then these feelings have never left me. What has, however, become a constant frustration in the ensuing years is the cruel fact that I, as an individual, can do little to conquer disease.

"To add to the frustration, I have not been able to convince a single person—not one person—to say, nor have I heard anyone say, 'I hate disease.' Have you guys ever heard anyone—in medicine, science, the government, foundations, the media, your friends—say, 'I hate disease; let's get rid of the mother-fucker, this monstrosity, this thing that can be beaten?' Has anyone every seriously and rationally tried to help establish a system in our great country to accelerate medical discovery? Not ever, believe it or not!

"The little girl died in 1959. I'm still waiting to hear these words, over forty years later."

Pussey Rapper leaned back and asked, "Spinuzzi, what you're saying is hard to believe. Do you know something that everyone in the U.S. doesn't know?"

Spinuzzi answered with surprising force in his voice. "That's a good question, and I'll try to answer it. The problem is simple to diagnose and the solution is clear. Have you ever asked yourself how you know that the medicines you take work? Answer that question, any one of you!"

"Since I asked you the questions," said Pussey Rapper, "I should be the first to try to answer yours." He paused and answered, "It's because the FDA or some government agency approves the medication. That's why it's available by prescription."

"Then why does the government approve the medicine?" asked Spinuzzi.

Pussey Rapper paused again and answered, "Because there is scientific evidence to show that it works."

"Not to belabor a point," continued Spinuzzi, "but what do you mean by scientific evidence?" After he asked the question he glanced at everyone around the table, trying to open up the conversation, because he had been here before and was rarely successful in getting the message across.

The Pig obliged and jumped in, "It's when scientists and FDA experts get together and agree on the scientific information."

Spinuzzi smiled and said, "Pig, that's what is known in rhetoric as a tautology or a kind of circular reasoning. You just said, more or less, that scientific evidence is scientific evidence.

"I'll stop the quiz now and get to the point. You can only know whether or not aspirin, insulin, penicillin or whatever works by testing these substances in people. This is known as clinical research. As a result of the thalidomide tragedy, Congress passed laws trying to prevent new thalidomide events. They forgot to address the need to encourage clinical research, which is the only way to discover whether potential new medical therapies designed to prevent and cure disease really work. In fact, the opposite occurred.

"Let me give you an example of the government's overreaction to the thalidomide tragedy. It happened to a friend of mine. These are the kinds of things that block medical discovery, and they happen every day, but escape national notice.

"There is a small company in Europe that specializes in extracting natural substances from the brain. This company is searching for new therapies to treat and prevent diseases and injuries of the nervous system. Their research scientists isolated a natural substance that had the potential of repairing and making new nerves grow. They did lots of animal studies that did indeed confirm that this substance could repair damaged nerves and make them grow.

"The company began clinical studies in Europe. They then asked my friend to supervise small clinical studies in the U.S., in patients with rare and fatal diseases of the brain, spinal cord and nerves that go to the rest of the body.

"There was a young nun with a rare brain disease who was bedridden and had a certain rendezvous with death within a period of a year. Her doctor found out about this potential new therapy and called my friend, requesting samples to treat her condition. My friend agreed to do so. But the law requires that you send information to the FDA requesting permission to send a drug that has not been approved by the FDA out to physician to treat a patient.

"So my friend sent out the paperwork and, much to his surprise and frustration, the FDA refused his request. He called the FDA to find out why the request was denied. They told him that, because of the thalidomide tragedy, no experimental drugs were permitted to be given to women of childbearing age. The government did not want any more problems with children born with birth defects.

"My friend then tried to reason with them, saying that this would exclude all pre-menopausal women from receiving the benefits of new potential medical therapies. They replied that they understood, but the new regulations prohibited this.

"He also told them that she was a nun and was bedridden and dying, making the probability of her becoming pregnant less than zero. The FDA replied that it didn't matter; she still was of childbearing age.

"With tongue-in-cheek, he offered a solution. He suggested to the FDA that if she were to undergo surgical removal of her ovaries, it would eliminate the possibility of her becoming pregnant, and she could then receive the experimental drug therapy. The FDA said that would be okay.

"Can you imagine that? When my friend called the nun's physician, he was incredulous. The surgery, of course, was never done and the nun never received the therapy. She died soon after, and, hopefully, has discovered that Heaven is a more rational and compassionate place than Earth.

"The costs and risks of conducting clinical research or studies have skyrocketed. Now mainly only organizations with big money, such as the pharmaceutical industry and the federal government's NIH, have enough money to test new medical therapies.

"As a result, medical discovery is being severely blocked, a tragedy far, far, and far greater than the thalidomide one. It pisses me off no end, thinking about those many, many millions of people who are needlessly suffering from their diseases or have died prematurely."

Pignachi asked, "Why isn't anyone raising hell about this situation? You're telling us that all those exciting new therapies that we read about—stem cells for Alzheimer's disease, transplantation of brain tissue after stroke, injections of heart cells for patients with heart failure—are a long way off before they're available to everyone who needs them? I find that hard to believe!"

"You better believe it. Not only are they a long way off, but many will never be tested. How's that for potatoes!"

Spinuzzi went for his wineglass and waited for some reaction from the group. None came. There was an interim of silence, as before. Mo then asked, "Spinuzzi, my sister has multiple sclerosis. Is there anything in the research pipeline that offers any hope?"

Spinuzzi suddenly jumped up and was clearly agitated. "Mo, no offense to you because you're doing the right thing in trying to help your sister, but what you just did is what happens a hundred percent of the time when I speak about the general need to accelerate medical discovery to help you, your sister, or anyone else that needs help.

"Look what just happened. I just told you guys that we now had the medical technology to cure or at least control the ravages of disease, in a couple of years, in some cases. I also told you that there are formidable barriers that block the necessary clinical research to test these medical breakthroughs. And how did you guys react? *Niente*! No curiosity, no anger, just dumb puzzling silence. This is the reaction that I always get. I can't figure it out. It drives me nuts. People should ask, 'What can we do about it or how can I help?' But what they say is what you just said, Mo. They ask about their particular medical problems or that of their family or friends. 'Should I get angioplasty instead of a coronary artery by-pass?' or 'Does gingko biloba really work for memory loss?' or 'Does Echinacea work for the common cold?' I understand that somewhat, but I'm frankly puzzled about the absolute lack of interest and enthusiasm when we are dealing with the need to accelerate medical discovery."

Spinuzzi sat down and looked at Genella.

Pignachi, forever the empathetic priest, sensed a bit of sadness and frustration in Spinuzzi's soul. At that particular point in time, he was thinking more of Spinuzzi's problems than those of the patients.

He gently asked, "What you've said doesn't speak well for us old-timers and the baby boomers. Why, in your opinion, are people not interested in your argument? To me, it seems that what you are talking about—making it easier to do clinical research—can have an enormously beneficial effect on our lives. You would think that people in every walk of life would have a high level of interest. In fact, there should be a revolution. Right?"

"Wrong," said Spinuzzi. "There's something about the reason why people fail to get excited over the real probability of curing disease in their lifetimes that I haven't figured out. What I do know is that there is a strong element of doubt or at least a hesitation to consider the issue seriously. Maybe they are afraid of hoping too much for something that they think can never be. There is a real Cartesian mentality of doubt. It could be that they think all is well and that I'm full of shit. Even the vast majority of my colleagues in academic medicine have been, in a complex way, brainwashed, and are happy with the present system. Pardon the old neighborhood language, but it is fuckin' unbelievable and fuckin' frustrating. There are no great visible leaders in medicine that the public can relate to.

The public knows about and worships the gurus, mostly non-physicians, who push unproven remedies, but not the professors of medicine who are trained to treat patients based on the results of clinical studies, combined, of course, with the art of medicine."

Pignachi, knowing that Spinuzzi was no dumb guy, respected his opinion and believed that it was probably true that Spinuzzi was onto something very important that others have missed.

Pignachi asked, "Your inference is that barriers to test new medical therapies block most of the creative physicians in our country from testing their ideas in patients by the process we call clinical research. You must have some evidence of this, *vero*?"

"Ah, Pignachi, what can I say, except to say that I have evidence but don't know how to get the message across. Americans have a very powerful suspicion regarding clinical research. Yes, we have had the great tragedies of Tuskegee, Auschwitz, and thalidomide, but these events are not enough to explain our national reluctance to embrace the importance of testing new therapies in people who have problems and want to get rid of them. Remember when President Kennedy said something like, 'Come hell or high water, we are going to the moon. We need our brave astronauts to risk their lives to get us there.' In a real sense, the astronauts were volunteering for clinical research risking their lives for a worthy cause. Everyone applauded and all of America was energized by this romantic and critical mission. When President Nixon, the guy that few people understand, announced his war on cancer, he didn't, nor did anyone else, know that *doctornauts*, like astronauts, were needed to volunteer for clinical studies to test new cancer therapies. I can't explain our national obsession with the evils of clinical research. All that I know is that it is stupidly powerful.

"If a physician—me, for example—wanted to volunteer for a clinical study to evaluate a very safe new anti-cancer therapy, let alone a dangerous one, I could not do it unless the establishment of hospitals, government, insurance companies, bioethicists, and the rest gave me and the clinical researcher permission. The government has robbed me of this right. Also, the costs and risks of going through this procedure discourage even the most patient clinical researchers, let alone me, from testing their promising ideas. The most brilliant minds hate barriers. If Da Vinci wanted to paint, he would simply pick up his brush and walk to his easel and begin. If Einstein wanted to write down a new mathematical equation, he would walk to the blackboard with chalk in hand and go to work. No barriers! If these guys had to go through all the paperwork and meetings with lawyers and regulators, bear the costs of doing unnecessary laboratory work as well as worry about and pay for the liability insurance, there would be no Mona Lisa or Theory of Relativity today.

"Look at our cultural mentality. We all know about a single patient—yes, one patient—who died in a gene therapy study at the University of Pennsylvania. The national shit hit the fan. The mass media, sensing the public's exaggerated suspicion of clinical research, trumpeted this story in a big way. Instead of calling the studies 'clinical research,' they used the fear provoking term, 'human experimentation,' questioning the ability and integrity of the physicians who had conducted the study. This, obviously, is not the stuff that encourages future creative physicians to try to find cures by doing clinical studies. The reputations of the clinical researchers, and they are excellent ones, by the way, respected by their colleagues, were heavily and maybe irreparably tarnished. Yet if people die from marketed drugs, and it happens a lot—many thousands each year— our society does not go bananas and accepts it. I can't figure it out.

"So the federal government, responding to the political pressures caused by this single death, suspended ongoing clinical studies. The result has been new rules and regulations that dramatically increase the costs and risks of conducting clinical research further delaying medical discovery. Who pays the price? All of us! Who's complaining? None of us!

"Now compare this to the reaction to the pilots who flew to the South Pole, as volunteers in formidable weather conditions, to rescue a lady doctor with breast cancer. They were free to do so—no stupid barriers. The media rightly praised them as heroic men risking their lives to save a patient. Why can't I, as a physician, take the same risk in clinical research, trying to discover new medicines that can save patients' lives, or at least diminish the suffering that is associated with their disease? Why the hell is there this lethal double standard?

"Guys, I'm getting carried away. Let's change the subject. But before we move on, it is important to note, for this indirectly tells us something about our national mentality, that Congress has never had a hearing on ways to increase medical discovery as a national policy. Let's forget about patient suffering for a moment. If we want to reduce national health care costs, what better way to do so than to increase medical discovery and reduce the amount of disease? I rest my case."

Genella suddenly asked, "What do you all think of abortion? Is it sometimes right or wrong or never right or wrong? Do you guys follow me?"

I looked around the table and observed that the boys were caught off-guard and uncomfortable with this question. In the old neighborhood, the topic of abortion was anathema. Like child molesting, it was simply not tolerated and rarely discussed.

Though I don't remember ever having discussed this topic at any of our annual dinners, I knew that some of the boys were pro-lifers while the others were pro-choice. I guessed that the boys that didn't go to Mass on Sundays were pro-choice, and those that did were pro-life. I subsequently found out I was right.

I decided to take tighter control over the conversation because I anticipated the high passions that would follow, even if the boys tried to be objective. These nights were nights of pleasure and enlightenment, not venom. And the topic of abortion often brings out the venom.

I said, "We will make this discussion very brief and follow strict ground rules. I want a crisp presentation, of no more than five minutes length, by each one selected to comment (and I will select), on the pros and cons of abortion. This will be followed by no more, and I mean no more, than a ten-minute plenary time period where those of you who want to can make very brief comments. But one thing is important. This discussion must not ruin the evening. You all know what I'm talking about, *vero*?"

With the exception of Genella and Pignachi, the boys all answered, "*Vero*."

I continued. "Why don't I start out with a personal overview trying to summarize the situation? Let's begin with the Catholic anti-abortion position. There are non-Catholic Christians, Jews, Moslems, and even people who have no religion, who are against abortion. But I don't know the reasoning behind their beliefs and cannot speak for them.

"It's tough to find anything in the New Testament that says Jesus was against abortion. It is silent on this matter. But somewhere along the line, the Church began to formulate its anti-abortion position. Bottom line, the message is a beautiful one, but with real big intellectual problems associated with it.

"There's no doubt that Yahweh, the God of the Old Testament, and Jesus, the God of the New Testament are—let's forget the Trinity for the moment—more or less the same entities, and were behind the Ten Commandments. I'm sure you remember the commandment, 'Thou shalt not kill.'

"Now in our times the issue is being raised almost on a daily basis. What did they mean and whom were they referring to when they talked about killing someone? Well, a romantic and somewhat logical argument is that anything that lives in the form of a human body should not be murdered. Of course, there were exceptions. There is the Jewish law of Talion—an eye for an eye and a tooth for a tooth—that made killing a person for having killed your loved ones, or whomever, acceptable. Bluntly stated, revenge is accepted. By the way, I love this law, and try to follow it. The Church also elaborated on this theme of justifiable killing, taking the position obvious to most (but, I'm puzzled to say, not all) that it's okay to kill someone in self-defense or when trying to prevent a potential murderer from killing your wife.

"Now the Catholic Church developed the highly elevated religious position that a fertilized egg is a human being and that aborting it is outright murder. Beyond abortion, the Church went so far as to take the position that preventing the possibility of birth by using contraceptives, be they pills or condoms, amounts to the same thing. Thus, if I put on a rubber and made love to one of Genella's girls, I would have committed murder for having blocked the birth of a human being. The same sin would be committed by Genella's gals who use oral contraceptives or wear a diaphragm when they make love.

"The proponents of this argument believe that the 'Thou shalt not kill' commandment is operative in these situations. They try to strengthen the argument by saying that the natural sexual act involves three steps: erection, vaginal penetration and insemination. Blocking any of these during a sex act is unnatural, and, therefore, wrong.

"Now arguments such as these, as well as others, in my opinion, all fail to pass the test of reason as well as that of religion. To repeat, the position that gives such an exalted value to a newborn is lofty and beautiful. But even St. Thomas Aquinas didn't believe there is a human being in the uterus until the moment of quickening, about the fifth month of pregnancy, when the mother feels the movement of the baby.

"But now we must address the issues of partial birth abortion and infanticide, for they are all part of the same spectrum. The majority of Americans, regardless of their religion, are against the brutal act of partial birth abortion. That's when a doctor, who's fucked up in the head, surgically aborts a baby during the late phase of gestation.

"Let's say that a mother decides, the day before she is to deliver, that she doesn't want the baby anymore. The fucked-up doctor then dilates the uterine cervix, inserts a forceps-like instrument through the cervical canal, and places the infant's head within the instrument. Next, he inserts a suction tube through the baby's skull, sucks out the brain, squeezes the forceps and crushes the skull of the living baby in order to make it easier to remove the baby from the uterus.

"It's not only the American people, but also Congress that are against this brutal act. The Congress passed a law against this procedure but President Clinton vetoed the bill. It's hard for me to understand why someone is not against this procedure unless, of course, the life of the mother is endangered. Even the Catholic Church is in agreement with the latter.

"Now let's look at infanticide, killing the kid a minute after he is born. That's against the law in our country. But what's the fucking difference that this minute makes?

"Infanticide is not an uncommon event in history; in fact, in some cultures it was routine. I'm sure it continues today but it is not as visible. If a Roman couple had a female or a deformed baby, they would not hesitate to throw it on the nearest dung heap and walk back to their home to prepare dinner. The poorer free Romans would check the dung heaps for these rejects. They would then take them home and rear them as slaves. I'm sure you know that almost everyone in Rome had slaves. Though I'm not absolutely sure, I think that there were more slaves in Rome than free citizens. I know that was true in ancient Greece."

Vinnie suddenly appeared out of nowhere and surprised us with his question. "*Piu vino, Signori?*"

"Sure, Vinnie, our glasses are just about empty," I said. I was trying to avoid interruptions that would inevitably lead to heated discussion, so I immediately pushed on. "Though I am sure that there are those who think there is nothing wrong with killing a baby that is significantly deformed, most Americans are against infanticide.

"In conclusion, the moral question for most Americans seems to be that it is not 'if,' but 'when' the act of preventing or destroying the life of the baby is acceptable. It is interesting that the founder of atheistic communist society, Karl Marx, believed, more than most Americans, in the importance of life and wrote, with a bit of tongue in cheek, that the state's responsibility extends 'from erection to resurrection.' I'm not sure, however, that he ever expressed an opinion on abortion."

There was a moment of uncomfortable silence at the table. Like automatons, everyone reached for their wine glasses almost in perfect synchrony, raised them to their lips and sipped.

I knew that I had to end this discussion *subito, subito*, and said, "Pignachi, *cinque minuti*. You have five minutes. Let's hear what you have to say."

Pignachi looked around the table and said, "This is an argument that is not to be made over dinner, wine and good food. But the rules are the rules, and I know I have to say something or lose my seat at our annual dinner.

"Please note that those who argue for abortion usually use the reasoning that a woman has a right to her body. Then the thinking gets fuzzy, like the philosophic issue of continuity versus contiguity. I'm not sure whether the fetus is considered a part of her body and therefore she has a right to get rid of it or if it is a foreign body in her body and, therefore, equally has a right to get rid of it.

"According to this argument, a pregnant woman has the right to starve herself to death along with the baby because she has a right to control her own body, and therefore, the baby's. I don't think the Supreme Court or any other court would permit this. But the principle is the same. Also, where did this right of a woman to her body come from? Certainly, God didn't give it to her. If God didn't tell her about it, then someone else did. Who is the person or institution with the legitimate moral authority to do so?"

Pignachi was on an intellectual as well as an emotional roll, and I was keeping a close eye on him in case things got out of hand. They never did.

"And don't forget that our Founding Fathers granted us certain unalienable rights, one of them the right to be free. In our country, neither a woman nor a man has the right to surrender themselves as slaves to someone else. At least we know where the right of freedom comes from.

"Anyway, Jesus Christ spoke about the importance and sanctity of each and every one of us, saying that in God's eyes, one person is more important than the entire universe. If you believe this beautiful message, then you'll understand why the Church is against abortion.

"My time is up!"

"What you said is certainly provocative and should give us food for thought," I said. "Okay, Pig, let's hear your point of view."

It was apparent that the Pig and the rest of the group were reluctant to continue this conversation. He knew that Pignachi had other arguments in his repertoire, but had cut his presentation short. Pig would do the same thing.

He began, "It is important to note that Jesus never touched on the subject of abortion. It was the Church's attempt to interpret the teachings of Jesus, by what is known as Church Tradition, that lead to the present position on abortion.

"And how's about this for food for thought? Close to sixty percent of the world's population is Asian, the vast majority of whom have never heard of Jesus' message or the Catholic Church's argument against abortion. Also, only about one percent of the world's population has graduated from a college or university. This means that very few people in the world can, even if interested, read and interpret the Church's position on abortion.

"In conclusion, if most of the world does not know what we have been taught, how the hell can these people even begin to consider that abortion is against God's will? Will God send to hell a lady born in Tibet who can't read and undergoes an abortion? Has God established what I call a 'geographic morality,' where if you happened to be born in the wrong place where you are not exposed to the right morality, you are doomed to go to hell?

"Pignachi, yours is the position of a mystic. You see things that simply elude practically everyone else in the world."

I was about to shut down this conversation when Pussey Rapper decided to make a comment. "Let me say something before we close the conversation. I was in Rome taking a leisurely walk after lunch, with two priest friends of mine. I was doing a story on the Pope. It was a beautiful spring day, and we were crossing one of those bridges that spans the Tiber River. We were halfway across when we decided to stop and gaze upon the scenery. As we were looking down toward the water, we saw three condoms floating by. One of the priests, with true sadness in his voice, commented on what an awful thing it was that within those condoms were three potential lives that would never come to be. He said that the sperm in the condoms were robbed of their chance to create three lives. Though not explicitly stated by the priest, the implication was that murder had been committed.

"It then struck me that this reasoning was beyond my comprehension. It was and remains inconceivable to me that God would punish a guy and a girl who want to make love for love's sake and not just to have kids. It also struck me that it was time to bring about a solution that most Americans could live with. We could never make the members of the left and right accept any compromise. There is something in the personality of those on the left that wants to give the government more and more power to snuff out the lives of human beings with problems. The opposite is true on the right. These guys and gals want to protect every form of human life to such a degree that some are against abortion even if the pregnancy will lead to the death of the mother. I disagree with both of these mentalities.

"Now, here is my proposed solution. It is nothing new but its time has come. A baby's organs are formed about the fifth month of pregnancy, the time of quickening. Let's draw the line here. The government or anyone else should not support abortion after the fourth month of gestation. Outside of these limitations, let everyone handle the situation for themselves. It is a personal matter that people themselves should decide, and it should remain so. Amen!"

Genella then said to me, "Don't shut down the conversation yet. Has anyone here had personal experiences with the abortion issue? Yourself, your family or others?"

There was dead, and I mean dead, silence. What Genella didn't know is that the boys in the old neighborhood, unlike the boys of today, never spoke about abortion to anyone except their closest friends. It was nobody's business, and if you violated this secrecy, you were considered a *numero uno* horse's ass. I knew that the conversation would go no further unless Genella did something. And so she did.

Sensing the situation, Genella said, "I'm not trying to pressure you guys to talk about what you don't want to talk about. My Rocco would tell me to be *zitta* and keep my goddamn mouth shut. But I thought you guys have rules and that when a subject is raised someone has to answer."

Mo broke the masculine silence and replied, "My father told me many times that there are exceptions to every rule. He also told me that somewhere in the Bible it says that rules were made for man and not man for rules. The case is closed, Genella."

"Then let me tell you of one of my personal experiences. It happened recently with my niece, my brother's daughter. She got knocked-up at the age of sixteen, while still in high school. We were all surprised because she wasn't like the rest of these modern bratty gals that are always into themselves thinking of ways to have a good time. These self-centered girls have a lot of freedom and are always away from the home looking for a good time. They don't give a shit how much grief they give their moms and dads, and they never wash the dishes or do anything to help mom out in the home. They are 'takers,' not 'givers.' My niece isn't like that. She's a good kid.

"My story is a classic case right out of a movie, you know, nice gal gets knocked-up by her first lover who happens to be the big star on the football team. Now though her father (my brother) is a kind and gentle man, he had no problems with getting even. I remember as a kid that when someone screwed my brother in a real way, he would patiently plot his strategy for revenge. He has a 'get-even' gene somewhere in his genetic pool.

"When he was a senior in high school, my brother had a mad crush on this chick. Her parents weren't Italian and gave her more freedom in the way that permitted her to show off her female attributes. She wore tighter-than-normal sweaters and wore a skirt short enough that half of her thigh was exposed, which was equivalent to a guy seeing a bare ass, in those days. She also wore heavy make-up, which, like the short skirt, just wasn't done. Both sent out the message, 'Would you like to fuck me?' To put it bluntly, she was a classic tease. I'm sure you guys know what I mean, and I don't have to explain.

"Anyhow, this chick flirted with my brother, and the idiot, God bless him, fell for her. But he didn't have any money, so he couldn't take her to the movies and buy her popcorn, soda water or even a hot dog.

"I know you guys talk about your neighborhood as something special, but mine was just like it. Anyway, there was a kid in the class that always had lots of dough in his pocket—much more than the other guys. One day, my brother's so-called girlfriend went after this guy, and this other idiot fell for her. He took her to a drive-in movie in his father's car. Afterwards, he took her to the local pizzeria, where he fed her—something that, as I said, my brother could not afford to do.

"My brother happened to be in the pizzeria that night watching everybody else eating and saw that the two of them were holding hands when they weren't holding their pizzas. He went home and got a hammer and some kind of tool. He came back and slashed all four tires and smashed the windshield of the guy's car.

"You guys better believe that I was really surprised by what my brother did. What was normal revenge for something like this in my neighborhood was maybe like slashing one or two tires, not all four, and not even thinking of smashing the windshield. This was big-time revenge, and this situation did not call for it.

"It was then that I learned that my brother was a big time Law of Talion man—an eye-for-an-eye and a tooth-for-a-tooth. But I can tell you guys that he didn't even know that this law existed. It came naturally to him."

Spinuzzi mused, "At least he didn't shoot the kid like the kids in our schools do today. And they shoot for thrills, let alone revenge. Hey, Pignachi, you're the guy here tonight that knows the most about the souls of Americans. How do you explain all these kid shootings in our schools?"

Genella didn't give Pignachi a chance to answer. She said, "It's because they don't get enough sleep. Now let me continue the story."

The boys were impressed with the agility of her mind.

Pignachi, however, felt obliged to answer and said, "It's a long story, Spinuzzi. It's part of the general change that's taking place. I personally believe that it involves kids with mental disturbances who go undetected because our society is more and more tolerant of abnormal behavior. We have shifted the line of normal versus abnormal behavior way left of center, so people with serious problems are now considered normal. Listening to rap music about how it's okay to kill somebody is now normal while in the old neighborhood it was a tip-off that kids had to be watched closely. Nobody is watching now. The kids are unsupervised.

"Genella, please continue."

"Getting back to my brother's daughter and her football hero boyfriend, their flames of passion got so strong that they finally gave in, and she got pregnant right after her first sexual experience. What a way to start womanhood!

"When my brother found out, the first thing to enter his mind, of course, was revenge. He called two of his closest friends, and they plotted how they would isolate the football player in a remote section of the neighborhood at night and break both his legs. This act would prevent him from ever playing college and pro football, and would meet the requirements of a just revenge.

"My mother got wind of this plot and told my brother that his priorities were all fucked up. She told him that it was critical to consider the impact of this pregnancy on the daughter and to have a plan to handle it. She told him that the two basic issues to consider were abortion or no abortion.

"Believe it or not, my brother was dumbstruck. This scenario had not yet entered his mind. He was temperamentally against abortion and could not conceive that his daughter would have one. But he was a practical man and could also handle difficult situations.

"There were many cons. If she had a baby at that age, she would limit her life and could make it a miserable one. It could, of course, also make the lives of her aging folks much more difficult. They felt no joy in becoming grandparents under those circumstances. In addition, even if the guy agreed to marry her, the probability of a long and happy marriage was not very good. He would probably leave her at a point in time, making everybody's life even more miserable.

"What is interesting is the fact that the snuffing out of a potential life, though it was considered a serious issue, became a secondary issue in their attempts to resolve what had become a practical problem.

"They then thought of the psychological impact that an abortion would have on their teenage daughter. After weighing the pros and cons of the abortion, they decided that abortion was the right thing to do. Religion and morality took a back seat.

"They told the daughter what they thought, and after much weeping and gnashing of teeth, the daughter agreed to have it done provided that her father would not break the legs of her lover, the stud. I think women are much less inclined to actually take revenge than men, don't you think?

"And that's the story, my friends. It wasn't easy, to say the least."

Genella, drinking away, seemed to want to continue the conversation on this downer subject. I tried to cut her off but she was too quick for me.

"What if," she asked, "we start modifying the genes of the sperm or the egg or wherever they modify genes, and the babies are made taller, blue-eyed, strong—you know, the Hitler thing—and something goes wrong, and we change our minds. How do we handle this?"

Mo then said, "Genella, baby, you are now entering the field of biotechnology and bioethics, which is not an item on our agenda tonight. My wife and I, believe it or not, were talking about this subject last week. She said that she would never want this option. We would never have had a happy life together.

"Over the whole nine months of pregnancy with each of our three kids, we argued heatedly about what their names should be. If we argued over something like that—important, perhaps, but not big-time—imagine what it would be like if we wanted to change the sex, increase the intelligence or the muscle mass of the kid. She said, and I agree, that it would be a nightmare. She said that our marriage wouldn't last, and that genetic manipulation of the fetus would become the major cause of unhappiness, divorce and destruction of the family in the United States.

"She also mentioned something that I haven't heard anybody discuss. If any one of us at this table were genetically manipulated to suit our parents' whims—and most of the manipulations will be whims, I can tell you that—then wouldn't the kids become pissed-off at their parents and have significant psychological problems? Wouldn't they ask themselves as well as the parents the question, 'Who am I?' Just imagine yourself being someone biologically other than who you biologically should be!"

I then said, "Bioengineering, as Mo said, is not on the agenda for discussion tonight. But it has arrived on the world scene, is big, and must be reckoned with. Since it will have a profound influence on mankind in the coming years we cannot ignore it, and we will talk about it at next year's dinner. But I am assuming that Pignachi has thought about this the most since it has profound religious and moral implications. Give us your thoughts, my friend."

Pignachi suddenly looked very sad and said, "My God, where will this lead us to?"

Mo, obviously agitated, then said, "I really don't want to talk about biotechnology and the future of mankind at this moment. The abortion discussion depressed me a little and this discussion will depress me even more. Let's liven the moment up a bit: Pussey Rapper, ask Genella a sex question."

Spinuzzi, with a tinge of anger in his voice, refused to put aside the subject of fetal manipulation. "I know where it will lead us. Many, in the past, have predicted what would happen to man in the future. Books like Huxley's *Brave New World*, and Verne's *20,000 Leagues Under the Sea* tell us the story. The message of the authors is that technology will not only change the way we live, but who we are. Even the optimistic religious philosopher, C.S. Lewis, had to admit that this would happen.

"Others are actually predicting an end to human history within the century, and the beginning of a new humanoid history. They believe that we will embrace genetic engineering, and, even if we don't, it will be forced upon us by the state. All our genetic natures will be altered, and we will become other individuals than we really are—you know, unnatural."

The Pig, with a look of wonderment, said, "Hey you guys, look at that guy over there. He's eating a hamburger with a side order of

131

home fried potatoes. Hey Vinnie, can you come over here for a minute?"

Vinnie came to the table and the Pig asked him, "What's with that guy? How come he comes to an Italian restaurant and orders a hamburger with home fries?"

Vinnie smiled and replied, "He's a wealthy guy that comes here one or two times a week and always orders hamburgers. He doesn't eat French fries for the simple reason that Mario doesn't *do* French fries."

Mo then said, "I heard about this syndrome of the wealthy and their weird patterns of eating. Warren Buffet and Bill Gates, I've read, eat hamburgers practically every day at both lunch and dinner.

Pignachi said, "I love hamburgers, but why does this guy come here to eat his, instead of going to a restaurant that specializes in making them?"

"Because Mario has a special recipe for hamburgers," replied Vinnie.

"What makes it so special?" asked Pignachi.

"I'm not allowed to give out the recipe, and he rarely gives it out. But since he had a good time with the sex conversation questions, and had a few drinks to boot, he may be more than happy to oblige." Vinnie disappeared and, about a minute later, reappeared with Mario.

"So you want my secret hamburger formula, eh? It's the best around, if I say so myself. *Va bene.* I will give it to you, but you must swear upon one of the graves of someone that you really love that you will never tell anybody. *Capito?*"

132

"*Capito*," we all replied in unison.

"It's really very simple and you guys should be able to remember it. But, *i miei amici*, you're getting old and the memory, like everything else (if you know what I mean), ain't what it used to be. *Vero?*"

"*Vero*," we once more replied in unison. Mario should have been a symphony conductor.

"Somebody should write it down," said Mario.

"I'll do it," volunteered Pignachi. It was obvious that the guy couldn't wait to get Mario's recipe. He must really love hamburgers.

Mario began, "These are the steps to hamburger paradise. Buy about two and a half pounds of sirloin and two and a half pounds of chuck—not lean. Then buy a quarter pound of pure beef fat. You can buy a little bit more, but that's according to your tastes. I often do. If you want to buy less meat, keep the proportions the same. Tell the butcher to put them all together in the meat grinder and blend them. Save a little bit of the fat on the side for later on.

"Now make your hamburgers a good size and don't pack them too tightly. I do not use the grill but the frying pan to do my burgers. I don't give a damn what those grilling chefs tell you, you lose fat when you grill, and the fat gives the burger the taste. Sure, I've had good hamburgers on the grill, but I've had better ones from the frying pan.

"Now you rub the fat on the cooking surface of the frying pan, covering it well. Make sure you use enough fat. Then you cook the hamburger *al vostro gusto*, the way you like it. I sometimes like it rare or medium-rare, but never well-done. After you take the hamburger out of the pan, dunk both halves of the bun in the juices in the pan.

"Some people like to put ketchup, onions and other stuff on the burger right away, but I would suggest that you taste it the way it is and then decide what you want to put on it.

"But here's a warning about those neurotic anti-fat health rules that govern what type of meat you can buy from the mass production butcher: If you go to the butcher in these big supermarkets, they are not permitted to give you what you want. Would you believe it? First of all they can't sell you really fatty meat. They have to trim off the fat to a certain maximum level. They can't even sell you a piece of meat where all the fat has been trimmed from the edges, if the fat content of the meat itself is high. They have a machine that measures the water content of the meat, which is an indirect measurement of the fat content. If it reaches a certain level, the poor butcher can't sell it to you. And would you believe this, he is not permitted to sell you pure fat by itself! He'll get fired!

"This is why we must, at all costs, keep the local butcher alive and well. We must prevent those big stores from destroying the taste of meat. They have already done that with pork, you know, those small pigs with less fat and lousy tasting meat. The small, independent butcher is free to give you what you want. Ask him to mix my recommended ingredients, and he will do it for you. If you have any problems, I will send you to my personal butcher, Mr. Erwin."

Mario, like a diva who's about to leave the stage, actually bowed and said, "I have now given you something that you can put on your happy-moments menu of life. You, my friends, are very fortunate, on this beautiful evening in New York City. Before I forget, did you notice there is a full moon tonight? In Italy, we call it, '*La Luna Stregata*,' or 'The Witch's Moon.'"

He then looked at Genella and said, "*Cara Signora*, I'm sure you are aware that the cycle of the moon is related to that monthly event experienced by people of your sex. In case you gentlemen around the table *non capito*, I'm talking about a lady's period.

"Now, I don't want to talk about a lady's period at the dinner table, but when *La Luna Stregata* is at the exact time as a woman's monthly curse, then that woman can become very interesting, *vero*, Genella?"

Genella smiled ever so gentle a smile, tinged with a very subtle pissed-off quality.

Mario, turning his eyes from Genella to the others, then said, "But, my friends, don't only think of woman when you observe *La Luna Stregata* in the evening sky. My grandmother used to tell me that my grandfather became very irritable and a very big pain-in-the-ass when there was a full moon. He hardly smiled, and lost his temper over even very small things.

"What I am trying to say is that I feel the power of the moon, tonight, and I feel it working on all of us, and if we direct it properly, it can be a beautiful thing."

Mario walked away, and Pussey Rapper, gazing at him, said, "There's a man whose entire life is spent on a stage. I wonder who the true Mario is?"

Genella, in what seemed an obvious attempt to defend both Mario and his observations, said, "Mario is right. In my profession, I always fear *La Luna Stregata*. My girls and I always check the horoscope in the newspapers to find out what's going on and what's going to happen. When I see that the full moon is coming up, I know that I'm going to have a hard time with some of the girls, and I know that some of them won't even show up for work. I haven't yet determined whether the full moon has an effect on our male customers. My gals think it does, but I honestly haven't seen it."

Spinuzzi then said, "Genella, you are biased."

Genella, somewhat hurt, answered, "No one has ever called me prejudiced!"

Spinuzzi laughed. "No, Genella, I'm not talking about minority groups. I'm talking about statistics.

"If you expect something to occur, you are mentally disposed to it and more readily inclined to observe it than you normally would be. You lose your objectivity. This is what it means, in the fields of medicine and science, when somebody says you are biased."

The Pig, visibly disturbed by what Spinuzzi said, made a statement that under normal circumstances would have created *beaucoup* ill-will among Anglo-Saxons. "Spinuzzi, stop playing your fuckin' dumb, intellectual games. We're not talking about fuckin' medicine and science, here. We're talking about the human experience, recorded in practically every human culture. The full moon, whatever the reason may be, makes people more difficult to handle."

All looked in Spinuzzi's direction, and he decided to remain silent. It was a dead-end argument, not worth pursuing.

La Strega was now in full bloom. The tables were full, and people were waiting at the bar to be seated. I figured they had at least a half hour wait. When I'm ready to eat, I have to eat. Waiting ruins the damn meal. Timing and proper rhythm are essential ingredients in experiencing life's beauty. I've always been curious about what the hell people talk about while they're waiting in line for an hour. It has to be a big downer.

As we were about to savor our wine, a middle-aged lady, who evidently spends a lot of time in front of a mirror, walked over to our table and stood behind Miserabile. He couldn't see her, but we did. She tapped him on the shoulder. He turned around and stared at her. There was a blank look on his face.

"Miserabile, evidently you don't recognize me. I'll give you ten seconds."

After plus-or-minus ten seconds had passed, Miserabile remained silent. A good politician doesn't forget names or faces, but it was obvious that he hadn't the slightest clue about the identity of this chick.

"I'll give you a hint," she said. "Think back to 1960, when you were at Fordham Law School."

Nothing clicked.

"Who did you take to the graduation dance?"

Miserabile, now clearly embarrassed, innocently asked, "You? Are you Elsa?"

"No," she replied. "Elsa is my sister."

Miserabile then let out a howl of real joy, most uncharacteristic of his personality, and I mean most uncharacteristic. Maybe at that point in his life, before his marriage and divorce, he was a happier soul.

"*Gesu Cristo, sei tu*, Kathleen?"

"*Si*, it's me!"

He jumped up from his seat, grabbed her, hugged her, and gave her a big, long kiss, right on her smackers. It was good to see a bit of joy in the joyless heart of Miserabile. The boys around the table exchanged glances of sincere satisfaction.

"Kathleen, you've changed. That's why I didn't recognize you. You've developed into a real beauty."

"I'll accept that explanation, even though you're full of shit."

Everyone laughed a laugh of contentment; this surely was a beautiful moment for Miserabile. But, like many such moments in life, it didn't last long.

"Is Robert with you tonight?"

Kathleen paused, and during this brief interlude, her facial expression went from joy to sweet sadness.

"Robert is dead. I really loved that guy, but he left me about six months ago."

Miserabile walked quickly to the table next to us and grabbed an empty chair. He took it over to our table, placed it beside his seat, and said, "Sit down here, next to me."

He then signaled Vinnie and requested the coldest white wine in the house. The brand didn't matter, as long as it was not sweet.

"Am I right, Kathleen? I remember you always ordered this drink. If your taste has changed, tell me. You don't have to be diplomatic with your old friend."

"Nothing has changed, Miserabile. I want to thank you for remembering."

Ever-so-subtle tears came to her eyes, and I wanted to say something to lighten the moment, but decided that there are certain moments in life that shouldn't be lightened. It took its natural course.

Miserabile said, "Would you like to join us for dinner? There's plenty of room, and I mean it. These are my very best friends, and I know they would love to have you join us. Here, try some of my red wine until the white wine comes; it will make you feel better."

Miserabile was now showing the kind side of his personality that I mentioned before, and which he hides so well. People are strange. Why hide kindness?

Kathleen took a healthy gulp of the red wine. Miserabile asked, "How did it happen?"

"It was a fast-growing cancer of the lungs," she said.

"But he didn't smoke, did he?"

Spinuzzi, somewhat irritated, interjected, "Not everyone with lung cancer smokes, Miserabile. The anti-smoking crowd, however, has convinced the public otherwise. They're even trying to convince us that second-hand smoke causes cancer, which may or may not be true, but the evidence certainly is not there. Smoking is like anything else. If you do a little, it won't hurt. If you do more, it may kill. It's a dose response phenomenon."

Miserabile looked at Spinuzzi, as if to say that his remarks, at this delicate point, were way out of order. But everyone knew that Spinuzzi is that way, and the inappropriate remark was overlooked.

Pignachi, forever the priest, asked, "How are you handling this greatest of tragedies, Kathleen? To lose someone you love and who you were together with for so long is tough to handle."

"Father, I am not a Catholic, but Robert was. Though he was a devout Catholic, he never pressured me to join the Catholic Church. He used to tell me that, since I was such a good woman and wife, that God would welcome me at the pearly gates of Heaven, even though I am a Protestant heretic."

The boys smiled at the "heretic" remark.

"But something strange happened to him, which has haunted me since his death. Here he is, a devout Catholic, dying of a dreaded disease, who should be making peace with his Maker. Right? Wrong! I don't want to dwell on the details, but he became a very angry man, and turned against God. He actually cursed Him. Sometimes, when he thought I was out of earshot, he would say nasty things to God, like, 'What, All Powerful One, have I done to deserve this?' or, 'I've been a devout Catholic all my life, and is this my goddamn reward?'

"He said many other things that really bothered me and I think about it almost every day. He refused to see a priest during his final moments, and actually challenged and cursed God, and I fear he may be paying the price."

It was clear that the boys at the table were not prepared for this. This uncomfortable moment came out of nowhere, and was having a profound impact on the tenor of the evening. But the boys are all really softies and empathize with her, even the ones who aren't sure a God exists, let alone a Catholic one.

Spinuzzi said, "Pignachi, how does your God handle Robert's lament?"

"Spinuzzi, sometimes you're a really insensitive man," Pignachi said. If you're referring to Cilea's aria, *Federico's Lament*, it is inappropriate. It is a trivial analogy. We are dealing with a man who knew he was going to lose his life. He had a beautiful wife, both on the outside and the inside, who loved him, and he knew he was going to lose her.

"And I can tell you, my old, sometimes cynical, friend from the old neighborhood, that God fully appreciates that Robert had a right to be pissed-off, and I can assure you that his anger over his fatal condition would not impact in the least on his welcome by God into Heaven."

Pignachi made his remarks with lots of old-fashioned Italian compassionate love, and nobody, not even Spinuzzi, would dare challenge the sincerity of this good man. This wasn't the language of some of these modern, phony, hairspray-using preachers, preaching shit that isn't real while raising lots of money doing it.

But something happened that surprised all of us. Kathleen turned her gaze to everyone at the table, and asked, "Is there a God? Is there a life after death?"

And, surprisingly, we all noticed tears come to Genella's eyes. There were none in Kathleen's. We were all beginning to become a bit nervous. We wished, at this moment, Kathleen had gone to another restaurant this evening.

Mo, always the guy that doesn't pull punches, asked, "Are we about to talk about religion? *Mamma mia,* not tonight! You guys know that we've been through this before, and we've never arrived at a consensus. Kathleen, it's nothing personal, but every time we talk about religion, we lose our tempers, and rarely conclude anything about God and life after death."

Since Miserabile had not yet introduced the dinner guests to Kathleen, she didn't know Mo's name. Miserabile, realizing this, said to Kathleen, "That's Mo, that just spoke. Going around the table, starting at my left, is Pignachi, who's a priest, as you probably know by the collar that he's wearing—by the way, he's Catholic, and not Episcopalian; then, there's the Pig, Spinuzzi, Pussey Rapper, and the mysterious guy, Lorenzo Baccalà, who organizes our yearly events. They're all good guys, Kathleen, but all of us have some screwed-up ideas about what's going on in this life and the life thereafter."

Kathleen, Genella and the boys smiled. Miserabile's remarks eased the tension somewhat. "Father," said Kathleen, "is my Robert in heaven?"

Kathleen went too far with that question. It sounded like a line from a television soap opera. I was a little pissed-off at her. You don't ask questions like this at a restaurant in New York City where wine is flowing and good food being consumed. The ball, however, was once more placed in Pignachi's court, again by a woman. None of us had the slightest idea how Pignachi would handle it. He, however, rose to the challenge. This is, after all, his calling, to help people that need help. And then, he began an almost Shakespearean-like soliloquy about Robert, God and Heaven.

"Kathleen, all these guys around the table have their own opinions. And, believe it or not, mistaken as some of them are, I do respect them. Many, many, and many times in the past, we have discussed whether God exists, and if so, in what way.

"I don't want to go into all of our heady thinking, but let me give you my opinion.

"Of course there is a personal God. Of course there is a Heaven. And, if Robert was the kind of man you say he was, of course he's now in Heaven in the presence of God.

"I can tell you, with the exception of Mo and possibly Genella, that nobody at this table is convinced that there is a personal God, let alone life after death."

Pignachi knew that the boys were very reluctant to discuss their thoughts about God and anything else personal in the presence of

Kathleen. The woman needed hope, and the boys knew it, and wanted to help her maintain her hope.

Pignachi continued, "You see, Kathleen, practically all the people in the world believe that death is not the end of our existence. To be sure, they don't all believe in the exact nature of the afterlife, but they all believe that one exists.

"Now, this isn't a coincidence nor is it the result of thousands of cultures communicating with each other and exchanging ideas. This belief in the hereafter sprung from the inner being of the minds of people themselves. Science cannot explain this phenomenon, and never will. It is beyond reason. The most influential philosopher in modern times, Immanuel Kant—who was not a Catholic—believed that in everyone's mind, there are categories already there, when they're born, and one of these categories tells us that God exists. You said you weren't Catholic, right?"

"That's correct, Father," replied Kathleen.

When she called Pignachi "Father," we all sensed its impact on him. This single word imparted to him a greater obligation than he normally would have felt if she had called him "Pignachi."

We were not surprised at all about this reaction. We had previously discussed the new phenomenon in the United States that has everybody calling everybody by first names, even older people. It's as if one's last name doesn't exist. We don't like it, for we sense that the reasons behind it aren't healthy. There is a loss of respect behind the misguided idea that first-name calling makes us equal, and that being equal is good. Though the boys all have different points of view about life, they all agree that first-name calling is an initial step to becoming a number, and when you become a number, you lose your humanity.

The boys continued to be concerned about the issue of respect, and why it is important. I wouldn't be surprised if the subject popped up later in the evening.

Spinuzzi was about to attempt to rebut Pignachi's condition that a personal God exists, when he looked at Genella. There were still tears in her eyes. Perhaps she was thinking of Rocco. Who knows? But it was Spinuzzi's feelings for Genella, and not for Kathleen, that made him change his mind. He instead said, "Kathleen, though we've all argued in the past, none of us doubt that there is a creator. The universe is a machine, and, if a machine exists, someone or something had to design it.

"Many cultures have different viewpoints about God, and in fact, worship many gods. Moses cut through all the confusion and mysticism by declaring that there is only one God, Yahweh, and that God gave us the Ten Commandments, which are the fundamental ground rules for doing God's will. The Jews, however, never had, and do not have a unified belief on whether there is a life after death. Do you remember the Pharisees and Sadducees in the New Testament? One sect believed in life after death, and the other didn't.

"Then came along Jesus Christ, the Messiah who was prophesied in the Old Testament. Let's not talk about the Trinity, you know, the Father, Son and Holy Spirit—that's another subject for another time, and it does not help you with your concern about Robert."

The doubter, the cynical physician, Spinuzzi, was apparently joining Pignachi to make both Genella and Kathleen feel at ease about the loss of their husbands. The bugger, in his own strange way, was trying to convince the ladies that Rocco and Robert were in Heaven, both alive and well. Remember, Spinuzzi's father was a religious Catholic, and his mother, a religious Jew. He knew both sides of the story better than anyone at our table tonight. He had lived and breathed in both religious cultures. His learning came not only from books but from his emotional involvement, almost on a daily basis, with this eternal question.

"And what did Jesus say?" continued Spinuzzi. "He said that everyone should love each other, and there is a heaven where the good people go after death. What is a good person? Well, Jesus was kind of loose in His definition. He even forgave the thief on one of the crosses next to him at his crucifixion. Was that thief a good person?

"And was Jesus for real? Did he exist? You bet your life! It is inconceivable that so many people could accept his message, if it were not true.

"I think that it is highly probable that Robert went upwards, and not downwards. From what you say about him, he surely was not a candidate for hell."

We were amazed. We knew that Spinuzzi didn't believe what he had just said. He was acting the role of a true physician—always comfort a patient, even if it requires a white lie. Why not?

Kathleen said nothing. The boys said nothing. All of us took another sip of wine. The noise level in La Strega was increasing. Sounds of laughter were everywhere.

Finally, Kathleen said, "Thank you, Father Pignachi, and you, too, Spinuzzi. I do feel much better. My dinner companion tonight is looking at me, and I think he's a little bit unhappy sitting alone. I'll have to leave you, now. Miserabile, let me write down my phone number, and please call me. Okay?"

"Sure," replied Miserabile.

She wrote her number on Miserabile's cloth napkin, and, without another word, walked away. I'm not sure, but I think she was wiggling a little bit more than one would expect.

Mo leaned back on his chair, and asked, "Miserabile, are you ever going to call her?"

Without hesitating, Miserabile replied, "No."

"Why not?" asked Mo.

"Give me a good reason why I should," replied Miserabile.

It wasn't his words themselves that signaled that the conversation regarding Kathleen was now over for the evening, it was the way that they were spoken. I knew this evening was the first and last time that Kathleen would be seen by any member of the gang.

Genella was still a little bit teary. "Spinuzzi," she said, "you lied to Kathleen, didn't you? You don't believe in a personal God, and you don't believe Robert is in heaven." Spinuzzi looked at her. Genella continued, "I hate to say it, but I think she's not an easy woman to live with. Don't ask me how I know. It's those vibrations that women sometimes get.

"What I think happened is that when her poor Robert got sick, she felt sorry for herself, and took it out on him. That's why he got angry with God—not because he was sick, but because God permitted that bitch to torture him."

If this were true, then the boys had really been fooled. Women do this all the time to men. Nature willed it that way.

Spinuzzi said, "Genella, what if you're wrong? Then you've dealt her a dirty blow, because now the guys believe she's a bitch, when maybe she's not."

"I just know," Genella insisted.

The case was closed. The boys believed her. Nobody was going to ask her any more questions about Kathleen.

Genella continued, "Getting back to the question of whether you believe in a personal God, you don't, and what you just said was done to help a lady in distress. This was a kind thing to do."

Spinuzzi smiled a gentle smile, and remained silent for a moment. He sipped his wine, and answered, "I spoke a half-truth, or white lie, you choose the one."

"But are you sure there is no personal God?"

"I'm not sure," he answered.

Pignachi, sensing that Genella was in a bit of a turmoil, entered the conversation. "Genella, I am convinced, in fact, I know, that there is a God in heaven, and I know that good people go there."

Mo added, "Genella, I agree with Pignachi." Mo and Pignachi were using the classic technique known as the argument from authority. In other words, if I say it, it's true. It is the weakest of all logical arguments, regardless of whether something is true or not. But that's not to say it's wrong.

"But the rest of you don't, am I right?" Genella asked.

Miserabile took the lead. "Genella, as we said before, all of us have been through the issue of religion many times, over many years. Do you know what the bottom line is, regarding belief? It's faith. You either have it or you don't. If you have it, you believe in God and the hereafter. If you don't have it, then you are either an agnostic or an atheist. We all agree on these points.

"Now, if you ask, 'Why do some people have faith, and others, not?' the simple answer is that no one knows. Faith comes from the heart, not the intellect.

"Pignachi and Mo have no problem understanding the faith of the common man. They also believe what St. Thomas Aquinas taught: that faith and reason, another way of saying 'religion and philosophy,' are compatible. He argued that if they both deal with the truth, they should not contradict each other. After all, the truth is the truth. The rest of us disagree. We believe that faith is blind, and don't believe it can be supported by reason. That's not to say that it doesn't have tremendous value or truth behind it. We can say the same thing about love—nobody knows why people experience it, and nobody knows how to define it. It's a matter of the heart, which is felt and not defined."

Spinuzzi joined in, "Well-spoken, Miserabile."

There was a lull in the conversation. This frequently happens after we talk about death and life after death. During this lull, I thought of one of my favorite arguments for the existence of heaven. It's called St. Anselm's Ontological Argument.

This guy Anselm was creative. He observed that in practically all cultures there is a belief that some afterlife exists, whether it's in heaven, with a personal God, or somewhere in the stream of universal consciousness. He also noted that people everywhere are not as happy as they want to be and all desire to be happier.

He then concluded that since all people are searching for happiness, it must exist—somewhere. And that somewhere, he concluded, is heaven.

Suddenly, a customer at the table near the restaurant entrance started to sing *Core Ingrato*. This is a passionate Italian song, usually sung by a tenor, about a female lover with an ungrateful heart. The guy's voice was big but ugly. Nevertheless, he was singing with gusto, and we enjoyed it.

When he finished, all of the folks in the restaurant applauded, including our group. There's something about the human singing voice that elevates our mood.

We were curious about this surprising outburst, so I called Vinnie over to ask him what it was all about.

"The guy just got legally divorced and he's happy as a pig in *merda*," he said.

Mo added, "In order for the guy to be that happy, he must have had a miserable marriage. He must have been married to a bitch."

Somewhat irritated, Genella said, "Or he's a son-of-a-bitch who drove his wife up the wall."

Mo smiled and answered, "Could be, could be."

Spinuzzi said, "Maybe she's a bitch *and* he's a son-of-a-bitch."

Miserabile smiled and said, "Could be, could be."

Pignachi said, "Tell me about it. It fills many of my working hours."

Mo said, "Now I'll tell you about my experience with my son. One night I took him out for a drink and dinner. It had just dawned on him that his marriage was *finito*. He really was very, very surprised when his wife told him that she wanted out.

"Pussey Rapper, you have three kids who have gone through a *maledetto* divorce. I've had only one. I don't know about you, but I learned a lot and have come to certain conclusions about modern marriage. It ain't what it used to be, that's for sure. In fact, it's almost the opposite of what it was in the old neighborhood.

"We used to come home and know that our honeybun was there, like forever. Not so today. You never know when a husband or a wife will suddenly, out of the blue, say that they want out. My son said that's what happened to him, poor bastard. He had no inkling that this would happen. Either she hid her feelings pretty well or my son is an idiot when it comes to women.

"I'm hearing more and more about this 'I want a sudden divorce' syndrome. I really can't figure out why so many people are surprised.

Can't they fuckin' see? Do they want it so much that they become blind to the obvious?

"I truly can't figure out my son. When his wife came home that night and asked for a divorce, he fell apart. From what I saw of their marriage, I already knew there was a high probability of divorce. I dropped him a thousand hints to get him ready for it, but the *testadura* did not listen to me. Genella, a *testadura* is a thick head."

"Tell me about it!" smiled Genella. "I knew your friend, Rocco, pretty well."

The boys smiled.

Mo continued, "You see guys, she was a pretty attractive piece of ass. She 'had it,' you know, the way that maybe one out of a hundred gals 'has it.' She also traveled a lot, and had been around. She was a buyer for some big retail clothing chain and used to go to Europe a lot, a couple of weeks at a time, a few times a year.

"I don't know about you guys, but I always thought that I wasn't a bad catch for the right gal. I don't want to go into details but I could sense this by the way the ladies reacted to me. I'm not saying this to pat myself on the back but only to make an important point. God knows how many times I was turned down but, more often than not, the ladies showed at least some interest in me.

"I always, let me repeat, always knew that there was a better man than me out there. But in the old neighborhood, the guys that were better than the other guys couldn't get their wives. One reason it didn't happen was because it was simply forbidden. There was virtually no mobility or freedom to hide. Everybody stayed home, and if anyone did go out, everyone knew where. If you disappeared for an hour or two, it didn't pass unnoticed, and you couldn't do it too often without being seriously questioned.

"Now in those days it was the guys that did the chasing. Sure, when the woman really wanted a guy, she did the chasing, but it wasn't easy. It was subtle and dictated by the culture of the neighborhood. Women didn't go to bars and nightclubs dressed to kill. Hardly anyone went on a dinner date, and when a woman chose and got her man, that was that. It was a forever deal. You guys remember the words at the altar, 'What God has put together, let no man put asunder.'

"My wife and I recently went to the wedding of our friend's daughter. The daughter was divorced once and the groom twice. They had a big wedding with about two hundred guests. The marriage ceremony was conducted by the local female mayor. When the mayor said, 'Until death do us part,' I almost had a stroke. But the idiot bride and two-time loser groom were not at all embarrassed. The whole scene was done in bad, bad taste."

Genella agreed with Mo. "It's as if, in a single generation, class has gone down the tubes."

Spinuzzi said, "You know, Genella, you can't lose something you've never had. I can't define class, but I sure can recognize it. Maybe we're wrong. Maybe class is a relative thing and what is considered class today was shitsville in our generation. Or maybe they haven't the slightest idea of whether class even exists."

The Pig said, "Spinuzzi, you're being the philosopher again, but it's a good point."

"Before you guys get into heavy epistemology and the definition of things, I'd like to finish my story," said Mo.

"You see, if my wife had a traveling job, I'd be jealous as hell, particularly if she's a piece of ass and pecker stimulator, like my daughter-in-law. There she is, with men all day long, and who knows what she's doing at night. Here I am, sitting with my fuckin' finger up my ass, wondering who she's with and what the hell they're doing. Remember what I said, there's always a better man than me out there. And even if the man is not a better man, a woman could give in at a particular vulnerable moment. I know for sure that my daughter-in-law is not in her hotel room every night having room service and watching television and kneeling at the bedside saying her rosary to give her strength enough to fight the temptations of her vaginal secretions.

"I don't know about you guys, but when it comes to my woman, I'm a very jealous man. I would be a very unhappy guy if my wife, beautiful or not, were out overnight, out of reach and out of sight."

"It's a double-edged sword," said Pussey Rapper. "You know the old story that when the cat's away, the mice will play. If my wife were out and about, I would not be at home watching television and saying my rosary before I go to bed. I'd be out and, more likely than not, meeting a girl I'm comfortable with. And who knows what the hell would happen after that. I could possibly become closer and closer to her, both mentally and physically, which is not the best thing, to say the least, for a marriage.

"Mo, you said you always assume that there's a better man than you lurking out there, somewhere, and that's a healthy position to take, when it comes to women. Don't take this personally, but there's always a better woman than your wife out there, too.

"Just imagine having a marriage where both the husband and wife travel. None of us has had this experience, but I'm pretty sure that none of us would tolerate it well. Why the hell should a couple like this be married?

"Genella, what do you think, as a woman?"

Genella remained silent. She's a good listener, and knew that more points of view would follow, and decided to wait before she put in her two cents. She got away with it; nobody put the pressure on her to respond.

Spinuzzi looked at Pignachi. "Pignachi, maybe God said that divorce is *verboten*, but even without the Almighty's marital command, all kinds of civilizations have accepted the reality that marriage is better for society than non-marriage. That's why the tradition of marriage was established.

"Though we still have this tradition, technology is making us more mobile and isolated, attacking the very foundation of a stable marriage. Technology creates too many options in life for people to handle. I don't care what anyone says, the more women men meet without their wives, the more the thing called sex raises its disruptive head—pardon the pun. The same principle holds true for women, although I think, in fact I know, that women are more choosey than men. But still, the more people of the opposite sex you meet, the greater probability there is of eating the forbidden fruit."

Mo then said, "I repeatedly told my son that a traveling woman spelled trouble for his marriage. He called me old-fashioned and reminded me that the world is changing. I then reminded him that, though the world may be changing, human instincts are not. A man, and I'm talking about a real man, cannot tolerate the possibility that his wife is fuckin' around. But guys, my son wouldn't listen, that *testadura*."

Pignachi smiled and said, "Mo, I wonder where your son got his thick head. I know his mother well, and she is a wise, accommodating woman."

The boys laughed. Mo is the most stubborn and strongest-willed member of the gang.

Genella said, "Not all traveling women mess around, Mo. You can't make that assumption."

Mo answered, "I know that, Genella. But the possibility—not the probability—of it happening is enough to make me jealous enough to become a very unhappy man.

"How would you guys handle this situation? About six months after my son was married, his wife took a buying trip to Paris. He called her at eleven at night, European time, to say hello. A guy answered the fuckin' phone. When he asked for her, the guy said he had the wrong room and that the operator made a mistake. Now, that rarely happens these days with modern telephone technology. You always get the right room. He immediately called her back, and the phone in her room rang and rang and rang. She never answered.

"Now that's no definite proof of hanky-panky, but it sure smells to high heaven. He called her back at midnight, and still no one answered. He then decided not to call back, in order to avoid an argument. He couldn't control his emotions at that point.

"He subsequently discovered that she frequently had late dinners with men in her business. He rationalized that this was a necessary part of her job, and I agreed. But I told him that if it were me, this would drive me nuts, and I wouldn't put up with it."

Genella said, "You mean she should give up her career?"

"You bet your ass. She has to do that, if she wants to save her marriage. If her traveling career comes before the marriage, fuck her. Get the fuck rid of her."

"That's called divorce," said the Pig.

"I know, I know," murmured Mo. "That's the hard and shitty part of it."

The Pig suddenly looked shocked. He leaned over and whispered, "Hey guys, look at the corner table, where Vinnie is serving. Isn't that Johnny Varese, the *ubriacone* from the old neighborhood?"

Ubriacone means a lush, or someone who drinks too much. You don't necessarily have to be a drunk to be an *ubriacone*. Johnny Varese was an outright *ubriacone*, but he wasn't a drunk. There's a fine but real line between the two. A non-drunk *ubriacone* maintains control over his life. A drunk *ubriacone* does not.

Ubriacone was a nice guy who never, we believe, read a book in his life. He was powerfully built, like Mo, but not as tall. He was into gambling, but didn't gamble himself. He arranged for the card and craps games, and was the only one to handle the "numbers" game. No one dared tread on *Ubriacone*'s turf. He was the king.

When we were young, *Ubriacone* would periodically meet with some older guys, not necessarily shady characters, but always serious ones, in the local pool room. They would huddle at a corner table, out of earshot of the crowd. It soon became apparent to all of us that *Ubriacone* was somehow involved in the underworld, the Mafia, the Cosa Nostra, the Black Hand, or whatever. He always had a wad of tens and twenties in his pocket, and was by far the greatest benefactor in the neighborhood. In those days, tens and twenties were big-time money. He always treated guys to drinks at the local bar and bought pizzas for the guys hanging around on the corners—which brings back interesting memories.

Small as the neighborhood was, there were about ten corners where the guys hung out that were all culturally distinct from each other. The guys on one corner used to talk primarily about gals or puntang; on the other corner, sports. On another corner, where the older guys were, it was politics, opera and, occasionally, religion.

I used to go from corner to corner, like the wandering Jew, and enjoy the best of the corner worlds. When I asked my father how it is possible to have corners so close together but with unique characteristics, he replied, "Birds of a feather flock together." I've never forgotten that, and it's been helpful to me at times, when I'm trying to figure out what the hell is going on in the world. There's another saying that contradicts this one, claiming that "opposites attract." I've found this to be true of individuals, but not groups. There's little room for opposing points of view among members of the ACLU or Ku Klux Klan, but plenty of room in the bedroom.

Getting back to *Ubriacone*: Though he drank a lot, he hated drunks. In fact, he wouldn't permit drunks to walk the streets of the old neighborhood. Though there were very few, they did pop up once in a while. When one of them left a bar obviously drunk, he would approach them and without saying a word, level the guy with a powerful left hook. Strangely enough, I never saw him use a right cross. Every time it happened, the guy was knocked out cold. Needless to say, within a very short period of time the word got out, and drunks were no longer seen on the street in the old neighborhood.

As time went on and the neighborhood broke up, everyone moved to the suburbs seeking a better quality of life. Later on, we heard on the grapevine that *Ubriacone* had become a big shot in the underworld. He was put in the clinker for a year or two for some minor tax evasion charge. When he came out, he resumed the career he loved.

One night, as he stepped out of his very modest row home for his usual nightly walk, someone approached *Ubriacone* with a shotgun and blew off his head. In one split second, he was gone forever.

The newspapers covered the story in a big way, writing about his life history and his wrongdoings. For some reason, television didn't cover it. The message was that *Ubriacone* was a bad guy, and good riddance to him. To my knowledge, no article ever mentioned how charitable he was. He helped a lot of people with their problems—and I mean a lot. He wasn't a famous Mafia capo, but he had a lot of clout.

This is why Pignachi was so surprised. Sure enough, the guy looked just like *Ubriacone*. I knew we were all thinking the same thing: Someone else, a stooge, had taken the place of *Ubriacone* that fatal night. *Ubriacone* knew he was being set up for a hit and probably invited one of his competitors, who he wished would go away, to dinner that night, realizing full well that when he left his home after dinner, the hit guy waiting for *Ubriacone* to take his routine walk would mistake the competitor for *Ubriacone*. After the hit, *Ubriacone* would go undercover, pretending he was dead, and then try to find out who wanted to kill him. He then would execute a plan to put a hit on that party.

We were all instinctively thinking about this potential scenario, but were also puzzled about why he would be sitting openly in a restaurant with a beautiful chick and without his usual bodyguards. Maybe they were outside, but there should be at least one or two sitting at a table near the door, which is where smart bodyguards always sit. We were looking for these bodyguards, but all the tables were occupied by men sitting with women.

Genella, observing all of us observing, asked, "What the hell is going on?"

I leaned over and briefly whispered the story in her ear.

In a loud voice, Genella said, "Rocco told me about *Ubriacone*!"

Miserabile jumped in and said, "Genella, *state zitta*, keep your voice down. His goons may be sitting right next to us, and in this goddamn day and age, the goons may not only be the men at the tables, but also the chicks sitting next to them. Women are becoming killers just like men. Just watch the television. Spinuzzi thinks this female personality transformation is the reason why there is a female heart disease epidemic in the United States."

Genella didn't answer.

Getting back to *Ubriacone*: We couldn't figure out what to do. One logical option was to do nothing. We could see little good in saying, "Hello, *Ubriacone* How the hell are you? We thought you were dead!" God knows what that would lead to. Perhaps the Feds were in the restaurant watching that night. We could become members of the Feds' list of suspicious characters—forever! On the other hand, this was a moment that one rarely encounters in life, a resurrected murdered Mafia kingpin who was a childhood friend sitting in a corner in a restaurant with a good-looking woman having a good time. *Mamma mia!*

Genella, with a big, warm smile, finally said, "Hey, you big wise philosophers of life. Am I reading you right? You can't you make a simple decision whether or not to say hello to the man who might be *Ubriacone* the great?"

Mo said, "Genella, don't bust our chops. There's a possibility that, if we identify ourselves to this guy, assuming he is *Ubriacone*, we might regret it. It's as simple as that."

Years of experience taught Genella when it was proper to keep quiet. In fact, everyone was quiet until Spinuzzi piped up. "I have an idea."

Everyone had lively curiosity in their eyes.

"I say let's have Vinnie solve the problem. Let's keep Mario out of this, because he has the capacity to fuck things up with his outgoing personality and big mouth."

"*Buon idea*," said Pussey Rapper. "But how the hell is he going to do it?"

"Vinnie can handle it."

I called Vinnie over and explained the problem, leaving out, of course, *Ubriacone*'s occupation. "*Niente problema*," he answered. "I will find out, right now."

We all became a little anxious. We thought Vinnie would take his time, and report to us later on in the evening. When he said he would do it right away, we almost wished we hadn't asked him.

We watched as he approached *Ubriacone's* table. He had the body language of a man on a mission. The couple was laughing heartily, obviously having a good time. Vinnie talked to the man at the table. Suddenly we heard an outburst of laughter. Vinnie shook the man's hand, kissed the woman's hand and then returned to our table.

Talk about anticipation, we were like little kids at a thriller movie matinee.

He arrived at our table with a broad smile on his face. "I have solved the mystery," he said. "The gentleman is not *Ubriacone*."

"Who the hell is he, then?" asked the Pig.

"*Non lo so*," replied Vinnie.

"What do you mean, you don't know?" asked the Pig.

"I don't know who he is, but I do know that he's not *Ubriacone*."

"How the hell do you know?" pursued the Pig.

"Because he's German and can't speak English very well. We spoke in German."

The idea did occur to me that the guy really was *Ubriacone* playing the part of a Kraut. But that was an ephemeral thought, for it was impossible to believe that *Ubriacone* had, in his voluntary captivity, not only developed a German accent but learned to converse fluently in German.

Pignachi then said, "*Grazie tanto*, Vinnie."

Vinnie replied, "*Prego*," and walked away.

"Thank God," said Pignachi.

"Amen," said Spinuzzi.

"*Beviamo*," said Pignachi.

And we did. We had now surpassed our usual evening's alcohol quota by about one hundred percent. I worried that tempers might flair up. There was simply too much controversy in the air to avoid heated debate. I became more alert than ever to head off any controversy that could create ill will. The boys loved controversy, but too much alcohol sometimes leads to negative instead of positive controversy. One must be like an operatic impresario, keeping the flow of the evening's conversation just right in order to have a successful show. I decided to start where we left off.

"Mo," I said, "did your son have any kids?"

"None," replied Mo.

"Is anybody around the table a grandfather?" I asked.

Pussey Rapper was the only guy to raise his hand. I felt that the guys were kind of pissed-off.

Pig then said, "Isn't it goddamn strange that except for Pussey Rapper, here we are, all in our mid-sixties, without grandchildren? This was unheard of in the old neighborhood. And the only one of us that has grandchildren has all divorced children. *Affanculo!*"

That remark confirmed what I thought: Pussey Rapper was not a traditional grandparent, as perceived in the old neighborhood, and I can assure you, he didn't feel like one. Grandparents in the old neighbor not only did not have, but could not conceive of having divorced children.

Pussey Rapper was about to go on the attack. His eyes were set for battle. There's an old Arab saying, "Least said, soonest mended." So I quickly changed the subject.

I was about to ask Mo to continue where he left off regarding his son's travails, but his desire to talk about his son's divorce had dampened.

So I said, "I wonder what the modern bride and groom are thinking about when they're walking down the aisle to become husband and wife. Pignachi, do they ever confide in you? We're talking about a Catholic wedding where the marriage vows are really supposed to bind the couple forever. Imagine being wedded in a civil ceremony by a female justice of the peace. I've been to a couple of those."

Pignachi sighed a truly big sigh, tinged with despair. It was obvious he didn't want to talk about it. He finally said, "I often wonder what the parents, grandparents and friends are thinking. I've spoken to more than a few, and it is a sad situation. The moment of marriage should be one hundred percent joyous. Negative thoughts should have no place on a wedding day. But they are often there. It's sad, my friends." Pignachi said nothing more.

"Pussey Rapper," I said, "you are the battle-scarred veteran of modern matrimonial problems. What's everyone thinking about, when the guy and gal are approaching the altar?"

Pussey Rapper smiled. "I knew this subject would eventually end up in my ballpark, since I'm the guy that's been through the most. I'm not pissed-off at being on the spot, since it is indeed reasonable that you guys should hear from me.

"Where to begin? I've been involved in many divorce scenes. It is like war. It is hell, where everybody takes sides. Every family thinks that its dingbat son or selfish daughter is in the right, and the other spouse in the wrong. The women are the more vicious ones, and they stick together like goddamn glue. In their minds, the husband is always wrong, even though they know that the wife has been screwing the milkman or their husband's best friend. By the way, the latter, my friends, is not a rare event anymore. It's fuckin' sick. But women somehow always place the blame for the woman's infidelity on the husband."

Pussey Rapper isn't a typical emotional liberal. Liberal males almost always take the side of the woman.

Pussey Rapper continued. "Men are a lot more objective and try to place the blame on the responsible person, whether it's the husband or wife, or a member of one family or the other. Women will deny this, but that's the way they are."

The boys turned their eyes upon Genella. She obviously didn't agree with Pussey Rapper, but she also knew that if she objected at that point, her ass would be in big trouble.

"Getting back to your question, I must confess that I don't know, firsthand, exactly what people are feeling while they're walking down the aisle, but I've heard some stories. My son told me about the wedding of one of his buddies from work. It has nothing to do with the couple itself, but with the guests sitting in the pews during the ceremony. As the bride was walking down the aisle, some of the groom's friends sitting next to him were very quietly laughing.

"My son is like his investigative reporter father; he's an extremely nosey person. He leaned his ear toward the giggling guests to hear what they were talking about. They were betting. One of the guys gave two- or three-to-one odds that the marriage would end in divorce within three years. And would you believe it? The bet involved big money.

"At first my son was understandably pissed-off at the bad taste exhibited by those fuckin' assholes. But he's a rational kid and thought it was not unreasonable to assume that there would be a divorce. After all, everyone knows that the probability of staying married is about fifty percent—and, knowing the personalities of the couple, one would not be surprised if the percentages were higher.

"Let me tell you a couple of other depressing stories. A gal about thirty years old went out to dinner with one of her close friends about a week before the gal was supposed to be married. As friends do, they not only talked about the wedding ceremony but also about the marriage and what the bride-to-be expected from it.

"Another one of my sons knows the gal's friend very well. They had a couple of drinks one night, and she told him the story. She was a relatively old-fashioned gal from a Jewish family which had experienced a number of bitter divorces."

Though we were all looking at Pussey Rapper, we were also, by hidden mirrors of the mind, observing Spinuzzi (it's a trick of the Italian trade). His body language showed a subtle change. The word "Jewish" set him off. Don't forget, his mother was a Jew, and a devout one. Spinuzzi has always been reluctant to talk about his Jewish roots, which really pissed all of us off. Maybe tonight, with all the good food, booze and open conversation, we could get him to lighten up a bit and talk about his Jewish experiences.

Pussey Rapper continued. "Well, the bride-to-be was really in love with the guy. You know, 'Goodbye logic, hello brain chemical attraction.' When describing what she wanted from her husband and the marriage, she said things like, 'I want to be able to debate my husband and I want him to help solve my problems,' and 'we must be able to effectively communicate,' and 'I want to be able to be open with him and shout at him when I'm pissed-off,' and 'I want to have babies and have him participate equally in rearing them,' and 'I want him to make me laugh,' and 'I want him to respect me.'

"I can't remember all the other qualifications she demanded from her husband. The fuckin' guy would have to be her full-time psychiatrist and servant at the same time. It seemed to me that a legal marriage contract would be required, to spell out the conditions of his giving and her taking. I repeat, it's pretty fuckin' depressing."

Pignachi knew that Pussey Rapper was hurt and somewhat of a lost soul because of the divorces of all three sons. He spoke from the heart. "The constant theme of the young lady is 'Me, me, me. What can my husband do for me?'" Pignachi said. "That's tough for any man to handle."

Pussey Rapper paused, and then continued, "Despite the fact that all of us around the table differ somewhat in our interpretations of life, I think we all agree—we've talked about this a million times in the past—that the secret to love is giving and not taking. Logically, you'd think it would be taking. You know, get what you want and you'll be happy. But for reasons that are imbedded in the primordial ooze of the mind, selfishness does not happiness make. I think it was the Greeks that believed that the worst punishment a man can ask of God is that God grant him his wishes, the implication being that most of man's wishes are selfish ones that lead to unhappiness.

"Christians and Jews—I don't know about Hindus, Moslems and other religions—hold the belief that giving is one of the great secrets of happiness. But do you know something? I haven't read one article, seen one television show or heard one radio program where they talk about the critical importance of giving. Of course, I'm not speaking about the religious media.

"Now I want to tell a confidential story; something I wasn't going to talk about tonight. I have no problem telling you guys, but Genella is here. Don't take this the wrong way, Genella, but this is a personal story, to be told to my friends tonight."

"I'll leave right now," she said, in a soft, accommodating way.

No one said a word; it was Pussey Rapper's call. Genella gracefully stood up and left the table. She did it with class, and the boys appreciated this.

As she was walking away, Pussey Rapper got up from the table and caught up to her. He whispered in her ear. She smiled, hesitated ever so slightly and returned to the table. Evidently, Pussey Rapper had changed his mind. We didn't know what he said to her, but we were happy he said it. There was little doubt that Genella was now a welcome member of the family, at least for the moment. She brought a lady's touch and wisdom to this table of strong men.

Pussey Rapper began, "One night, after my third son was married, and divorce was becoming more and more common, I took him out to dinner, just the two of us.

"I learned as a kid that it is good for family members to pair off once in a while, to be alone—you know, mother with daughter, father with son, mother with son and daughter, whatever. You learn things about those you love that you would never have learned otherwise. I think it's necessary for family communication, particularly in these times.

"Anyway, we were in a meat mood that night. There's a little restaurant in Greenwich Village that serves suckling pig on the spit. I remember as kids, all of the family loved pork. At least with a whole suckling pig, you can get enough tasty fat to offset the insipid, tasteless pork."

Spinuzzi—the eternal physician—interrupted. "I've got a hot nut against this anti-meat mentality in the United States. It's a long story, but there's absolutely no evidence that meat is bad for you. There is evidence that too much meat, and too many vegetables and fruit are bad for you. But that's another story, for next year's dinner."

By now, alcohol had had its impact, lessening the rules of disciplined discussion.

I interjected, "Pussey Rapper, what did your son say to you, that night, while you two were pigging out on the suckling pig?"

Pignachi and Genella were exchanging visual messages. Perhaps they had more of a feeling than the rest of us did about was going on in Pussey Rapper's mind.

Pussey Rapper continued. "I asked my son what the hell he was thinking when he got married. He appreciated how I said it, laughed, and told me something that, to this day, boggles my mind.

"He said he thought it would be dangerous to his mental stability to give one hundred percent of himself to his bride. If he did, and she later left him, then he'd be up shit's creek. As he was talking, I remember thinking that the bride-to-be had probably thought the same things my son did.

"Then I asked him whether he was considering the financial aspects of marriage. In the old days, the courts favored the woman in divorce cases. Today, they favor the male, but the question of finance still remains. He thought, as one example, that if he put a down payment on a home and put the ownership in both names, she would have the right to half of the value of the home if they divorced. He concluded it was best to keep everything separate. These thoughts all occurred to him while he was walking down the aisle.

"And then I asked him—and I had to do it—if he didn't feel like a real, bona fide traitor, telling the bride that he would be hers, forever, when just a few seconds before he had been thinking about how to handle a divorce.

"He told me that he really was disturbed by it, but he couldn't help it. The thoughts just jumped into his mind. He had thought about those things before, but never dreamed that they would be replayed during the one-minute interval it took him to walk from the vestibule to the altar."

Miserabile, understandably hesitant at first, finally decided to join in the conversation. "Look, you guys, I'm the only divorced one in this group, and I know what it feels like. When I got divorced, it was a difficult thing to do. There's nothing worse than to totally love someone and then lose that someone. I couldn't conceive of even thinking of contingency plans when I got married. 'What if this happens or that happens,' never entered my mind. My commitment was total."

I knew what the boys, and perhaps Genella, were thinking: 'If he was so committed, why did his divorce happen?' But no one wanted to ask that question, because we knew it was the result of a pernicious type of jealousy. If he were jealous in the old days, where male competition was at a minimum, imagine what he would be like today. He made a wise decision. He remained single, and he's paying the price of being alone. Pignachi frequently says that except for priests, God said it's not good for men to be alone. Spinuzzi says that women can handle being alone much better than men. We all agree, and it's good news for women, since men are dying off at younger ages than women. Ninety percent of patients in nursing homes are women.

Things were getting a bit too heavy, and I wished Genella would do something. I decided to invite Mario back, so I called Vinnie over to ask Mario to come to the table. He told me that Mario was helping the chef because of the full house and probably wouldn't be able to come to our table for a while. So I told Vinnie to tell Mario that we were about to continue our sex conversation with Genella. Vinnie smiled a big one, and said, "I'm sure Mario will be here soon. Please don't start until he comes, or my *culo* will be in big trouble."

Everyone laughed. The thick ice was beginning to thaw, and lighter moments awaited us, I hoped.

I was wrong at least for the moment. The discussion of marriage and divorce was not over. Sex would have to wait.

Mo led the way. "You know what else my son said about what these modern guys think about when they get married? He told me that quite a few of the young guys would love to sign legally-binding pre-nuptial marriage agreements, but don't have the balls to do so, for fear that the future bride would blow her stack and walk away. These guys have moved marriage from the bedroom to the courtroom.

"Genella, do you have any idea what the future bride is thinking?"

Genella promptly said, "Yes, I do. And, as always, the woman is way ahead of the man when it comes to things that involve the emotional commitment."

Mo said, "Let me interrupt you, Genella. I totally agree with you that in the old neighborhood it was that way. But I'm not so sure about today. I don't see much difference in the maturity level of young guys and gals today. Which, by the way, bothers me."

Genella answered, "It may look that way, but it ain't. There's no question about it, these modern young gals have the same instincts as the older chicks. The problem is that they can't trust them—their instincts, that is. How the hell can you trust them when we live with all the turmoil we've been talking about all night? These gals have got to be scared shitless to commit themselves.

"I'll tell you what she's thinking. She's also thinking of a possible divorce, and she's indeed thinking about having children. She's thinking she should postpone having her children until she's sure that the marriage won't break up. She knows, despite all the bullshit she reads and hears about, that, with the passing of the years, it's tougher for a woman to find a serious spouse than it is for a man—particularly, as we said before, if the woman has children.

"A man of thirty, forty, fifty, sixty, seventy, and even eighty, has many more options of marriage than a woman of the same age.

Younger women flock to older men, seeking a secure haven. Younger men simply do not flock to older women. Don't you think that the younger women see that there are tons of women in their thirties and forties, many with children, living alone, working to support themselves? Their ex-fuckin'-husbands are either dating or married to younger chicks, and seem to be happy."

Pussey Rapper commented, "Genella, you're not going to like this. One of my sons told me that his friends realize that here, in our country, where bravery and masculinity were always admired, things have changed. In the old neighborhood, masculinity meant taking care of your loved ones and friends by working and putting food on the table and clothes on the backs of your loved ones. That doesn't exist anymore.

"Many of these young guys know they've been on the baby milk bottle all their lives. They've never had to work until their mid-twenties. Even if they're brave, they can't punch a bully in the mouth because they might go to jail. They're forced by these goddamn universities to take courses that teach them that the strong male of the past was a misfit, that men should be considerate and kind, feed the baby, clean the house and treat their women as equals. In other words, as someone said earlier, they should sit down and pee. They've been robbed of their masculinity."

Genella, with fire in her eyes, said, "Well, that's not what I hear from the gals when they're relaxed. They want strong men. Even though they say they want the sensitive type, deep down many women despise them. Though they want the strong guy, they always challenge men and try to beat them down. If the guy gives in, the woman loses respect for him. If the guy doesn't take her shit, and draws the line, then she respects him. Of course it's not always that clear-cut, but that's the basic force behind women and men. It's a duel. I could go on and on. It's a mess out there."

Pussey Rapper looked at Genella in a strange kind of way. "This brings back memories of a night I spent with one of my sons. We had had dinner, and it was late at night. We were sitting in my study, drinking cognac and listening to a tape of many of the great tenors singing the arias that they sing the best.

"He told me something very sad. You guys know my temperament. I'm very flexible and I try to understand and appreciate people's predicaments.

"We were talking about modern marriage, and he mentioned one of the main reasons his buddies want to get married.

"He said, 'They know they're immature and that they've been protected and never had to face the challenges of life as American men did before them. They think that getting married is a way to mature and grow up. It's a way to end their delayed puberty.'"

"Jesus Christ," said Genella.

"*Gesu Cristo*," said Mo.

"Amen," said the Pig.

Pignachi, forever the romantic, said, "I cannot believe this. In all my years, no one has ever said anything like this to me."

Miserabile said, "Pignachi, that's because you're a priest. Can you imagine the groom-to-be coming to you and openly confessing that he wants to get married primarily to be able to grow up and become a real man? That he's already preparing for divorce before walking up the aisle, that he's already tried to figure out ways to get out of the marriage without being financially crippled for the rest of his life, that he cannot fully commit himself to his honeybun because it may become too emotionally unbearable, that he's thinking that his wife is thinking the same thing that he's thinking; that, despite all that shit about how over fifty percent of the wealth in our country is in women's hands and that well over fifty percent are working, women know, deep down that 'it's still a man's world,' that he knows that she's thinking that if the marriage is destined to end, it's better that it happens sooner rather than later, because her options decrease as her age increases, and that it's just the opposite for the man?"

I sensed that, hidden in his comments, Miserabile was harboring memories and thoughts about his first wife. I subsequently learned, as the months passed by, that the rest of the boys sensed it, too. Such is the Italian intuition. There is no need to be trained as a psychiatrist to develop this know-how. It is learned, in the old neighborhood, from the time a child is first able to observe the observable.

It was time for the *pietanza*, or the main course, and I decided to bring this serious discussion to a close and begin a lighter one. I couldn't do this, however, without some type of conclusion. I was about to ask Spinuzzi, who I knew would have thought it through thoroughly, but changed my mind. I asked Miserabile instead.

"Okay, you guys," I said. "Let's wrap this thing up and go on to other topics. I think the best way to do this is to compare how people perceived marriage in the old neighborhood as compared to today. Miserabile, sum it up in less than five minutes."

"It will take me much less than that," responded Miserabile. "In the old neighborhood, when you got married, it was forever—and it was! Because of this, you gave yourself totally to the marriage bond. You never thought to prepare yourself for the possibility that the marriage wouldn't work out. Because of this, you tried harder, much harder, to make it work. And that's why you see married couples celebrating their thirtieth, fortieth, and fiftieth wedding anniversaries. Sure they've had problems, but they worked them out."

"Amen," said Pignachi.

"Amen," said Genella.

"Time for the main course," said Spinuzzi.

Everyone laughed, and from the corners of their eyes, they saw that Mario was watching. He knew it was *pietanza* time, and he and Vinnie once more came to our table.

La Pietanza

"Tonight, my good guests, I have prepared *straccetti*, the traditional Roman dish, for you. I'm sure most of you have had it, or something like it, when you were kids, but probably didn't know it was called *straccetti*.

"Do you know what *straccetti* is, Genella?" asked Mario.

"Rocco loved *straccetti*, Mario," said Genella.

"I am happy that Rocco loved *straccetti*, Genella. I would be even happier if you love *straccetti*," said Mario.

"I love *straccetti*," answered Genella.

"Mario," Spinuzzi said, "you will be pleased to know that we all love *straccetti*."

"I hate *straccetti*," said Miserabile, "and I can't eat it."

Mario's face paled. He wanted to please everybody.

Genella, trying to soften the blow to his feelings, said, "How can you hate *straccetti*? There's nothing to hate!"

"I agree," said Miserabile.

Genella pursued. "But you just said you hated it."

Miserabile answered, "I wasn't telling the truth. I just wanted to shake Mario's apple cart a little, so he doesn't always take us for granted."

Mario smiled and said, "I may get even with you tonight, my friend. Wait until I bring the unexpected plate tonight. You really might hate it, but for reasons I will explain later on, I believe we should all try it."

Mario was truly an expert. He piqued our culinary curiosity, which is a wonderful thing to experience.

The Pig asked Mario to tell us how he prepares his *straccetti*."

"It's probably a little different than the others you've had. I cut the steak into little slices. I put some good olive oil and lots of fresh garlic in the pan over a low flame and then add the steak. I wait about a minute and then add one-third cup of red vinegar. Please note that I do not recommend balsamic vinegar, but good old-fashioned red vinegar. This country is going bananas over balsamic vinegar. It's really wonderful, but it has its place, and it shouldn't be used every time a recipe asks for vinegar.

"Anyway, if you really like vinegar, you can add a little more. *Si giocca al orecchio.* If you don't like vinegar, then add a healthy cup, even a little more, of red wine. Some of my friends tell me they use both red vinegar and red wine. I've never tried it, so I can't recommend it. I cook it for almost ten minutes, then I add *crescione* to the frying pan and mix it up."

Genella asked, "What's *crescione*?"

Spinuzzi said, "Does anyone know what *crescione* is?"

Pignachi raised a hand. He said, "I know what *crescione* is."

Genella couldn't stand it any longer. "All right, already. I'm dying to know. Pignachi?"

Pignachi replied, "Watercress."

Genella said, "I don't know anyone who uses watercress in their cooking."

Mario said, "That's good news. That means you have a lot to learn, and there's nothing like beginning to learn about cooking. Do you like to cook, Genella?"

Genella said, "It's none of your business, Mario."

Spinuzzi said, "Genella, by our annual dinner rules, you must answer the question unless there's a compelling reason not to."

Mario said, "I withdraw my question."

Genella said, "Yes, I love to cook."

Spinuzzi said, "You're truly a beautiful woman."

Miserabile said, "But a difficult one."

I said, "What else are you serving tonight?"

Mario said, "A light *insalata* and a special dish that you don't find in Italian restaurants. In fact, you probably can't find it in any New York restaurant."

Genella, now full of piss and vinegar, asked, "Does its rarity make it good?"

"Beautiful lady, that's for you to decide."

There was now little doubt around the table that Mario was very comfortable with women. The fact that he never married is probably a reflection of too much female know-how.

I decided to end this banter and get to the point. "What is this special dish?"

Mario answered, "Turnips!"

Genella said, "Do turnips go with *straccetti*?"

Mario said, "I don't know; I've never served them together. But we will soon find out! Do you see the elderly gentleman at the table in the corner?"

He nodded in the direction of the table of the *Ubriacone* look-alike. Our pants almost dropped. I can't speak for Genella's skirt.

"That man is from Germany, and he loves Italian food. But he has been away from home a long time, and naturally, he misses the taste of the food of his country. So he called me yesterday and asked me if I could prepare him some turnips. I told him that I had prepared it many times. You see, one of my uncles married a lady of Italian-German descent. She was from Trento, a city in the north of Italy, near the Austrian border. And she used to cook the best turnip dish that I ever had. It's truly *meraviglioso*, a knock out.

"I told him that I would cook it for him, tonight. And because it's such a rarity, as Genella says, I thought it would be an interesting dish for you to have tonight, too, even if it doesn't quite go with *straccetti*. *Sono un uomo molto fortunato*. How lucky can a guy be? Such an unusual group, you are. And here is Genella, *una vera donna senza dubbio*."

"Why do you think I am a real woman? What does that mean to you? I'm curious, Don Mario."

I could see that small alarms went off in the minds of the boys when Genella spoke the word "Don"—it was a confirmation that she was really interested in this guy. And we all suspected that it might be more than a casual interest.

181

Also, we all knew that Mario sensed the same thing. But he was no idiot. He knew that if he behaved like a *rimbambito stupido*, she could easily change her mind and consider him a low-life not worthy of her attention or affection.

But Mario was a smart guy. The opposite would occur, too, and we all sensed that Genella knew this. The second Genella-Mario round was about to begin.

Mario turned to me and said, "The restaurant is now under control. All the guests have arrived and most of their orders are being prepared.

"I am now making a request, not in the Arab style that I usually use by simply suggesting it. I will now be like my German guest in the corner, and be direct. I would like to join you for the rest of the evening. I have much to learn."

This was my decision to make, not his. Normally, I would be uncomfortable with it, for Mario's presence could either elevate or ruin the evening. It would be risky. Though I knew that sex and Genella were on his mind, I believed that he was really sincere in wanting to join us. Guys who run restaurants have very little free time and have few moments to talk to others in an open way.

I decided that his company was worth the risk. He and Genella were the two most open people at the table and that was supposed to be an essential characteristic of our annual dinners. To be honest, I also knew that if I rejected his request, it was highly probable that an offended Mario would make life miserable for us for the rest of the night.

I said, *"Perché no?* Please join us. Your food has made us happy, and it would also make us happy for you to share in our appreciation of it."

I suddenly realized that I was talking the talk of *The Godfather*, and wondered if I sounded like a horse's ass. But do you know what? *Me ne frega.* I didn't give a shit. Such is one of the positive behavioral effects of alcohol.

Mario sat down and there was a brief period of silence and uneasiness. It didn't last long. Pignachi said, "If you guys are ready to talk about sex now, please feel free to do so. I'm not going to excuse myself."

At that moment, Vinnie arrived with the *straccetti*, turnips, *insalata*, four bottles, would you believe, of a red wine and one bottle of white. Pig asked Vinnie for some ice to put in his wine glass. Vinnie asked if there was a problem with the wine. The Pig said it was good, but not cold enough. I thought of Alexis Lichine, the great American oenologist who, many years ago, had his own vineyard in France. He was married to the beautiful actress, Arlene Dahl. He once said that Americans were born with a refrigerator in their mouths. What he meant is that Americans drink and eat too many cold things.

I remember when I used to go to Europe in the 60s and 70s, it was difficult to find a bar or restaurant that carried ice cubes. Most Europeans drank things at room temperature. Things have definitely changed now. Our neighbors in South America are currently like the Europeans used to be, but things will also change there.

I could see that Vinnie was disappointed at the Pig's request. If the Pig were a billionaire and asked Vinnie for ice in his wine, Vinnie would smile and excuse him for it, because all billionaires had the right to be eccentric. But since the Pig was probably not even a one-hundred-thousand-aire, he didn't have that right—an example of human thinking that defies logical explanations.

As the impresario of this great evening, I knew that Mario and Genella's preoccupation with sex would always be on the guys' minds and could distract them from the evening's conversation.

Now that Mario had joined us, I decided it was best to get to the subject of sex immediately, though I wasn't sure how to get started. I didn't want Genella and Mario to monopolize the discussion. But God is good. He sent me a coincidence. By the way, everything that I was thinking happened in the brain within a few seconds. Can a computer ever match that type of thinking? An interesting question, indeed.

A gal in her forties with a pretty good figure and a very tight dress waltzed by our table and stopped to greet the folks sitting in front of us. Her dress was very low-cut, and her silicone breasts were in full view, big and symmetrical, not to be ignored by men that are still interested. She bent over to kiss the people at the next table. When she did this, her tits almost overflowed the confines of the dress and her hemline rose to about six inches below her pubic zone and bordered on her ass. She looked like a "hoochie mama"—one of those fleshly, sensual, busty Hispanic gals in Florida that let it all hang out. In South Beach, Miami, a "hoochie mama," is young, in her twenties, maybe early thirties. This gal was in her early forties. Nonetheless, she looked like she knew a lot about orgasms, and did a good job making them happen, despite the fact that she was over-the-hill.

I decided to initiate the subject of sex by asking the boys questions. Hopefully, Genella and Mario would tactfully join in.

"*Mamma mia!*" I said. "That's the type of woman I can be with in the sack all night, provided she's not a dingbat. She's really got it. She's got that sensuality that Tony Soprano's car salesman gal has. She knows how to turn a man on by her body language and the look in her eyes.

"But I have one problem, my friends: It's my pecker. The best scenario would be to take her to dinner and simply observe her throughout an evening of good conversation, food and drink. We should drink only enough to really enjoy the moment and place it on an upper level.

"But now the problem: When I have more than two drinks, it kills my pecker!"

Genella giggled and said, "That's normal. Don't worry about it."

"What do you mean, 'Don't worry about it?' Certainly, I worry about it. Don't forget, it's all about the orgasm, and without the orgasm, it's not the same thing."

Genella said, "You're right. You are definitely right. I understand."

I continued, "Don't get me wrong. Some of the most beautiful moments that I've had with women were at lunch or supper, where the give and take of body language and verbal language was beautiful, but there was no sex. But it wasn't platonic just because sex wasn't involved. It was like if I made a move on the woman to take her to the sack for orgasm sex, the beautiful moment would have been ruined, I can't explain why. Mario, have you ever experienced something like that?"

"A few times, my friend. I know what you are talking about and few people have ever talked about this, let alone explained it.

"Genella," he asked, "have you ever experienced anything like that?"

"A couple of times," she replied. "They were really beautiful moments that, in a funny kind of way, can never be repeated at such a high level with the same man. The ladies who work for me usually talked about this kind of relationship—lunch or dinner with nice guys—after they had experienced a session with a guy that behaved like an animal. These animal guys, we could do without. Thank God there aren't many of them, but our establishment sees about two or three a week—enough to make you appreciate better scenarios."

This was Mario's opportunity to get details. Believe it or not, I don't think the main reason for his curiosity was to get verbal sexual highs. I really believe he was curious for curiosity's sake.

He said, "Genella, tell us some things that the ladies enjoyed— just a couple of examples, in order to give us the flavor."

"All right," said Genella. "Why not? We're all here to learn, right?"

"Right," said Spinuzzi.

"Right on," said the Pig.

"*Sempre Avanti*," said Mario.

"Amen," said Miserabile.

"*Un brindisi*," said Mario. "Let's toast to the remainder of the evening. I must warn you that I will mainly listen and not offer many opinions. I am sorry about that, but I am a student among the teachers." I can tell you that all the boys hoped that this would be true, but they had already read the guy; he simply cannot stay quiet. The strategy would be not to stop but to limit his participation in a way that was hopefully productive.

"I'll now give you four or five examples of what both my girls and clients enjoyed together.

"There was one big shot high up in the government of a big country in Europe. He kept a gal in New York City. When he came to the Big Apple, he would take his girlfriend to our place. One of our ladies joined them. Both ladies put on black stockings with red garters, and high heels. They then dressed him up like a girl with high heels and everything else. They also put a lady wig on him. He's a guy that obviously didn't prefer blondes, because he always asked for a black wig with long hair. Both gals took turns spanking him and he jerked off while they were spanking him."

Mario asked, "How do you masturbate when someone is hitting you on the *culo*?"

Genella replied, "Use your imagination, Mario."

She continued. "A regular customer of mine used to live at the Waldorf Astoria. It was Halloween, and he asked me to arrange a party for him. I invited six gals to dress up in various Halloween costumes. In situations like this, gals frequently take drugs to get rid of their inhibitions. Incidentally, there is little doubt that most ladies of the night prefer *ménage a trois*, usually two girls and a guy; more than that usually ruins it.

"This guy loved big breasts, and he loved to watch the gals rubbing against each other and doing cunnilingus. While the gals were kissing each others' you-know-what, he would walk over to the gal with the biggest breasts, jerk off, and come on her breasts."

"Pardon me, gentle Genella, but I don't understand this man," said Mario. "Why did he use his hands instead of asking one of the women to use her hands?"

Genella looked a little bit confused and amused. She thought that this Mario guy was either pulling her string or was a bit naïve.

She said, "I never ask these customers what's going on in their minds."

"Do you guys want to hear a couple more stories?" asked Genella.

"Go right ahead," I said.

"There's a couple that were regulars. They used to come to our place twice a month, in the afternoon. She had big tits, and loved to be with gals that have big tits. We always had two big-breasted women for them.

"They would watch sex videos, and while the gals would do cunnilingus to his wife, he would masturbate. The gals would take turns helping him masturbate. After his wife came a few times, then he would come.

"I'll tell you two more, then call it quits. There were a couple of guys who liked to hear stories about how one of the gals would go to buy a dress and the sales lady would touch her and make a play for her. The guys would either masturbate themselves or they would have the gal telling the story do it for them.

"A high roller used to come, about once a month, with his wife. She was always dressed to kill. One of our gals would hold hands with her, caress her and kiss her, while another of our gals would beat him with his own belt. He would jerk off during the beating."

"*Mamma mia*," said Mario. "Such complicated sex. Didn't anyone do it the old fashioned way—you know, like the animals do on television shows?"

Genella laughed. "Many times, Mario, but that was straight sex, and we're not talking about that tonight."

Mario said, "What were some of your favorite situations, *cara mia*?"

"I believe it is out of order for me to discuss my preferences tonight," answered Genella.

Mario, a guy that never quits, then said, "Genella, tell us just one, and then the quiz is over."

All the boys looked at each other. I knew they were all thinking that this guy Mario has balls and is a curious son-of-a-bitch who may be asking for trouble. But we were all, to be honest, just as curious.

Genella grabbed her glass, lifted it to her lips and finished it off. For reasons that I cannot explain, that act and the look in her eyes were disturbing. These were signals that she was losing her feelings of pleasant relaxation and conversation, and instead seriously concentrating on unpleasant sensual moments. A potentially negative scenario was on the horizon, and I had to do something about it.

But before I could put my thoughts together and make a move, she said, "Though I don't do it anymore, I used to enjoy getting involved in certain types—and I mean real selective ones—of high-class domination. It was not so much the physical kind, but kind of a sexy, mental kind.

"I only did it with the very strong men, like Mo. They could walk away from it and not let it bother them."

I was right. Genella had crossed the Rubicon and made her first and hopefully her last major error at the annual dinner. She had just pushed the sex subject too far in the wrong direction by choosing Mo, the most private man at the table.

Silence reigned. No one said a word, simply because no one knew what to say. I looked at Mario and observed that he hadn't caught on. It was probably because he didn't know the personalities of the boys, particularly Mo.

Strangely enough, I had a funny feeling that his feelings were hurt. Could it be that it was because Genella correctly mentioned Mo as the strong male, and not Mario? We shall never know, because Mario, being what he is, would never admit it.

Everyone was now looking at Mo, who was looking intensely at Genella. We did not observe one blink of his eyes. Mo wasn't pissed-off. It was more than that. He was offended—big time!

Being pissed-off doesn't necessarily require a counter-attack, but being offended does, particularly in the old neighborhood.

The silence and the staring continued. It was obvious from Genella's facial language, that she knew she had fucked up. For the first time tonight, she didn't appear truly sure of herself.

Mo leaned forward and with a voice that commanded attention, said, "Genella, you are the lady of my good friend, Rocco. If you were not, I would throw you the fuck out of here. Listen, baby, you can talk this way to whomever else you want, but not to me. Do you fuckin' understand?"

Genella remained silent. As we had observed before, she knew when to keep her mouth shut. But Mo's anger was visibly beginning to skyrocket, and we all feared that he was about to further reprimand her and ask her to leave. Someone had to stop this, and, as usual, it was Spinuzzi.

"I don't know why, but I'm reminded of Xanthippe, the wife of Socrates," he said.

The Pig decided to join in and lend a helping hand. He added, "I didn't know Socrates was married. I don't remember reading that."

Pussey Rapper joined in. "Socrates may have been versed in the ways of the world, but he certainly didn't understand women."

Miserabile, the student of history, added, "How can he be wise in the ways of the world, when the fuckin' weirdo committed suicide?"

Spinuzzi continued, "Let me tell you about Xanthippe. She was a real cunt. But, on the other hand, maybe she had no choice but to be a cunt because she was married to a weirdo. I guess it's like the proverbial chicken and egg. Which came first?

"Well, anyway, one day they had an argument. She threw him out of the house, and he went down and sat on the stoop. Xanthippe got the garbage can, leaned out of the window and emptied it on poor Socrates' head. He looked up and came forth with the famous saying, 'After the thunder comes the storm.' And he was right. You always pay the price!"

The boys were doing a good job trying to lighten up the moment.

Spinuzzi added, "Speaking about paying the price, let me tell you something that happened to me during the Vietnam War.

"I was a hot clinical research doctor, and was investigating some interesting new drugs, when I received a letter from President Lyndon Johnson. It was a nice letter, but the basic message was that I was drafted, and I that had better get my ass to Fort Sam Houston in San Antonio, Texas.

"Well, when I got to Fort Sam Houston's training camp, I met some of the other drafted physicians. We all thought there was a reasonable probability that we would be killed in combat. I was standing in line to register and a guy behind me asked me a question, I've forgotten what it was. But it started a brief conversation between us. He was a nice guy, and we wished each other luck, which meant serving our military time without being killed or maimed by the Viet Cong or a Chinese nuclear bomb, let alone malaria or some other infectious disease.

"We had a choice of staying on the military base or getting our own lodging. Well, I remembered what the poet-philosopher Santayana once said: 'Whatever are the reasons that we exist, it is a privilege to experience it and we should make the most of it.'

"So I decided to make the most of it, and signed in at the fanciest motel in the area, Howard Johnson's. I got the key from the front desk and, as I was unlocking the door, I sensed someone behind me. I turned around and saw a man unlocking the room across from mine. And do you know who it was? It was the guy I'd met in the sign-up line at Fort Sam Houston.

"Well, he turned around and we both laughed. This was more than a coincidence. Perhaps God was trying to tell us something and wanted to hook us up.

"We decided to go out for dinner that night, and did so about seven or eight times during training camp. He had a keen mind and understood much of what makes people tick. He was a psychiatrist from one of the great institutions in our country, Yale Medical School.

"To complete the series of coincidences, everyone in our group went to Vietnam, except for me and him. And, would you believe it, we both ended up in the same U.S. Army Medical Facility, he in the psychiatry department, and I in the drug research one.

"Now, the point of my story: The guy had a constant mantra. When we talked about the pros and cons of doing certain things in this life, he said, 'You always have to pay the price when you do something you want to do. If you want to become a doctor, you give up the time to enjoy the many pleasures of youth. If you want to be a leader, you can't talk to anyone about your problems and insecurities. If you lie and cheat to get what you want and get away with it, you have to live with a guilty conscience. You always have to pay the price.'

"And he was right. When I used to cut military classes because they gave me *agita*, I felt better, but when the chiefs found out, they gave me a hard time, which made my *agita* come back. In other words, I paid the price.

"When he and I used to eat and drink a lot, and have a wonderful time, we frequently woke up the next morning with a headache, indigestion or both. He would then invoke his mantra that one always paid the price. If you want pleasure, be prepared for the inevitable compensatory pain.

"One night just before the end of training camp, we went to fairly good French restaurant and decided to pig it out. At that time we were convinced that we were going to be shipped out to Vietnam. After a couple martinis, we drank two bottles of the great French white burgundy, Corton Charlmagne.

"We got on the subject of sex, and he waxed philosophic. He was not only speaking as an analytic psychiatrist, but as a normal man, subject to the influence of hormones and other natural substances that make us what we are.

"He spoke about a patient and about the male and the institution of marriage. He said, as we all know but try to hide, that man is naturally polygamous. When I brought up the subject of polyandry, where women have multiple mates, he dismissed this as an uncommon phenomenon. When I reminded him that it commonly happens in certain minority groups in the U.S., he responded that there are exceptions to every rule.

"Getting back to his patient. He was a middle-aged male who was sexually vigorous. His middle-aged wife had lost interest in sex, not one hundred percent, but enough where she had ceased to be interested in playing the role of the sexy butterfly. She would consent to sexual acts because of his needs, but she did not encourage them.

"Then he met this attractive young chick who had the hots for him. She was used to weak modern pretty guys who used blow-dryers and read clothing ads for men in magazines.

"To make a long story short, she finally gets him in the sack, and he really likes it. She'd been around, and she has a lot of sexual know-how.

"Well, what happens? He's happy as a pig in shit when he's with her. Remember, he's a nice guy and he loves his wife. So when he goes home he feels guilty. The more he sees the young chick, the more guilty he feels when he goes home; and the more guilty he feels, the less pleasure he has with the young chick.

"He was paying the price for his sexual fling, and, according to my friend, many Americans are paying the price of their increased freedom to follow their pleasures."

Pussey Rapper said, "I agree with Schopenhauer and Freud."

Mario said, "I know about Freud, but who the hell is Schopenhauer?"

"Schopenhauer was a brilliant but pessimistic philosopher. He never married, and probably never got laid. He lived alone and he hated his mother. When he approached middle age, he fell in love with a teenager and wanted to have an affair or marry her, I don't remember which one. The young lady was repulsed by this guy—so much so that when he touched her she immediately withdrew.

"The poor guy just couldn't handle women and sex. He got himself a dog as a companion, and I think he died before the dog. But the son-of-a-bitch was a keen observer of what goes on in life. He wrote that sex is the driving force behind all behavior, from marriage to business careers to politics. He believed it was vicious but necessary in order for the individual and mankind to survive. Spinuzzi, as your friend would probably say, with sex you always pay the price."

Spinuzzi added, "Philosophers and artists almost always have problems with sex. Francis Bacon, one of the keenest analysts of human behavior, married a teenage girl when he was approaching middle age in order to get her dowry.

"The modern philosopher, Bertrand Russell, fell in love with a lady and wrote her love letters. The guy was sexually off-the-wall, and extremely inhibited. You knew, by reading these letters, that he couldn't say to her, 'Come on, baby, let's go to dinner and make merry.' One can guess that he relied on hand relief and not on the sexual act itself."

With tongue in cheek, I asked, "Spinuzzi, what do you mean by 'hand relief?'"

He answered, "Ask Genella," and continued. "The sex life of artists and philosophers is frequently one of celibacy and perversion, and normal sex is uncommon. Renoir was one of the few happily married artists. Aristotle, unlike Socrates, was a happily married man, too. By the way, he probably was a physician."

The Pig jumped in, "I know about Freud and his feelings about sex. Yes, he did agree with Schopenhauer, that sex drives all. He wasn't, however, just talking about screwing, but all the factors involved in the relationships between men and women."

We all observed a broad smile on the face of Miserabile—a rare event indeed. He said, "The power of sex reminds me of my early days as a politician. Some of the members of my congressional subcommittee took a trip to France to meet with some of its leaders to discuss certain economic problems between our two countries. One of the members knew a very famous hero of the Middle East who lived in Paris. The Congressman and I met the hero for dinner at a little bistro at Montmartre. It was a lovely night, and the charming square was full of life.

"There were a few pretty girls at the restaurant, and we could not help but take notice. The hero smiled and told us that these pretty girls reminded him of an experience of his youth, when he had an affair with a very pretty gal.

"She lived in a village about ten miles from his home. There were many large hills separating their homes. One night, he received a phone call from her. She told him that she would be alone until about midnight, when her parents would return.

"He didn't have a car that night, but found a bicycle in the garage. He jumped on his bike, full of piss and vinegar, and raced over the hills to her home in no time flat.

"She was waiting for him in a sexy outfit with a bottle of wine in her right hand, a sexual symbol that she was ready to go. And so they did. He had a wonderful time for a few hours.

"He heard the clock strike eleven, and decided that it was best not to take a chance and wait around any longer.

"He kissed her goodnight, jumped on his bike and headed home. He told us that it was the longest journey of his life. He huffed and puffed and could barely make it over the hills. In fact, he thought he wouldn't make it, that night. When he finally got home and into his bedroom, he collapsed. But he swore to himself that any time he had sex in the future, the pleasure of the sexual act would never be followed by unpleasant moments. He told us that sex was too powerful and beautiful a thing and that it had to be nurtured and respected or one would not appreciate it to its fullest.

"We all laughed, ate well, and wondered about life. Toward the end of the meal, he became somewhat introverted, and withdrew from the conversation. I liked the guy, and had no problem asking him what was bothering him.

"He said, 'Do you know what? I found out later that this young lady was a lesbian. I can't figure it out. We had a wonderful time. She responded the way most normal passionate women that I've met respond. But she's a lesbian, and I felt sorry for her.'"

The Pig, somewhat irritated, said, "Why the hell did he feel sorry for her?"

Miserabile replied, "I told you, because she was a lesbian."

Pig answered back sharply, "Why should that fuckin' womanizer feel sorry for her? One could make the argument that the fucker should feel sorry for himself."

The boys and Genella stiffened. It was obvious that a sensitive nerve had been touched. I knew that all the boys were convinced that the Pig is a homosexual. Whether he is bisexual and enjoys the company of women is something we never did find out.

Because he treated the subject of homosexuality in such a forceful way, it demanded follow-through. I decided, without hesitation, to pursue the subject in a very brief and somewhat indirect way. As you know, this is the style I use to avoid subjects that bring more pain than light in the exploration of truth. My strategy failed.

I said, "Speaking of homosexuality, it's big-time, now. As in the olden days of Rome, they're coming out of their closets. I'm not saying this in a pejorative way, but only to say that they are all over the place trying to become part of the mainstream of American culture."

Trying to be strictly objective, I continued, "You know that different societies at different times in their history have treated the homosexual issue in different ways. I…"

The Pig interrupted. "No fuckin' shit. Brilliant observation! Let me write it down."

Under the influence of alcohol, the Pig was beginning to get out of hand, and only strong Mo could put the lid on this boiling pot. We knew it and Mo knew it.

With a formidable aura, Mo virtually commanded, "Pig, cool it. If you can't talk about the subject without losing your cool, then keep your fuckin' mouth shut."

This was the second crisis of the evening, and both involved Mo. It's a curious thing how conservative minds have an innate capacity to judge when things are getting out of hand and know when to apply the brakes. I think it was former Senator Daniel Patrick Moynihan, a liberal, who made this observation regarding conservatives and their concern for freedom. It seems that modern liberals have the opposite mentality.

The Pig knew that Mo was right, and he remained silent—which was not good. Not entering the homosexuality discussion would isolate him from the group. But good old Spinuzzi got things going again. "I had a homosexual experience, once. Does anyone want to hear about it?"

Genella, her eyes sparkling, was the first to reply. "I'd love to, Spinuzzi."

Trying to move the conversation as far away from the Pig as diplomacy would permit, Spinuzzi pursued the issue with Genella. He said, "I'll tell you what, Genella: If you tell me about one of your homosexual affairs in general terms, I'll tell you about mine, in detail."

"I just can't do that," answered Genella.

"Did you ever have one?" pursued Spinuzzi.

"Yes," said Genella, "but I can't talk about this, tonight."

Her remarks definitely left the door open; she would be inclined to talk about it another time, but definitely not now. Miserabile said, "Spinuzzi, leave Genella and the rest of us out of this. You made the statement. It's your ball. Tell us what happened!"

Spinuzzi answered, "Are you really curious, Miserabile?"

Miserabile answered, "You bet your ass, I am, and so are the others. Don't forget, everybody was curious in the old neighborhood. Gossip was one of the mental fuels that kept everyone going."

Everyone smiled except the Pig, but the intensity of his facial expression, though still there, had diminished. I knew that the homosexuality issue would not go away from the evening's conversation, and I feared that the Pig might crack up at some point in time. Though things heated up, thank God it didn't happen.

"When I was in college," Spinuzzi began, "I had no college buddies, nor did I date college girls. It's a long story, but that's the way it was. My friends were the working guys and gals who were generally four or five years older than I.

"There was no postponed puberty syndrome with my friends. Nobody supported them. They had to work to earn their way in life. And that gave most of them a quality of toughness that I like.

"Anyway, I used to meet these guys every Friday night at a local bar where we drank beer and threw darts until closing time, which was about midnight.

"Now, you've got to appreciate that this was a tough young group of working-class guys, so when a middle-aged, well-dressed gentleman entered the bar one night, everyone noticed and wondered who the hell he was.

"He ordered a round of beer for everyone in the bar, and though it is hard to explain, that was the tip-off that this guy was a queer. As you guys know, in the old neighborhood queers were not tolerated unless they were extremely discreet.

"Speaking of the word, 'queer,'" Spinuzzi continued, "do you remember some of the other words we used, like 'dago,' 'kike,' 'harp,' 'nigger,' 'spic,' 'limey,' and all the rest? They certainly ain't politically correct, today."

"Spinuzzi," Mo said, "I am assuming that some type of homosexual episode happened between you and the well-dressed man, which was politically incorrect in those days, but might be considered politically correct, today."

Spinuzzi laughed, picked up his wine glass, and finished off about a third of a glass. I noticed that, in order to protect the Pig's sensitivities, he took careful note not to direct the discussion at him.

"It was not only very politically incorrect, but a very dangerous act. If you made an obvious move on one of the boys, you risked being punched-out and beaten-up.

"It's funny, though we talked about it, we never knew of a homosexual lady in the old neighborhood. I haven't the slightest idea what happened with these ladies, if anything at all. We knew who the fags were, but they were discreet and kept their activities hidden.

"Anyway, that night, I was hot at darts. Generally speaking, those guys were much, much better than I was, but that night I was hitting the bulls-eye like never before. When you're hot at darts, you drink more. And when you drink more, you pee more.

"Well, I went to the john just after I hit two corks out of three darts. There were two urinals in the john. As I was finishing my *pisciata*, the well-dressed guy came in the john, reached for my pecker, and shook it. Now, if he had done that to anyone else in the bar, they would have beaten him mercilessly, and the guy knew it. But, except for a couple of times when I had little choice, violent acts are not part of my nature, and that son-of-a-gun had the sixth sense to know it. He had been around and could read the cast of characters extremely well."

Genella, still emboldened by the martini-wine effect, said, "Don't be modest, Spinuzzi. You're an attractive man. Did you enjoy it, when he grabbed your 'thing?'"

Spinuzzi laughed heartily, and said, "Not really. What crossed my mind was a feeling of sorrow. The poor son-of-a-bitch was seeking a relationship in an almost suicidal way, risking his own well-being. I told him this and also, by the way, told him I wasn't interested, and that I wouldn't tell anyone else in the bar what had happened.

"Believe it or not, he continued to come to the bar for about a month, but made no moves on me or anyone else. The boys grew to like him. Then one night he didn't show up. We later got the word that he'd committed suicide. The boys were sad, and for the first time, I began to wonder what it is like to be a homosexual."

"What did you conclude, Spinuzzi?" Mo asked.

Spinuzzi smiled, and answered, "Mo, I really didn't say it right. I not only began to think about homosexuality itself, but about all sexuality that we consider abnormal, and what it all means."

"I repeat, what did you conclude?"

"I concluded that sex, both obvious and not so obvious, drives practically everything. Sex is good. Sex is dangerous. And the secret of sex, both for individuals and societies, is knowing where to draw the line between acceptable and unacceptable sex."

Pussey Rapper added, "And who decides?"

Pussey Rapper was the liberal of the group. I turned to him. "Pussey Rapper, where would you draw the line between acceptable and unacceptable sexual behavior?"

Pussey Rapper wasn't prepared for this question. I could see he needed more time to put his thoughts in order.

"My wine glass is empty," he calmly remarked. "Please pass me the bottle."

Genella, sensing the strain, decided to help Pussey Rapper in his rather difficult position by changing the subject. She said, "Hey, me too. Please pass it on, when you're finished. Hey, Mario, you never told us about the wine."

Mario answered, "It's a good wine. Are you complaining?"

"No," answered Genella. "I'm just curious."

Mario playfully shot back, "Curiosity killed the cat, you know."

Spinuzzi said, "That's the best way to die."

And to my surprise, the Pig answered, "I agree."

I breathed a sigh of relief, and so did the group. We weren't quite sure what Spinuzzi and the Pig agreed upon, but the Pig was now more relaxed.

The group was back in sync, and the conversation was now in Pussey Rapper's ballpark.

He began, "That is a tough question, my friends, and you all know it. Honestly speaking, I've never asked myself this question directly, and I have to think about it while I'm answering it. After being with you guys all these years, I've learned to do that, but I have a more productive idea.

"Spinuzzi, since you told us that you began to think about this issue as a young man, I'm sure you've continued to do so. Why don't you summarize your thoughts, and then we can respond to them. Does anyone disagree?"

No one said a word. Judging by the look on everyone's face, this meant, in a way that is difficult to explain to people who never lived in the old neighborhood, that there was strong, unanimous agreement, and Spinuzzi had the obligation to lead off the discussion.

Spinuzzi said, "*Mamma mia.* I didn't expect that to happen tonight, but why not? It's one of the critical issues of the times and should be addressed by us. *Vero?* We can never be politically correct at our dinners or we will lose sight of the truth."

"Amen," said Pignachi.

We were all a bit startled by Pignachi's "Amen." I had a feeling that he would be an active participant on the sex subject. Yet I feared for him a little because of the issue of homosexual and pedophilic clergy. But the boys did well that night. It was never put on the table, though it is a real issue. Once during the evening's conversation, Genella was about to bring the clergy-homosexuality issue up, but Pussey Rapper kicked her under the table to shut her up. She does have a tendency to create problems.

I don't give a shit what anyone says, women create big problems. Today, to be politically correct, one should say that men also create big problems. But there's a real difference: The problems created by American women far exceed those created by men. They say that men start wars. I say that often it's because of the women behind them. But that's another subject.

Spinuzzi, would you believe, began to address the issue of homosexuality as his first subject. This guy is unpredictable. "Now, what I'm going to say does not involve my personal opinion. It is simply based on social, medical and scientific phenomena.

"A man has nipples, and so does a woman. Why does a man have nipples—to make him look good? Of course not; they probably exist for the same reason that a woman's nipples exist—to feed babies. There's a common biological basis for their existence.

"A man has a pecker and a woman a clitoris. Stimulation of each causes excitatory moments and enlargement of the stimulated structure. Is this a coincidence? You know, they're in about the same place on the body.

"Most men are more aggressive than females, but many women are more aggressive than men, and many men are more passive than women.

"So you see, there is an overlapping of the mental and the physical characteristics of men and women. So why is anyone puzzled by the fact that some men are attracted to men, and some women are attracted to women? Biologically and psychologically, sex is not a black-and-white phenomenon! In other words, the phenomenon of homosexuality is simple and understandable and a natural part of the sexual spectrum.

"But, with occasional exceptions, different cultures throughout history have encouraged monogamous married relationships. In other words, the family. It is a profound, irrefutable fact. Those with peanut brains claim that the custom of marriage is simply a way of encouraging a stable society in which babies could be produced and protected, in order to propagate the species. And that's all it is. I think it's much more than that; there is more to the critical dynamics of monogamous family life."

Pignachi seemed somewhat saddened—in fact, very much so. We all noticed this sudden change of mood. He was deep in thought. He seemed to not have noticed that Spinuzzi had stopped talking and that there was silence at the table.

Spinuzzi decided to take a break from his dissertation on homosexuality and asked, "Pignachi, where the hell are you?"

Genella said, "Let's leave Pignachi alone. Every man is entitled to his own thoughts."

Mario said, "How about women?"

Mo said, "That depends whether she's cheating on her husband or not."

Genella said, "The same goes for the husband."

Mario said, "*Brava*, Genella!"

Mo said, "Mario, your pecker is getting in the way of your brain."

Mario said, "That's sometimes a good thing, Mo."

Mo laughed and said, "Touché, Mario. You're right, and I stand corrected."

This is what I loved about these annual get-togethers. Though everyone had his firm convictions about the positive and negative forces of life, we listened to each other and were open to criticism. Though no one ever changed his fundamental philosophy of life, we broadened them to include other points of view.

For example, Mo was a conservative but sincerely supported welfare, as long as it did not destroy someone's will to go forward in life and try to be independent. Pussey Rapper, the liberal, was in agreement with Mo's viewpoint. The problem, however, has always been where the line should be drawn.

Spinuzzi said, "Hey, I stopped my spiel because I wanted to hear what was going on in Pignachi's head."

Once more, there was silence. Pignachi, it seemed, was not inclined to speak. It seemed to us that he wanted to talk, but needed a little bit of encouragement.

"Hey, let's have a little wine," I said.

We all picked up our glasses and imbibed a healthy quantity of red wine, except for the Pig, who stayed with his white.

I sensed that what was on Father Pignachi's mind was important for us to hear. One could see that it was not strictly an intellectual position but an emotional feeling that was fueling his mood. He was clearly disturbed.

I said, "Pignachi, unless there's good reason not to talk about it, tell us now what's on your mind."

Then I knew that Father Pignachi was now thinking of us as the general sheep of the Church and not as individuals letting off a little steam while having a good time at Mario's restaurant.

"I was thinking about a beautiful thirty-three-year-old, one of my parishioners. She is a good kid with a good heart. But she just can't handle the instability of modern life.

"She got married in her early twenties and then got divorced, soon after. Over the next ten years she moved in with three different guys, expecting to marry each one, but none of them worked out.

"She and the guys she lived with drank a lot and took good amounts of coke and smoke. During the intervals between her affairs with the three men, she slept with others, and continued to drink heavily and take the coke and smoke.

"The funny thing about it is, she never realized that there was something wrong with her. I've seen this a lot—people who lead screwed-up lives but don't realize that they're screwed-up. I occasionally convinced her that she did something wrong, though she always put the blame on the guys and our society. It was never her fault, and nothing I said or did could convince her otherwise.

"Well, I think it was with the second or third man. They moved someplace down south where the sun shines more and the warm weather is better for your mood. And what happened?

"They lived in an apartment complex with a swimming pool, tennis courts and clubhouse with all kinds of gadgets to do your exercise."

Spinuzzi interrupted. "Pignachi, was she really beautiful, I mean physically or spiritually beautiful? It can make a difference, you know."

"What do you mean, 'It can make a difference'?" asked Pignachi.

"As a physician, I have observed that good-looking women in today's United States are more fucked-up than average-looking women. It's always been that way, but it is more than ever now. It's a result of the relaxations of sexual prohibitions, better clothes, better figures, and being the most sought-after.

"Bottom line, what I want to say is that the more options in life people have, the more fucked-up they are. It makes sense, if you understand the nature of man."

"How about the nature of women?" asked Genella.

Mo jumped in, "God, you know, Yahweh, took my fuckin' rib from my body and made women because he thought that is was no good for man to be alone. So whether you like it or not, women are really like men when it comes to basic behavioral principles."

Spinuzzi said, "Are we getting back to the subject of sex?"

Mo smiled and said, "Pignachi, go on with your story."

Pignachi continued. "Well, when she lived with that guy in the south, she made a number of friends, not like old neighborhood friends, but the kind that are quickly made and quickly disappear.

I've forgotten all the bad things that she told me, but let me tell you a few that stick out in my mind.

"Her so-called 'closest friend' was divorced and had three children. She liked younger guys, and she invited a guy ten years younger than she is to move in with her and the three children. The guy was a big drinker, coker and smoker. She joined him in his habits and much of their life was spent with their minds outside of reality."

The Pig asked, "How did the kids handle this situation? Kids are not so dumb or naïve, you know. They know when something is wrong and, thank God, they're extremely flexible. They manage to adapt to the most bizarre situations. This trait is a godsend in our unsettling times. But, my friends, there is always a limit to flexibility!"

Pignachi said, "Pig, you hit a big nail on the nose. To make a long story short, she discovered that this guy was an incestuous bisexual pedophile. He was having sexual encounters with her daughter and one of her sons.

"What could be more tragic? What, in God's name could be more tragic?"

Spinuzzi became coldly clinical and said, "Pignachi, by the judgmental tone of your voice, I see you have now made two assumptions. The first is that pedophilia is evil."

I knew what Spinuzzi was up to. He was preparing for the discussion of other types of sexual behavior, most of which, up until modern times, were generally considered unacceptable.

Pignachi was in a priestly emotional mood, and Spinuzzi was in a philosophic-logical mood. Logic had no role in Pignachi's observations, so I decided to ignore Spinuzzi's remarks because they didn't fit the situation.

I said, "Pignachi, what happened when the poor lady found out?"

Pignachi answered, "She threw him out. While she was trying to dry out from the drugs and the booze, she met another much younger man and had an affair with him. People just don't learn, do they? Anyway, he was a health nut and he got her into all kinds of physical exercise programs. She loved it, but then the guy left her for a younger, sexier gal. After that, she went back to the bottle and gave up the coke, simply because it was too expensive, but took the inexpensive smoke."

Mo interrupted, "Pignachi, how the hell can someone be a good mother dedicated to her kids, while behaving this way and taking all this shit?"

Pignachi was too emotional to even consider this question, and he went on. "There was another couple, with two children—a boy and a girl. They were in their late forties and got along reasonably well. Like Lady Chatterley, she became involved with the gardener who, by the way, was about ten years younger than she. Evidently, she loved her husband but was only having this affair to fulfill her sexual appetite.

"Now listen to this: The kids were highly suspicious of this guy, but didn't say anything to their father. The father often came home while the gardener was still working on the lawn and the shrubs.

They would all be together in the presence of the wife and the kids. Can you imagine what impact this contemptible behavior had on the minds of the kids? Can you imagine what they will think of their parents? This could never, never happen in the old neighborhood.

"I remember one other story. A couple with three kids who settled in America. He was a faithful guy and a hard worker. She didn't work, but insisted on having a nanny to take care of the kids. Well, the guy did it in order to keep the peace, but when he came home at night she would either be high or drunk, and dinner was never pleasant. He finally got fed up and told her to drink within her limits or pay the price. I don't remember whether he told her what the price would be. Usually, in my experience, such threats are empty ones. I wish the husbands and wives giving these ultimatums would live up to them. It might resolve the problems and make a positive difference in family life.

"Anyway, he got fed up and found himself a woman he could relate to. The wife, sensing that something like this was going on, dramatically reduced her drinking. But it was too late. She had burned her bridges, and the guy was happily in love with the other woman. He left his wife, with little feelings of remorse.

"I remember what my Uncle Bruno told me when I was a youngster. He said that even the deepest love could be destroyed by negative behavior. I couldn't accept this idea as a young kid. I was sure that love was an immutable part of family life. It could not be destroyed. Then I learned the lesson I didn't want to learn. You can destroy even the deepest love, and this is becoming quite commonplace in modern family relationships."

Pignachi, with a touch of tears in his eyes, was obviously distraught.

Genella said, "Father Pignachi, I know what you're saying, but don't get too upset or else you'll get a heart attack. There's little you can do about this except on an individual basis with the people in your parish."

Spinuzzi then said, "There's no doubt that women are drinking and drugging too much, and that's playing a big role in screwed-up families."

Genella quickly added, "But so are the men."

Mo said, "*Mamma mia*, this conversation is getting depressing."

Spinuzzi said, "Don't forget the first miracle of Jesus Christ, performed at a festive drinking occasion. When the wine ran out, he turned water into wine."

No one commented on this off-topic observation. Once more, it was typical Spinuzzi.

Genella then made another mistake. She asked a personal question which was far too personal. "None of you guys has been divorced. You've been married for well over a quarter of a century, and you're still with your wives, or should I say, your wives are still with you."

(Just for the record, neither the Pig nor Pignachi were ever married)

"Maybe if each one of you guys would tell the reasons why your marriages have lasted so long, we could get a clear idea of what getting along in married life is all about."

Stone silence followed. The boys would never talk about their relationship with their families. In the old neighborhood, this was private territory, and nobody's business.

Spinuzzi, ignoring Genella's remarks, said, "Pignachi, you're making the assumption that there's something wrong with this general pattern of sexuality, by calling it deviant and perverse. In rhetoric, this is called begging the question. You've made the assumption before you've made the argument." Spinuzzi was obviously trying to goad his companions to discuss their thoughts on this complex issue.

Pussey Rapper took the bait. "I would like to reiterate that sex is perhaps the most powerful mover in human behavior. Two examples come to mind, which cover the spectrum of its power. Though they had their differences in the hay-day of their careers, Thomas Jefferson and James Madison, after they retired from their roles as public servants, became good friends and started writing letters to each other.

"One letter talked about the great Benjamin Franklin's sex life. Though it wasn't mentioned in the letters, Franklin had thirteen illegitimate children. Imagine that happening today!

"Well, Jefferson wrote to Madison that Franklin, 'in the company of women, loses all power over himself and becomes almost frenzied.' Now, this was one of the most stable and wise statesman in U.S. history.

"Now, let's jump to modern times and these homosexual guys. They have an unequivocal Thanatos or death wish. They know that AIDS is a fatal infectious disease transmitted by sexual contact. Yet, these guys make love with other guys like it was nothing. One study reported that a single homosexual male can have up to a thousand different male partners in a lifetime.

"The life span of a heterosexual or non-homosexual American male is almost seventy-three years of age; that of a homosexual male is forty-three years. These guys are sick mothers and—"

Genella interrupted, "What about lesbians, Pussey Rapper?"

Pussey Rapper answered, "There's much less known about female homosexuals. They are much more quiet and private about their lives. Also, they have very few lifetime partners, compared to males. I don't remember the exact number, but I think it is less than six."

Spinuzzi remarked, "I knew a medical doctor who told me one day that he was a homosexual. Why he told me, I'll never know. In certain cases, the less I know, the happier I am. In my experience, the more one knows about the details of human behavior, the less happy one is."

Mo said, "That's bullshit, you know. One must know and understand things in order to handle the difficulties of life."

Pignachi said, "I don't think you guys really disagree. I think the basic principle is not that people shouldn't know things, but wanting and trying to know too many things often brings unhappiness.

"You guys remember that we all lived in the old neighborhood where gossip reigned supreme. Everybody talked about everybody.

But most of the gossip was about petty things, and brought a bit of innocent excitement into neighborhood life. 'Who will Giovanni marry?' 'Maria is pissed-off at her husband because he spent ten dollars at the bar on Friday night and came home with a smile on his face (which, by the way, didn't last long!).'

"But today, the gossip is about who's taking coke and smoke, who's knocked-up, who's getting a divorce, and who's screwing who on the side. It is not uplifting, but down-pulling knowledge that occupies our current gossip stage."

Spinuzzi said, "I remember when I was a medical student, I attended a debate between two psychiatrists on the value of psychotherapy and the belief that getting the patient to know more about himself is a good thing.

"I won't bore you with the details, but one of the psychiatrists was an old-timer who spoke with a heavy German accent. His point was that many people have enough problems handling what they already know. Adding to this knowledge about themselves and the people they deal with can only add to their confusion and mental problems.

"Though I don't buy this argument one hundred percent, the guy hit it on the nose for a lot of people who have mental turmoil, ranging from mild to severe."

Mario, instinctively sensing that things were perhaps getting too heavy, looked at Genella and said, "I love your dress."

Spinuzzi, smiling, said, "Mario, isn't this a funny time to bring this up?"

Mo said, "But I agree with Mario. The dress is beautiful."

Pussey Rapper said, "I believe that the beauty of this woman far exceeds the beauty of her dress."

I said, "Let's take a vote on that. Do we all agree with Pussey Rapper?"

All smiled and raised their hands.

Mario, becoming increasingly playful, asked, "Genella, can you stand up for us old-timers, so that we can see the dress in full?"

Considering everything, I sensed it would be the right move for Genella to stand up. She does have a sensual figure, and it would be good for the boys to behold her sensuality and lighten the mood. After all, we were talking about sex, and she had it! Also, speaking frankly, Mario didn't give a shit about the dress, but about what was in it.

Trying to protect her, the Pig said, "Genella, you really don't have to stand up."

But without hesitation, she answered, "But I want to." And she did.

The old bag really looked good. I don't know about Pignachi, but I knew what the boys were thinking. "Who the hell needs Viagra with a woman like this?"

And Mario, who loved to play, said, "Genella, would you turn around?"

Everyone knew that Mario wanted her to pose and show off her rear end. He was a real "ass man," as we used to say in the old neighborhood.

Genella slowly turned around and all the boys, like in a military drill but without the command of the sergeant, raised their glasses and partook. Genella obviously was enjoying it. This chick has certainly been around.

Though enjoying the moment, I decided that things had gone far enough. *"Grazie tanto, bella Genella.* You're a beautiful woman, and we can't take much more looking at you because it will destroy our concentration. Please be seated, and let's continue with our conversation."

Genella, the pro, knew I was right. She sat down, but slowly and sensually. No wonder Rocco was the first one to die!

I then said, "We were talking about male homosexuality. We are in America. Doesn't a person, homosexual or not, have a right to his or her private sexual life? I remember that President Clinton equated homosexual rights to the civil rights of blacks."

Mo, in his booming voice, answered, "Does a homosexual have the right to stick his pecker up your kid's ass? If Clinton had a son and if you gave him a choice to send him on a trip with a white homosexual male adult or a black heterosexual male adult, would he say, 'It doesn't matter?' Of course he wouldn't, unless he's totally fucked up.

"This bullshit about broad sexual rights has got to stop, but nobody in Washington or the media is saying a fucking thing. These fuckin' liberal moralists are trying to convince people that everything goes. They've got keen sexual hang-ups.

"How would they like it if an adult male sodomized their ten-year-old daughter? How would they like it if the fuckin' plumber periodically fucked their wives? Would these fuckin' liberals support the civil rights of these guys, or would they take action to get even or at least try to stop these acts?

"And let's talk about responsibility and fault. More and more, the liberal press is taking the position that sexual as well as other behavior is genetically determined. Those fuckers are trying to undermine our country's great tradition and strength that a man and a woman are responsible for their actions. Years ago, they started by blaming the disturbed behaviors of sex offenders and other criminals on their childhood experiences, and particularly on their parents. 'The mother didn't show enough love,' or 'the father was distant and cold' explained why the guy raped the gal, slashed her breast and beat her up. As we talked about before, they're blaming everything on the parents these days. Even parents are blaming themselves for their kids' behavior, these fuckin' weak idiots.

"Everybody and everything is to blame, except the person committing the act. And the liberal media is slowly winning the battle."

Spinuzzi leaned forward and commented, "But Mo, there is some truth in this type of reasoning. Certainly your genes and your childhood experiences influence what you finally become. Sure we can't predict it because we don't know enough about genes.

"Let's take an obvious example of how genes, one's environment or the interaction of the two can influence what you are—depression and suicide.

"Depression and suicide run in families. Not all people with a family history of depression and suicide, however, end up that way. This is a powerful argument that there is a gene that is inherited by some and not others in families with such histories."

Mo rebutted, "Then you're saying that there is no fault in behavior, that if someone raped and mutilated your wife, he's not responsible and shouldn't be punished?"

Spinuzzi replied, "No, I didn't say or imply that. I'd cut off his balls and torture the mother-fucker over a twenty-four-hour period, then I'd stick him in a cauldron of boiling water and take great pleasure in pushing his head under until the son-of-a-bitch was toast."

Genella then said, "But, if you believe it's not his fault, why kill him?"

Spinuzzi answered, "That's a fair question, Genella. The answer is, if you assume that people are not responsible for their actions and, therefore, not held accountable, then anything goes! If every crime and abuse were forgiven, then the floodgates of crime and abuse would be opened. And you know that that would not be acceptable to any society. No society has ever adopted this policy; a society could not exist if it did.

"Listen: take communism. It's a long story, but Karl Marx based its principles on the thinking of two guys, Hegel and Fuererbach. Tonight is not the night to get into the details, but basically, communism is the extreme version of materialistic determinism. No one has free will. History, people's behavior, is determined by forces that have nothing to do with free will. So, in communistic countries, nobody is really responsible for their actions because they have no free will. Right? Wrong!

"Communist governments everywhere punished and killed people for having hopes and dreams that were born from so-called determinism and, according to their thinking, not their fault. In a society that preaches communism, there should be more tolerance of unacceptable behavior, because people are not responsible for their actions."

Genella interrupted. "I can't follow you, Spinuzzi. Are you saying that even though a person is not responsible for his actions, he should be punished?"

Spinuzzi, almost contradicting himself, answered, "Not at all. What would Rocco have done if someone raped and beat your brains out?"

Genella thought a moment, took a sip of her drink and answered, "He would have had him killed!"

Spinuzzi smiled and so did the rest of the guys. They remember Rocco. You never fucked around with Rocco. He was the classic example of the Law of Talion guy.

Genella, in an expansive mood, wanted to talk. She said, "Speaking of behavior, I can't understand why we're all losing respect for people, our government or whatever. I feel that this is not such a good thing. My gals talk about this a lot."

Pussey Rapper commented, "It's funny you bring this up. I was thinking about it last night, and about the time my son and I were out to dinner, just the two of us. While we were talking, we heard this commotion at the next table. There was a well-dressed old-timer sitting with his distinguished looking wife. Yeah, guys, I know what you're thinking, 'Was it his wife or his girlfriend?' I can tell you, it was his wife."

Spinuzzi asked, "How do you know it was his wife?"

I saw the look in Pussey Rapper's eyes, and it wasn't one of love for his buddy from the old neighborhood. Spinuzzi made a mistake by raising a dumb question at this sensitive point. It was not the issue, and it detracted from the importance of what Pussey Rapper was saying. I decided to step in before Pussey Rapper took off against Spinuzzi.

"Pussey Rapper," I said, "what the hell happened with the old-timers?"

It worked. Pussey Rapper looked away from Spinuzzi and continued, "The old man was telling the waiter that he brought the wrong main dish for his wife. He brought her salmon tartare instead of the broiled salmon that she ordered.

"Now the fuckin' asshole waiter insisted that the old-timer's wife ordered salmon tartare, and the fucker also spoke with a cold tone. He was an ignorant son-of-a-bitch, the kind we used to punch out in the old neighborhood."

Spinuzzi, undaunted, commented again, "Was the waiter a hostile male homosexual?"

Though the liberal Pussey Rapper did not like to speak or even think in those terms, he did have the impression that the waiter was a queer. He replied honestly, "I think so."

Then the Pig said, "How do you know that he wasn't a hostile male heterosexual?"

We all looked at each other, feeling that somehow we had forgotten our friend's sensitivities and were now debating instead of discussing.

Pussey Rapper, sensing this, replied, "Who the hell knows? What we do know is that there are too many hostile mother-fuckers in this world, be they male or female, heterosexual or homosexual."

The beauty and wisdom of this statement was that it both spoke to the truth and assuaged the hidden hurt feelings of our old friend, the Pig.

Pussey Rapper continued, "Well, the bitter and unpleasant give-and-take between the shit waiter and the old-timer continued for too long. It was a kind of mini-battle where the waiter was seeking war and the old-timer, peace."

"Now, I said to my son that he should put himself in the place of the old-timer at the next table. The couple appeared to be in their early eighties and in pretty good physical condition; their years to further experience the privilege of life are limited. Let's assume that he deeply loves her and wants her to enjoy herself at dinner. He's the kind of guy that looks after his wife.

"Both of them are having a good time and she claims to have ordered broiled salmon and the waiter brings her salmon tartare.

Then she politely tells the waiter about the mistake. At this point, I want you to take the place of the husband.

"The waiter says to your wife, in a cold, uncaring way, that he heard it right the first time. She ordered the salmon tartare and not broiled salmon. She's the one that made a mistake, not he. Once more, he does not offer to replace the tartare with the broiled salmon.

"Now, what's your wife thinking? She's thinking that maybe the waiter is right because she has had recent problems with her memory and may have had a 'senior moment.' But she believes that she did indeed order the broiled salmon.

"But, deep down, you're both unsure. Then your wife is thinking that the waiter is thinking that she is old and decrepit and can't remember what she ordered. And this, my friend, is a depressing moment for the woman you love.

"I asked my son what he would have done in this situation. He said he would call the owner or whoever was in charge, complain and insist that they bring his wife the broiled salmon. Then I asked him whether this scenario would increase his and his honeybun's *agita* level, not only eliminating the pleasure of the evening, but leading to indigestion. I then told him to sneak a look at the couple. They were holding hands, looking uncomfortable, but united in their battle against the *schmuck* or *stronzo* waiter and the lack of civility in the modern world.

"Then I said to him that the entire fuckin' evening was ruined for these old-timers by a fuckin' hostile waiter who, in the old neighborhood, would have been told by one of the guys at the nearby table to apologize to the guy; if he didn't, someone would be waiting for him outside of the restaurant at closing time to teach him a lesson.

"'Remember, son,' I told him, 'in the old neighborhood the elderly were very much respected. They earned it. You always treated them with deference.'

"My son was silent. I told him I would now give him an alternative scenario and that I would like him to choose between the two. The other scenario went as follows:

"Wife: 'Sir, there must have been some misunderstanding. I believe I ordered the broiled salmon and not the salmon tartare.'

"Waiter: 'Madame, my mistake. It's been a rough day. Please excuse me for having made this error. I will ask the chef to prepare your broiled salmon immediately, so that you and your husband can enjoy the main course together. In the meantime, I'll keep your husband's dinner warm.'

"'Son, that's respect. For a lousy ten-dollar piece of fish, the evening is easily converted from shitsville to a night of relaxed pleasure, and that's very important in life.'

"Then I asked him what scenario he would have preferred, calling the owner of the restaurant over and fighting over the fuckin' salmon or enjoying the meal with the woman he loved because of the respect shown by the waiter.

"My son, an honest lad, said that there was no contest. Surely the respect scenario was preferable.

"While we were talking I thought of something that Jesus Christ once said. It kind of sums it all up. I told my son that I knew that the guys in his generation that are making tons of money aren't particularly religious, but the secret of a fruitful life is to listen to the advice of those with wisdom. I then told him of the Golden Rule of Jesus—'Do unto others as you would have them do unto you.'

"My son then said, 'According to the Golden Rule, McVeigh should not have been executed for the bombing, but released from jail.'

"Now, I told him that I am not much of a religious man and that I don't want him to be a smart-ass about my feelings for the Golden Rule.

"He said, 'Dad, I'm not being cute. If I were in McVeigh's shoes, that's what I would want.'

"I got a little pissed-off at him and told him he was doing exactly what a lot of these smart-asses are doing today. They are ducking the issue by demonstrating that there is no perfect world, and that there are exceptions to every rule. I told him that one of the Ten Commandments states, 'Thou shalt not kill,' but that does not prohibit us from killing in self-defense or in the defense of our country. I also told him to smarten up because he has his life to live, and he should make every effort to make it a happy one. It's tough enough as it is, and it's the supreme idiocy to create unnecessary problems to add to life's travails.

"Then something really unexpected happened. You've got to remember that he had just been beaten up by life. His wife left him, probably for another guy, and she had probably been fucking around with this other guy while my son thought everything was fine with his marriage, embracing her under the covers at night, telling her that he loves her, and she saying the same thing, back.

"Well, getting back to what happened. He became extremely relaxed, as if someone had given him a drug. I hadn't seen that look on his face for many a moon—too many moons, my friends.

"He said, 'You know, dad, I remember what you told me time and time again when I was a kid. There are problem solvers, problem creators, and those who live in ignorant bliss—and only about ten percent of people are problem solvers. I didn't believe you then, but now I see it. And I remember that when I asked you why most people are problem creators, you told me that you hadn't the slightest idea, because you couldn't read the mind of God, who created these people. But you also told me it was critical to accept this fact, so that I could prepare myself in life to handle it. You told me that it was a waste of life to be dragged down to the dregs by the downers, and now I see it. But, dad, you told me to get rid of the problem creators and surround myself with the problem solvers. I don't know how to do it.'

"I said to my son, as strongly and convincingly as I could, that I didn't know, myself, how to do it, a hundred percent of the time. Yes, I do succeed in getting rid of many of them, but as soon as I get rid of them more problem creators appear. It's an inexorable process, but if you give up, you lose. You have two choices—to try or not to try. I told him that if you don't try, you're a horse's ass in spades, and a weak chicken shit, to boot.

"As I mentioned before, my son was really down because he's one of those guys that needs a warm body next to him at night. There's nothing wrong with that. I imagine that most guys would like to have warm bodies next to them every night. I'm not so sure about women. I guess I'm a little bit odd. If I were divorced, I wouldn't mind sleeping and being alone about half of the time, and I'd be happy the other half, being next to a warm body."

Miserabile said, "I haven't slept against a warm body for quite some time. I can tell you, Pussey Rapper, that it ain't much fun sleeping alone."

Frankly speaking, we were all a little bit surprised, first of all, that Miserabile would be without a woman at night for any significant period of time, and second of all, that he would publicly admit this, particularly in front of Genella.

Something was fishy here, and my old neighborhood vibrations told me that Miserabile's surprised, open behavior had something to do with Genella's presence. He was playing up to Genella's mother instincts, and most women have them, though they seem to be diminishing these days. I had the feeling that he was making a play for Genella and would try to push Mario out of the picture.

Pussey Rapper continued, "Well, guys, I want to continue with my story regarding respect.

"My son said, 'Some of my friends would question why the waiter should show respect for that complaining couple? Why the hell do they think they're something special? In fact, my friends believe that this respect shit is overblown, and would question why anyone should be respected.'

"Well, you know this fuckin' idiot remark really caught me off guard. I was about to answer when I suddenly realized I couldn't put the answer into words., In the old neighborhood, no one ever asked anyone to explain the reasons why one should show respect. It was, as Aquinas would say, a self-evident truth."

Spinuzzi then said, "Epistemology is the part of philosophy that deals with definitions and what we can know. For example, an epistemologist would want to know what a chair is or when a chair stops being a chair or when a dog is a dog no more. If, for example, you cut off one or more of the dog's legs, he's still a dog. If you cut off his head, he's no longer a dog. Now the conclusion is that a dog's head makes a dog a dog more than a dog's legs. An epistemologist, like those in the Enlightenment, Genella, would even go a step further. He would question whether there is such a thing as a dog or whether we exist around this table, tonight."

Spinuzzi was off on one of his mental journeys into outer space, so I decided to cut it short. "What is your point, Spinuzzi?"

"Well, I want to let Pussey Rapper know that there's nothing wrong with not being able to define things with the right words. It's frequently impossible. If someone asked me to define love, hate, friendship, goodness or evil, I could not, nor could anyone else, do it adequately.

"Most things in life are felt and perceived but not defined. We do not have nearly enough words to describe what we know."

The Pig said, "I agree with Spinuzzi but the reality is that, in this modern era of communication, everyone wants to know 'why.' They don't just accept things, as we do.

"Remember? A horse's ass was obvious to us in the old neighborhood. No one even thought of defining him with words. All you had to do was hear him speak and see how he acted to know what he was. The modern generation will ask us why so and so is a horse's ass, when it is obvious that the son-of-a-gun is one. Our society is very verbose and frivolous, you know. It talks a lot about life instead of understanding it."

Miserabile looked at Genella and asked, "What do you think? What is respect, and why is it important?"

Genella smiled at Miserabile. There was already little doubt in our minds that she was impressed by Mario, but now, judging by her smile, there was little doubt that she was also impressed by Miserabile. Mario was bravura, short term. Miserabile was steady, long term. Both are strong men. Genella evidently likes strong men, in whatever form they come.

Genella said, "You know what is life all about? Isn't it important to reduce your strife and get what you want? I'll never forget what my mother told me about the importance of respect. It had nothing to do with epistemology—did I pronounce it right? It had to do with the practical things in life that help us get by. She told me time after time that you catch more bees with honey than with vinegar, and I've never forgotten that. You have little to lose by showing respect, and much to gain."

"*Brava*," said Miserabile.

"*Veramente brava*," said Mario.

"It makes life easier for everyone," added Pignachi.

"Isn't anyone going to ask me what I finally said to my son?" asked Pussey Rapper.

Spinuzzi then asked, "Pussey Rapper, what did you finally say to your son?"

Everyone laughed, including Pussey Rapper. That remark made him relax a little bit more.

"While I was searching for words, I ordered another drink for both of us in order to bide my time. Then I remembered what my father said to me when I was a young lad. It's much the same as what Genella said. He told me once that you have little to lose and much to gain by being nice to and respecting people."

"I also remember him saying that people like to be recognized and treated well, and that I should make it a habit of mine to do so. He told me it was also a beautiful thing and not to be practiced just for selfish reasons.

"He asked me how I would like to be treated by the banker, doctor, plumber, electrician, and government employee—whether I would prefer them to greet me with a smile and say, 'Good morning, sir. Please have a seat and I'll be with you in a minute' or greet me rudely, hardly recognizing my existence, and let me sit on my *culo* until I get an anxiety reaction."

The Pig jumped in. "You guys ain't going to believe this. *Affanculo*, it's true.

"After I turned age 65, I got a call from a gal from Social Security. I was all set to handle a rude daughter-of-a-bitch: You know, the kind of miserable personality that government employees are noted for.

"Well, will wonders never cease? The gal was a sweetheart. She sensed I was a dingbat about details, so she followed up with at least four or five phone calls.

"Then I went to get a photo driver's license. These government offices are usually packed and tension fills the air. I was expecting the worst, but then it happened again. *Affanculo*!

"The receptionist and the other employees were cordial, told me what to do and got me out of there in less than an hour.

"Why the hell did I bring this up? My goddamn mind is beginning to go. Oh, yeah, I remember. I had two good days, because I was treated well. It could have gone the other way if those people had treated me like shit."

Dolce

Mario decided it was time for dessert. Before he spoke a word or made a sign, Vinnie walked over to the table and stood by his side. There was some kind of telepathic communication between these two guys. Vinnie was just too busy to notice that the last leg of our meal, the dessert, was due.

What the hell did we care! The timing was right, and the approach impressive. That was good enough for us. We were all curious about what Mario would recommend: Probably something fancy that would be an impressive finale to the eating part of the evening.

"*Cara* Genella *e signori*: Let me tell you what I have in mind for dessert. Do not forget, I am a *contadino*, a peasant who has peasant tastes. Tonight I will serve you something rare that you will fall in love with.

"You guys all know what it is but probably haven't had it for a long time. By the way, it's not easy to make well, so if you do find it, most of the time it stinks to high heaven."

Pignachi turned to us all and asked, "Does anyone want to guess?"

It became immediately apparent that no one was in a guessing-game mood. After a few hours of emotional and intellectual give and take, the sharpness of their minds had been almost spent. They all needed a moment of mental respite. They knew they had to discuss a few more serious issues and didn't want to spend their remaining intellectual energy guessing what goddamn dessert Mario had selected.

Mario had been expecting a playful reaction from the group: It didn't happen. Not wanting Mario's disappointment to lead to a significant downer moment, Pignachi decided to reverse the negative momentum.

"Mario," Pignachi said, "I know what it is."

The boys and Genella seemed to be suddenly energized by Pignachi's declaration of clairvoyance. "How the hell does this guy know?" they were all thinking. Maybe it was Vinnie who told him, I thought.

Mo then said, "Pignachi, you're full of shit. You can't possibly know."

"Yes, I do," said Pignachi, with a broad smile on his face.

Mario, somewhat flustered, remarked, "My friends, I haven't the slightest idea how Father Pignachi could possibly know. Vinnie, did you tell him?"

Vinnie, with feelings hurt, answered, "No."

"Then," Mario continued, "there is no way on God's earth that Pignachi could know, unless God sent him a message from Heaven."

Pignachi rebutted, "But I do know, Mario. I do indeed know. I'll tell you what: If I'm right, I'd like each of you to contribute one hundred and fifty dollars to our charity project which helps feed poor children."

Mo said, "What if you're wrong?"

Pignachi smiled and answered, "If I'm wrong, I'm wrong. Do you really expect any money from me? *Vergogna!*"

Everyone smiled. I said, "I'll take that bet. How about the rest of you?"

All raised their hands in the affirmative. Genella didn't join in. In the old neighborhood, it wasn't ladylike to bet. Or maybe, like most women, she's just plain cheap.

Mo then said, "Shouldn't he tell us now?"

I then said, "Let's prolong the mystery. Pignachi, write it down on a piece of paper, fold it and put it in the center of the table."

Pignachi did as he was told. He was having a real good time playing this mental game with his buddies.

"*Mamma mia*," Mario said. "*Mi sono dimenticato.* I forgot. I promise you an hour of opera, and the time has come. It is getting late, and most of my guests will not mind a bit of opera at this time. If they do complain, my friends, I'll pick up their checks and tell them to leave. *Va bene?*

"I made a tape of my favorite arias and duets, and I'm sure you'll like most of them. I included Cilea's *Il Lamento di Federico*, by Gigli, the Verdi *Otello* baritone-tenor duet with Caruso and Ruffo, Del Monaco singing, would you believe, Wagner, DiStefano and Callas in a duet from Puccini's *La Boheme* and Pinza singing Mozart's *Don Giovanni*. There are others that you'll like. *Va bene?*"

Mario turned and made a signal to someone with his hands, and within a few seconds the glorious tenor voice of Gigli was heard. It was as if a sorcerer suddenly appeared and sprayed a tranquilizing solution on the group. Though I could not be absolutely sure—because of her professional ability to fake things in life—I truly believed that Genella was really enjoying it, too. Nothing gave us more pleasure in the old neighborhood than watching someone truly enjoying herself. The reason? Who the hell knows! Some people, thank God, are built that way!

But I thought that Mario's timing was a little off. He should have saved the music for after dessert, when he brought the *grappa*. We could then light up our annual Cuban cigars and listen to these glorious sounds like we did as youngsters at Victor's Cafe in Philadelphia. Who the hell needs dessert after that? Besides, I'm not a true dessert eater.

The famous combination duet-quartet of Puccini's *La Boheme* was just beginning. Rodolpho, the tenor, was being sung by Giuseppe DiStefano, and Mimi, the soprano, by Maria Callas. DiStefano had perhaps the purest and most beautiful voice of any recorded opera tenor. Callas had one of the most enchanting female voices I've ever heard. Interestingly enough, both lacked real solid high notes. They were, however, good enough to get by.

The part of *La Boheme* that we were listening to reflected Puccini at his romantic best. I rate it in the top five opera moments ever written. It is a modified duet-quartet scene, where two couples sing their hearts out regarding their problematic relationships. It is pure schmaltz, and I love schmaltz. It always amused and irritated the boys when they read the reviews of opera critics. These critics do not like, and look down on schmaltz. We love schmaltz! What is life without schmaltz? It brings out the good in you. The boys often noted that women are much nicer to them after they've seen a tear-jerker movie or read a love story.

Opera critics don't go for this. They look down on schmaltz. If schmaltz means tender and open feelings, they're not comfortable with tenderness and openness. We all agreed once that one cannot be both mentally healthy and an opera critic. Opera critics have major problems. Spinuzzi says that it's all because of their childhood sexual experiences.

Getting back to Puccini, DiStefano and Callas: We had stopped dead in our conversational tracks. The most romantic of music and the most romantic of voices had an impact. Who wanted to talk? We just listened.

Then it happened: As the voices flowed, Genella reached out and put her hand on Miserabile's forearm. She was not looking at him but gazing, it seemed, into space. She isn't a woman with big tits but she wore a low-cut top and a type of brassiere that squishes them and makes them bulge out and look bigger and more sensual.

Speaking of big tits, we discussed this modern phenomenon during our last dinner in 2000. We all concluded that, though it has an initially favorable impact on the cerebral-penal axis, it rapidly fades as foreplay begins. We unanimously agreed that silicon breasts are good for photos and movies but a disaster in the bedroom. Like women faking orgasms, they are cock-killers. Women don't even like them to be touched. Just for the record, I'd like to state clearly that

Pignachi did not take part in that conversation. All he did was sit back and sip his wine.

Getting back to Genella's tits, they began to heave—not big-time, but enough to notice. The boys became a little bit uneasy. Here they were, sucking up the beauty of Puccini and the singers and observing Genella's yo-yo breasts and Miserabile's reaction to her hand on his forearm at the same time. Speaking of mental and emotional conflicts!

Though I hate to say it, Genella's hand and breasts, coupled with Miserabile's reaction to them, defeated Puccini, DiStefano and Callas. We could always listen to this opera again but this Genella-Miserabile scene could never be replayed. I'm sure the boys were thinking, as I was, of Freud, Schopenhauer and the power of sex.

There was little doubt in our minds that Genella had turned on the hormones of Miserabile, the Stoic. And there was little doubt in our minds that stoical personalities are that way because they need barriers to expressing and feeling emotion in order to function well in life. The reason? Who the fuck knows?

"It is what it is," my father used to say, when confused by complicated situations that involved people. My mother often used to say, "It's better that way!"

Frankly, we were all kind of surprised that Miserabile didn't gently remove Genella's hand from his forearm. He apparently liked it too much to do so. And though I don't want to give the impression that the boys lack a romantic streak, we thought it was a mistake for him to like it, or at least to show that he did. She was the kind of woman that any rational man should take lots of time before letting himself go for. Not that Miserabile had let himself go, but that possibility wasn't a long way off—tonight, tomorrow or within the next month or so. We knew it wouldn't take long, if this pace continued.

Silence reigned and things were beginning to get uncomfortable. To our surprise, Miserabile took the lead. We couldn't fuckin' believe it!

"Genella," he said, "you're one of the most interesting and, let me say, beautiful women that I have met since I grew hair on my chest."

We waited for him to continue. He didn't.

We waited for her to respond. She didn't. She was a smart chick who knew when to talk and when not to. She was afraid that if she said something she could hit a sensitive spot in Miserabile that would shut him down. She gambled that being silent was the best way to encourage him to continue.

The boys decided to stay out of it for the moment. They were thinking about what Miserabile's next move would be. The seconds of silence were palpable.

Miserabile then said, *sotto voce*, "I believe I said too much already. Let's listen to Puccini."

Bravo, Miserabile! He'd thrown the foreplay back into Genella's ballpark.

She accepted the challenge. "Miserabile, a lady, particularly at my age, appreciates a compliment that is obviously from the heart. *Grazie tanto*, my friend. Now I would like to pay you a compliment."

240

Mario panicked a little. He thought he had Genella all wrapped up, but now this miserable personality, Miserabile, was taking the lead and Genella was encouraging it. Mario decided he had to move in.

He said, "Miserabile, when do you return to Washington and the Congress?"

"Next week," he answered.

"And how long do you stay?"

"It depends. Why do you ask?"

"It takes a pretty loyal and patient woman to get married to a politician," said Mario.

Mario had just crossed the Rubicon and declared war on the Roman Senator Miserabile. There was no turning back.

Nobody knew what to say about Mario's ballsy move, including Miserabile. Mario, appreciating the temporary confusion, continued with the Genella initiative in order to maintain his advantage.

"Genella, though I am not a literate man, I do love poetry. When I first saw you, tonight, I thought of a line from a poem that stirred my senses when I first read it in high school. I've forgotten the title and the exact words, but it deals with a lady called Julia, a name similar to your own. The part I like the best is the beginning. It goes something like this:

'Whereas in silks my Julia goes

Methinks the liquefaction of her clothes

Puts a fire in my *coglioni*.'

"When I saw you tonight, Genella, I thought of those lines."

Miserabile smiled. Mario had made a serious blunder with that last line. It was unlike him. He had openly talked about his balls, and we could all tell that Genella didn't like this crude type of foreplay. But her eyes also showed amusement rather than disappointment or disdain. That's the problem with eyes. Though someone once said they are "mirrors of the soul," it ain't always true. If you know how to read them well, they can reveal the innermost feelings and thoughts of the brain behind them. But there are times when the eyes mask one's true feelings and thoughts. Tonight was such a moment.

Miserabile, realizing that he now had an advantage over Mario, decided to overcome his reticence and speak. He said, "Genella, have you ever thought of living a different life, like that of the wife of a poet, a businessman, a doctor, or even a politician? If you fell in love with such a man, would you give up your profession and become a classic housewife, taking care of your husband and family?"

Genella was in the driver's seat and she knew it.

"I certainly would," she said, "if he were the right man."

Instead of shutting down the conversation, as she would have done if she had no interest, she'd spurred it on.

Mario jumped in. "How about the proprietor of a great restaurant?"

Genella smiled another teasing smile and didn't answer. She was inviting increased competition between Mario and Miserabile and, in doing so, perhaps inviting some trouble.

Mario became visibly uncomfortable. He wisely changed the subject back to that of eating, as if nothing had happened.

"And now, my friends, and also you, Pignachi, it's time for the *dolce*. *Dolce*, Genella, means 'dessert' in Italian." This condescending remark, we thought, would turn Genella off like the *coglioni* one had.

Small covered plates were brought to the table.

"*Siete pronti?*" he asked.

I replied, "Yes, Mario, we are ready." Mario stood up from the table, and he and Vinnie divided the chores and removed the covers in perfect synchrony.

And there it was—good, old fashion *spumoni*, the Italian ice cream of yesteryear.

Mario began. "These *maledetti* American chefs got fancy and removed two of the most commonly eaten Italian foods in America from their menus: spaghetti and meatballs, and *spumoni*. These two dishes were, in those days, the symbols of the oil and garlic peasant image Americans had of Italians. The chefs wanted to change Americans' taste and bring more Italian cuisine into their restaurants. So what they decided to do is what Aristotle taught Mayor Giuliani to do: Change the specific habits of the people and, by doing so, you create the pattern of general behavior that you want. By cracking down on crime, dirty streets, noise-making, intrusive beggars and blowing of car horns as well as all the shitty behavior that disrupts the rhythm of daily life, the city will become a more civil one where people can generally live more comfortably and be more productive.

"I believe, however, that if you put spaghetti with meatballs and *spumoni* back on the menus and make them taste good, people will enjoy them. And do you know why? Because both dishes are really good if prepared properly."

Mo laughingly remarked, "Hey, did anyone around this table follow philosopher Mario's pitch?"

Everyone laughed. The *spumoni* sat there before us, and no one said a word. Mario had transformed this simple Italian ice cream into something highly symbolic, something Gestalt-like. The *spumoni* was now more than *spumoni*. It was, at that moment, and in a real sense, something to be respected and preserved rather than consumed. Why? It brought back beautiful memories. It was a powerful reminder of things past. Shades of Proust!

Mo looked at Mario and asked, "Where the hell did you get this?"

Mario smiled and, with obvious pride, replied, "There's a *gelato* maker right up the street in Little Italy. He doesn't make *spumoni* because he thinks there's no market for it. Now he makes the *gelato* only for my restaurant. Last year, I asked him to make me, as a favor, some *spumoni* in small quantities. I paid him something extra to do so, because there's no money in it for him to produce small quantities of a particular *gelato*.

"I put it on the menu and very few people ordered it. I had to take it off the menu because I was losing money. It was one of my few marketing failures.

"But when I knew you guys were coming, I told the old *gelato* maker to make a special batch for you for tonight."

He looked at Genella and said, "And now that you're here, I know God planted the idea in my head. *Cara mia*, I'm sure you'll enjoy. If you don't," he added, "please fake it well, and don't tell me."

Genella had a hurt look in her eyes. I wondered whether it was because Mario used the word "fake," a characteristic adjective that describes the service she provides in her nighttime profession. This was the second time Mario had unknowingly made a diplomatic error. It was undoubtedly a result of excess booze. We all, including Mario, were over our limits. (Vinnie later told me that Mario was uncharacteristically drinking a ton of wine in the kitchen.)

I looked at the Pig and observed him staring intensely at Pignachi. I don't know what it was, perhaps a sixth sense, but I concluded that his look meant that he was a full-blown atheist who had something anti-clerical to say. To repeat, I can't tell you how, but I knew. It was like Genella knowing that Kathleen was a *rompiscatole* ballbusting chick without knowing any details about her.

Then Pig coldly said, "Pignachi, we haven't forgotten about your piece of paper and the dessert."

Pignachi felt the subtle hostility in the Pig's voice but couldn't figure out why it was there. He thought to himself, "Is he or anyone else at this table tonight crazy enough to think I believe God spoke to me in a revelation about Mario's dessert?" This guessing game had upset the Pig for reasons that are hidden deep in the inner circles of his mind, reasons that not even the Pig was aware of.

Pignachi decided to hasten the process of revelation and get on to other subjects. He said, "Mo, you're the non-believer. Unfold the piece of paper, and then behold!"

Mo did, and there it was, "*SPUMONI*," printed in capital letters." He passed the paper around and everyone except Spinuzzi was amazed.

Spinuzzi said, "You hit the lottery, that's all. It's simply a matter of probability."

How did Pignachi know? When Pignachi left the table to avoid the initial sex talk of Genella and Mario, he didn't really have an urgent telephone call to make. He stood hidden from view beside the door to the kitchen where the waiters go in and out in constant rhythm. He overheard one waiter say to another that Mario had ordered *spumoni* for his guests at the special table, and that he had tasted it and really enjoyed it, but could only have a couple of teaspoons because of the limited supply.

"I read somewhere that the greatest minds are those of atheists," Pig said, out of the blue.

We were startled. We didn't know where the hell this statement came from and what was behind it.

Mo asked, "Pig, why the hell did you bring this up, now?"

"Because Spinuzzi was talking about probability. If no one told him, then either he guessed, with an inconceivable probability of being right, or God told him. Now we know, and he knows, that God didn't tell him; he simply guessed right. Most things that are attributed to God are due to chance. In fact, if you think about it, everything in life is a matter of chance."

It was obvious that the Pig wanted to talk about God and religion. And it was just as obvious that he was, as usual, in a mood to attack both of them. There was also little doubt that God and religion must have let him down in a big way, in the past. The boys were thinking that perhaps it was the other way around!

I decided I would take the back door approach to the subject.

I said, "Listen Pig, I can't buy your argument. There are too many coincidences in life for them all to be true coincidences. Do you know anything about statistics?

"Anyway, you hear about two people dreaming more or less the same dream at the same time. You think about someone you haven't heard from in years and then the phone rings and there's that person, on the other end of the phone.

"Listen to what happened to me and my wife only last week. She was reminiscing about a childhood friend who went abroad to study after high school, over forty years ago. My wife never saw or heard of or from her since.

"The next day, my wife received a letter from that very same friend we had talked about the night before.

"Pig, I don't think that's mere probability. And there is no way for you to be positive about it either, unless you have a contact with God and *spumoni*, which even Pignachi claims he doesn't have."

Miserabile added, "Pig, I think he's right. Many people, almost always materialists or atheists, who believe these things happen by chance, want to believe that as a kind of personal mental self-defense. If they would admit to their own uncertainty, it would go against the grain of their positions on religion or the supernatural and make them uncomfortable.

"You can't explain everything by science. Some things have to make you think. Why become an atheist and absolutely convince yourself that God doesn't exist? Why not be agnostic, and simply admit to yourself that you don't know? There's a psychological component to being an atheist that agnostics and believers don't have. I don't know what it is, but it's real."

"I know what it is," said Spinuzzi. "It has to do with sex."

Pignachi got visibly upset. "How, in the name of God, do you know that has anything to do with it?"

"Because," answered Spinuzzi, "I agree with Schopenhauer, Freud and everyone else who says that all behavior has a large sexual component behind it. Didn't we agree on that?"

Then the Pig exclaimed, "Enough with this theoretical language shit! Listen to the real world. Let's listen again to DiStefano and Callas singing the love duet from *La Boheme*. Behold true metaphysical beauty. It's the hormones and their message of something ethereal, not the intellect, my friends, that makes the world go 'round."

"Speaking of hormones," Mo said, "this *spumoni* is out of this world! *Bravo*, Mario!"

"What the hell does the *spumoni* have to do with hormones, Mo?" the Pig asked.

Mo looked toward Spinuzzi and asked, "Spinuzzi, aren't hormones substances that float around in your blood and make you feel good?"

"Mo, you've got part of the story right. But yes, they do make you feel good."

"Well, this *spumoni* makes me feel good."

Pignachi said, "Mo, I knew it would be the best *spumoni* you've ever tasted."

The Pig sarcastically asked, "Pignachi, how the hell did you know that?"

Pignachi smiled, looked at the gang, then looked the Pig straight in the eyes and said, "Because God told me."

Everyone laughed—except the Pig. But after two or three seconds, the Pig gave in and burst out laughing, too. He said to Pignachi, "*Touché, mon ami, touché!*" Thank God the Pig had not lost his old neighborhood sense of humor.

Mario spontaneously extended his hand to Miserabile for no obvious reason. Miserabile did not hesitate to shake it. It's funny how small events can change tense moments to pleasant ones. And, I should add, vice-versa.

Speaking of breaking the tension, not too long ago I had a late lunch in Little Italy in the Big Apple. It was stinking hot and as humid as could be. I headed for the Holland Tunnel, where there was a humungous traffic jam. I was stuck in traffic for at least an hour when I noticed that the engine was getting hot. I turned off my air conditioner, turned on the heater and opened the windows on both the driver's side and the death-seat side.

Then I heard an old neighborhood-like exchange of heated words. There were two guys in a truck to my left and two guys in an old car to my right. Evidently, something happened that had pissed all of them off. I had the feeling that a fistfight or something more serious was about to happen, and I didn't like being caught in the middle.

The truck driver shouted to the car driver, "You were born with shit for brains!"

I don't know why, but this remark really struck my funny bone. I had never heard it before, and I had a hearty fit of laughter.

As I was laughing and looking at the truck drivers, I noticed that the expression of anger on their faces had suddenly disappeared. Now they looked puzzled. I looked to the right and saw that the guys in the car looked puzzled too. Suddenly all four guys—the two in the truck and the two in the car—burst out laughing along with me. All four got out of their vehicles and shook hands. No one said a word to me, but the truck driver walked over and patted me on the back. And that was it.

All the *spumoni* was gone, and it was now time for *espresso*, *grappa* and some good cigars. The Pig was the only guy that smoked a pipe, and Genella smoked cigarettes.

Espresso and Grappa

I suddenly realized that it was already beyond our usual witching hour and decided to begin the discussion about what is usually the most controversial topic at our dinners. When we talk politics we don't just talk about the platforms of political figures—that's what the idiots do. We speak about the entire spectrum, forces that drive people to vote the way they vote and behave the way they do. We go from divorced women to the elderly population, from gays to the messages of mass media, from political correctness to the redistribution of wealth. We debate—and it is a debate—what our national policies should be.

I said it before, and I'll say it again. Though these guys have firm beliefs, they will listen to the other side of the story and learn from it. But I must warn you that, with the exception of Pussey Rapper, none of the boys is a true liberal. In the old Italian neighborhood, most folks voted Democratic but few were liberal. Mo is the one true conservative. Pignachi has strong liberal tendencies because of his great capacity for empathy, and Spinuzzi has strong conservative tendencies because of his intellect and his personal vision of a strong America. The Pig slants a little to the left, Miserabile a little to the right. I don't know about Genella, but we would find out. I am to the left of Mo and to the right of Pussey Rapper. Let's say I'm to the right of center, where all clear minds should be! How's that for objectivity?

I began, "Lady and gentlemen, the night is coming to a close. The food, spirits and conversation have been better than ever. Mario—a special thanks to you for being such an *in gamba* and wonderful host. Now, let's get on to the subject of politics.

"We're all tired…"

"Who's tired?" asked Mo. "Is anyone tired, here?"

"I'm not tired," said Pignachi.

"I'm not tired," said the Pig.

"I'm not tired," said Miserabile.

"I'm not tired," said Spinuzzi.

Genella remained silent. We looked at her. The guys still had an old neighborhood soft spot for the ladies. If Genella were tired, they would make an attempt to limit the time of the discussion. Except for Mo. If she said she was tired, Mo would ask her to go home so the boys could talk without having to worry about her. When somebody in the old Italian neighborhood became a downer at a festive occasion, be it a lady or a man, they would be asked to leave or straighten out, before they ruined a beautiful time. It made sense then, but I'm not so sure it makes sense now. Does age really make one wiser or just too tired to make tough decisions?

We all still were waiting for an answer from Genella. It finally dawned on her that she should say something.

"I'm full of piss and vinegar," she said.

"Well," I said, "the hour is late and our gas tanks may be empty, even though we guys don't feel it yet."

"I'll fix that," said Mario. "Vinnie, *portaci un giro di grappa*. A round of grappa, my friends, should make us last through the discussion on politics."

I thought that everyone, including me, was "high" enough as it was. God knows where *grappa* would lead us. I didn't want to risk having the group driven by alcohol rather than by common sense reasoning. This could cause bad blood among the boys. I knew it was my responsibility to control the debate and put a time limit on it. I decided to ask five or ten specific questions and then close the evening with a fond farewell.

It didn't work.

I said to Genella, "Tell us why you voted for Kennedy."

Instead of bringing just another round of grappa to the table, Vinnie brought out two whole bottles with yellow raisins in them, which gives a smoother "hit" to the *grappa*. We all looked at him, and he didn't say a word. He put one bottle at one end of the table, and the other bottle at the other end. It was as if he was telling us, "*Ciao, bambini!*"

"Do you really want to know, guys?" Genella looked at Miserabile with eyes that seemed to be seeking help. Cool as Miserabile is, we all saw by his body language that he responded to the "lady in distress" syndrome. It was almost impossible to resist this in the old neighborhood, because it was part of the Italian code of gallantry. And let's not forget the sex part. He softened—visibly so.

No one thought it necessary to respond to Genella's question; we expected her to go on with her thoughts. But Genella could not accept the silence. She felt uncomfortable and made a move on unsuspecting Mario. She looked at Miserabile again, then turned her eyes from him to Mario, put her hand on his forearm, and asked, "Do you really want to know, Mario? If you don't, and you want to talk about other things, I won't be offended."

What the hell this meant only hormones could interpret. She did it in a very sensual, teasing way. Mario probably got a hard-on, and Freud, Schopenhauer and the orgasm principle probably jumped into everyone's mind. Mario broke the male silence and replied, "*Cara Genella, certamente.* We all would like to hear your reasons why."

Miserabile, who probably also had a hard-on, because of the tease-turn-off syndrome and the fact that she was playing one guy off the other, turned toward Mario with cold eyes and said, "How the hell do you know that we all would all like to know the reasons why?"

Then came Miserabile's most characteristic moment of the evening. He wasn't going to play Genella's game anymore. By old neighborhood standards, she had taken it too far and, desire her though he did, he said to Mario, "I personally am not interested."

"*Bravo,*" we all said to ourselves.

Besides sending a message to Mario that he didn't give a shit and that Mario could also have the chick, Miserabile was also sending an indirect message to us all about whether she had a future in our annual dinners. She was now robbing the evening of the important give-and-take of ideas and, instead, making it a night tinged with the cerebral *fetor soma* of sex. He was also telling us that, although he had succumbed momentarily to the allure of sex, he had realized his mistake and didn't want it to interfere with the beauty of the annual dinner. The boys read Miserabile's message—and they agreed. It was implicit that henceforth Mario would also be *persona non grata*. He had blown his debut as a potential permanent member of our annual dinners. The boys were already thinking that they had to find a new restaurant next year, where they wouldn't have to worry about an intrusive proprietor who let puntang interfere with the purpose of our evening.

Genella realized that she had made another big boo-boo. She wisely remained silent. I knew she was apprehensive, believing that she really may have blown her welcome. Though I wasn't sure who it would be, I knew that one of the guys would make excuses for the lady's unacceptable behavior, as they used to do in the old neighborhood. He would probably blame the newness of the situation and too much drinking.

But, to tell the truth, those wouldn't suffice. We had talked many times in the past about people having excuses for their behavior, even legitimate ones. In the old neighborhood, making excuses was generally heavily frowned upon and you paid a price for screwing up. It was not uncommon to hear, after someone screwed up, "*Affanculo a te e tutti i quanti.*" I remember when I was a teenager working in the produce section of a large supermarket. One day I was late for work. I had a good reason: My bus was late. I told the boss the truth and thought that would be enough to get me off the hook. You know: "The truth shall set you free." Boy, was I wrong!

"Son," he said, "you being late, for whatever reason, doesn't do me any good. If you ain't here, I can't get my job done. And when my boss sees that I can't get my job done, I'm in deep shit. And I have a family to support. So you see, son, stick your excuses up your ass and never make this mistake again, or you're out of here! Take an earlier bus!"

Instead of thinking that the guy was an unreasonable, miserable son-of-a-bitch, I agreed with him and learned an important lesson.

Genella would have to pay the price too. I didn't want to offend Miserabile, but the question had been asked and Genella had an obligation to answer. I said, "Let's get on with the conversation. Genella?"

Genella hesitated and looked around the table. She saw encouraging facial and body language from the group. The boys are softies. Even Miserabile, strangely enough, seemed to be somewhat *simpatico*, though more like a father than a lover. Of course, he could have been faking it to convince us that he was back on track and in charge of himself. Who knows? He has the most complicated of emotions, because they are largely suppressed.

Genella then said, "I'm sorry guys. I was just pulling your chains to stir the waters a little bit. I'm a little bit younger than you are, and I wasn't old enough to vote in the Kennedy-Nixon election."

"You were old enough to vote for Nixon the second time around, *vero*?" I asked.

Genella blushed a little. "I had just come of voting age. Now you guys know how old I am. That wasn't supposed to happen tonight or any other night."

The boys smiled. Genella was a Pirandello-type woman, with many aspects to her personality, the expression of which depended on the moment and the time of day. We were sure she could be a hard-nosed businessman at work (we wouldn't use the term "businessperson" or "businesswoman"; we're slow to change our ways, and nobody could dictate what words we used), but she was in a very playful mood and the boys were not. This was the main problem. The boys were not inclined to play games, particularly sexual ones, at the annual dinners.

Speaking about play: We'd talked about the importance of play many times in the past: How young animals, even the most ferocious ones, like lions and polar bears, love to frolic and play. It seems to be related to the energy level and brain biochemistry of youth. Philosophers may question whether animals can be happy; one can question whether human beings can be happy. No one can define happiness, but we all know when we see someone having a good time. Play defines itself, and no one would question that there is joy in play. Of course, there are moments when those that play too much become irritants, but that's like everything in life: Too much of a good thing may not be good at all.

A few annual dinners ago, we talked about why this wonderful characteristic of youth markedly diminishes with the passing of years. Of course, no one had a clue, but we all agreed that the capacity to

257

play doesn't completely disappear but becomes dormant. There's nothing like a good party with the proper mix of good food, good spirits and uplifting music to bring out the play in adults, including the depressed and the elderly. But come the next day, the joy of play begins to fade away. For some inexplicable reason, nature has placed a strict time limit on this wonderful gift of life.

People were leaving the restaurant and it was quieter, with the exception of the German guy and the guy who recently sang *Core Ingrato*. They were drinking a lot and having a ball. The *Core Ingrato* guy also had a good-looking chick with him, like the German turnip guy. We figured that Mario served turnips to him, too. Vinnie confirmed that our hunch was right. He said the guy was a turnip freak.

Spinuzzi asked, "Are turnips better than Viagra?"

No one laughed because we were wondering if it was a coincidence that two guys who love turnips have young, pecker-stimulating chicks with them and are having a ball. Spinuzzi commented that Viagra makes the erection happen but doesn't stimulate the desire. It seemed that the turnips were doing that. Maybe turnips plus Viagra should be patented. Man has been waiting for this combination since the day he emerged from earth's primordial ooze!

Genella, God bless her, urged us to take the combination and test the theory. No one volunteered to try it, but I was sure that one of the boys would. There's an orgasm and there's a wonderful orgasm. As one gets older, as the boys have, the latter becomes harder to achieve.

For some reason, nature has dictated that the orgasm, like play, must gradually fade away. Is there, as some say, a cruel God?

I said, "For the record, I wonder what would happen if I tried the Viagra-turnip combination. Would I get indigestion and blurred vision? If that did happen, how would my wife handle it? Would she take pity on, or laugh at me? It would be a sexual psychological mess. But, as they used to say in the old Italian neighborhood, 'What the hell can you do about something you can't control? Just accept it!' Shades of Epictetus!"

Genella asked, "Who is Epictetus?"

"Epictetus was a Roman slave and a stoic philosopher. A stoic is a person who believes that he can't control the forces that impact on his life. Forces that make us unhappy constantly assail us. The stoic believes that one should not fight these forces, for the effort is useless and frustrating and will only make us unhappier than we are. The secret of life is to just grin and bear it. There is some wisdom in this philosophy, but it can be carried too far.

"Let me give you an example: One day, Epictetus' master was really pissed-off at him. He began to twist Epictetus' arm until it really hurt. Epictetus, like a true stoic, made no move to free himself, saying to his master, 'Master, if you continue to twist my arm, it will break.' The master didn't give a shit, and continued until the arm finally broke. Epictetus said, 'Master, didn't I tell you so?'

"The most interesting stoic, in my opinion, was the last great Roman Emperor, Marcus Aurelius. His wife was fucking around with other Roman bigshots, and he had a psychotic asshole of a son,

Commodus, who wanted his father dead so that he could become Emperor.

"Now, Marcus was a very wise ruler of the Roman people, but he put up with the shit his family put on his plate.

"The barbarians of the north, in Gaul, were threatening to invade Roman territory and even the city of Rome itself. Marcus had to leave Rome for seven years to—very successfully—battle the barbarians of the north.

"The fuck-head left control of Rome to his unfaithful wife and psychotic son, believing, as stoics do, that there's nothing one can do about these forces in life. Well, the stoic philosophy backfired on the Roman people.

"Aurelius died shortly after his return to Rome, and Commodus became Emperor. He was a mean, perverted, incompetent son of a bitch, and the Roman Empire declined rapidly."

"For a period of time," I continued, "the leaders of mighty Rome realized that the Emperors would automatically pass the Empire to their weak and incompetent sons. Before the great stoic Aurelius, there were a number of great Emperors who ruled wisely and strengthened the Empire, and who weren't succeeded by members of their families. So Rome adopted the custom that the 'best qualified man' should take over the Roman Empire after the death of the Emperor, and it couldn't be anyone from the family. It worked well, Miserabile, and there's a lesson to be learned."

I wanted to get on with the subject of politics, which covers everything from religion to war to cloning. I decided that the practical politician, Miserabile, should lead off with the discussion.

Since the hour was late, I decided to change the give-and-take format of our discussion and just let Miserabile give us his opinion of present and future politics and world events—all in one shot. No interruptions unless it was deemed very important or simply due to an irresistible urge to speak out—which is not uncommon at our gatherings. I asked him to give us his ten-minute overview of what's going on in the U.S. and the world and what's going to happen in the future. I said I would add on a little time, if the remarks from the gang were not too lengthy.

Miserabile welcomed the challenge to briefly summarize the world and where it is going. In our hearts we all knew that he would take longer than ten minutes to do it, but it didn't matter. We were all at La Strega to learn.

"You guys knew my father. He was a kind man. But behind this kindness, he was a hard-nosed realist; he wasn't cynical, but he called the shots as he saw them. My father always had some type of saying on the tip of his lips. One of the first that I remember kind of summarizes the general situation of life. He said, 'Remember the Eleventh Commandment: Fuck them before they fuck you.'"

We all noticed that the pecker center of Miserabile's brain was now, thank God, dormant. Though not a high-powered intellect, he is a supreme pragmatist and keen observer of mankind's behavior both as individuals and within their cultures.

"In the old neighborhood," he continued, "there was a guy that used to deliver an antiseptic liquid women washed clothes with. He claimed that this medicinal liquid would prevent all viral and bacterial epidemics, such as smallpox and typhoid fever. For legitimate historical reasons, the fear of high-fatality epidemics was justified. But there was no way that this phony antiseptic liquid could prevent the bubonic plague or an influenza epidemic.

"There were no washing machines in those days, and the women used to soak the clothes in this solution called *Aqua Pura*, then scrub them by hand on corrugated washboards. They'd repeat this process until they were satisfied that the clothes were clean enough to wear, the sheets clean enough to sleep under, and so on. It took a lot of energy. Practically everybody in the old neighborhood did the wash on Mondays. I never knew why.

"Anyway, the guy that sold *Aqua Pura* was Mr. Gozzo. I remember his face and eyes very well. For some reason, I didn't like or trust him. As you guys all know, this sixth sense was learned from daily experiences in the old Italian neighborhood.

"Genella, in those days no one was starving in the old neighborhood, but no one had extra money to spend. Any little money left over from the paycheck was put in the bank. And, unlike today, with people making tons of money, the old neighborhood families saved money instead of blowing it on things that were not essential in life. They sought very few of life's experiences outside of the family community.

"Now one day I was shining shoes outside of the Italian club, the Sons of Italy. I used to do this every Friday and Saturday afternoon and night, and on Sunday morning. Mr. Gozzo's house was right next door, and one Saturday afternoon he was sitting outside on the sidewalk with his family. A lot of homes in the old neighborhood had porches where people would sit outside after dinner, and families, neighbors and passerby friends would talk. Mr. Gozzo didn't have one, so he put chairs on the sidewalk. What he did have was a big mother-fuckin' car. I believe it was a Packard, one of the great monster cars of the past.

"Well, I wasn't busy with my shoe shining that afternoon, and I had nothing to do. Mr. Gozzo began talking to his family, and I listened to what he had to say.

"He said that business was very good. The women in the old neighborhood bought into his marketing trickery. I've forgotten the exact details, but he said that it cost him this much to make the *Aqua Pura* but that he sold it at ten times the price. His family members shouted, '*Bravo!*' I was about to walk up to him and say, 'You fuckin' shit,' but I learned in the old neighborhood that this would have been a stupid move. It would have put me out of the shoe-shine business, which was situated in a lucrative location. Instead, I said to myself, 'You fuckin' greedy son-of-a-bitch...you fuckin' shit, robbing your own,' and so on and so forth.

"Boy, was I pissed-off that night. It was my first experience with greed. I was going to tell my father about it, but he was going through a difficult period, and I decided to keep my mouth shut. He didn't need any more *agita*."

Spinuzzi joined in, "Speaking of greed, Miserabile, I remember when I was in my early teens and there were a few poor people in the neighborhood who needed a helping hand. My parents would send over a big bag of groceries every week to this one poor family with five or six kids. There was a guy next door who made a lot of money selling furniture. Except for the boys of the underworld, he was the richest guy in the neighborhood. The fucker never gave away a penny to anyone.

My father tried to convince him to help *La Spaventosa*, an obese lady that lived alone and was in ill health. The poor lady couldn't afford to pay her medical bills. She just stayed in the house, suffering silently, waiting for her final hour to arrive.

"Do you know what the fucking *stronzo* said? He said, '*Quello che faccio io sono i miei affari.*' In other words, 'Mind your own business.' My father persisted, but to no avail. The *stronzo* hoarded money and didn't give a shit about anyone. I remember seeing him pull a thick bankroll of ten-dollar bills, a fortune in those days, out of his pocket, with a rubber band wrapped around it. He sat on the stoop and counted the bills twice. I thought he would turn into a gold statue.

"My parents told me that greed is a natural characteristic of mankind. They taught me that it has many faces, some of which are vicious. My mother told me to read a short book written by John Steinbeck called *The Pearl*.

"It's about the poor Mexican pearl diver, Kino, who finds a pearl the size of a sea gull's egg which is as 'perfect as the moon.' Boy, is he happy. The pearl, he figures, could bring himself and his wife and young kid wealth, happiness and security. Then the shit hits the fan. To make a long story short, he experiences a series of attempts on his life by those who want the pearl. He even kills someone to defend his family, but he cannot prevent someone from shooting his kid's head off. Kino finally concludes that the pearl is what led to greed and violence. He and his wife Juana—a beautiful name—decide to get rid of it. They walk to the Gulf of Mexico, where Kino hurls the pearl as hard and far as he can into the water."

The story had its impact. There was silence around the table.

Mo broke the quiet. "Hey, I remember *La Spaventosa*. She was one of the biggest ladies in the old neighborhood. I'm no talking about fat, but muscle. What the hell ever happened to her?"

Spinuzzi answered, "Well, my father went to Alfonsina, the lady who owned the grocery store and was well-respected by almost everyone in the old neighborhood. She used to sneak extra food in the grocery bags of her poorest customers. She had a heart of gold.

"They came up with a plan to make a collection from her customers and other charitable people in the neighborhood. They were pretty successful, and took the money and some homemade wine over to *La Spaventosa*. She cried tears of joy, and they all had a drink together.

"*La Spaventosa* smiled and thanked them. She died a week later. No autopsy was done, so we never found out the cause of death. At her funeral, my father told me that almost all wealthy people are greedy, and one reason why they're wealthy is their love of holding onto money. Though I think he may have exaggerated, I have frequently observed the same thing.

"Hey, Miserabile, sorry for the distraction, but I got carried away with this greed thing. I hate the mother."

Miserabile answered, "*Pure io, mio amico, pure io. Ma la vita e cosi.*"

Genella asked, "What did you say, Miserabile?"

Miserabile ignored her question and went on. "I also hate greed. But getting on to the larger picture about mankind and his governments, history is clear on these matters. Man is not only greedy but he is avaricious, selfish, cruel, untruthful and murderous. And the governments that govern him share the same characteristics. Plato said that the state is a macrocosm of the microcosm of man's mind. States go to war, kill their so-called enemies and enslave those that remain alive, without remorse. In fact, there is pleasure in this type of act. Someone once said that war is a nation's way of eating. These facts dawned on me when I was a kid, reading about ancient Egypt. The Egyptians were a very happy people. They had a wonderful family life. But then they would go to war with their neighbors, slaughter all the males and take the women and children back as slaves. This seemed like a contradiction to me, but history has proven me wrong.

"I was out to dinner one night with one of the senior senators of Congress. He was a very wise old-timer who had been through many battles in his life and had witnessed many more. I was in a philosophic mood that evening, talking about why people are miserable, why there are wars and why people don't learn any lessons from the past. Dostoevsky was right when he wrote that people love to be miserable, and Freud was also right about people having a death wish. I asked my senator friend whether he had the answer, full well expecting that he would say that no one has the answer to the riddle of mankind. But the bugger surprised me.

"He said, 'Sure, I have the answer!'

"I smiled and told him he must be pulling my chain, but he insisted he was not. He said, 'It has to do with the scorpion and the frog.' He then told a story that goes something like this:

"A frog was about to cross a large pond. Just before he started to swim across, a scorpion approached him and asked him whether he could climb on his back and hitch a ride to the other side of the pond.

"The frog told him, 'I'm not a stupid creature, my friend. You want to kill me.'

"The scorpion replied, 'I'm not stupid, either. If I sting you, I'll sink into the water and die, too.'

"The frog thought about it and concluded that the scorpion made very good sense. So he invited the scorpion to get on his back, and they took off.

"Halfway across the lake, the scorpion stung the frog. The frog said, '*Affanculo*, why the hell did you do this? Now we will both die!'

"The scorpion answered, '**I could not help it, my friend. It's in my nature**.'

"That, Genella, is the best answer I can give you. I agree with the Senator *cento per cento*. It is that way because it is that way."

Genella then asked, "You're pretty pessimistic about the future of the world, aren't you?"

"It's tough not to be," answered Miserabile. "Look around you, and what do you see: Weapons of mass destruction, biological warfare and genetic manipulation are increasing at a rapid pace. We are scorpions, and we will use them, no doubt about it. The part of the Bible that I really believe in is the Apocalypse. Natural catastrophes may have ended the era of the dinosaurs, but man-made ones will end ours. Though many in the past have written that Armageddon is about to arrive, the weapons to bring this about did not exist. Now we have them."

This conversation was getting too depressing. I didn't want to end the evening on the downside, but Miserabile was on a roll, and I couldn't stop him.

He looked at Genella and said, "President Eisenhower had a rare moment in history to solve the problem, but he blew it."

"What should he have done?" asked Genella. It was obvious to everyone that Genella and Miserabile were again beginning to light each other's fire.

"After the Second World War, we were the only superpower in the world, and we were the only country with the atomic bomb. Eisenhower should have taken the position that no other country in the world could develop atomic weapons; if anyone did, we would attack it with our own and destroy them. In fact, Einstein took a similar position. The two great Italians, Julius Caesar and Napoleon—Napoleon was Italian, you know—would also not have hesitated to do so. Most great leaders would have done so. But for some reason our democratic country has its weaknesses. We don't act to prevent, we react.

"I don't give a fuck what anyone says, we are the greatest and most benevolent nation in history. Those who say we would have become cruel tyrants of the world if we ruled it are dumb fuck-heads. Immigrants are streaming into our country and very few in our country are leaving to go to other countries such as Russia and China. That tells the story about how great our country is. What more do we need?

"Getting back to the point: Such diverse personalities as Einstein, Hemingway, Huxley, Pauling and others all agreed that science would drastically impact mankind. Einstein and Pauling were absolutely sure that the world would end in a nuclear fireball."

The Pig interrupted, "*State zitti*, you guys. Be quiet. Speaking about the power of mankind, Del Monaco is singing the death scene in *Otello*."

It's very tough to judge the greatest anything. But if one had to judge what is the greatest opera of all time, practically all opera lovers would rate Verdi's *Otello* in the top three.

Verdi was an old man when he wrote this powerful, dramatic opera. He surprised everyone. He was already old when he wrote

Aida. Everyone thought that *Aida* was his swan song. Suddenly, *Otello* springs from the aging brain of the greatest operatic genius of all time.

After we all passed sixty, our annual dinner conversations turned more and more to the issue of aging. We did discuss the aging and its impact on life when we were younger, but then the discussions were intellectual, not emotional. We had not yet arrived at the threshold of the twilight years. But now we were there, and detached emotional syllogisms were replaced by deeply felt reality.

We were all, thank God, in relatively good physical shape and none of us showed signs of losing our functioning brains to Alzheimer's or any other disease that would rob us of being involved in and enjoying the world.

None of us has a daughter, which presents a problem. My grandmother used to say that, "A son is a son, until he gets a wife; a daughter is a daughter for the rest of your life." That used to be very true in the old neighborhood. It is less true today. Daughters ain't around as much anymore.

In the old Italian neighborhood, it was the daughter who took care of her aging parents. This was never questioned. If daughters-in-law also got involved in the helping, it was an unexpected blessing. In fact, my mother—the daughter-in-law—took care of my father's parents, but that was the exception, not the rule.

There was no assisted living, no nursing homes and no primary care givers in the old neighborhood. Everybody was taken care of within *la famiglia*. But then came modern medicine, modern technology, wealth, and the unexpected phenomenon of old-timers, particularly women, living much longer. Increased mobility and the disintegration of the family made old-timers feel as though they were not welcome at home and had no place else to go.

Before I forget, Spinuzzi is a sometimes misanthrope. He has a hard time loving or respecting either men or women. But more recently he has become a sometimes misogynist. He tries to hide it, in order to maintain his image of being logical and objective about all that is going on in the world, but sometimes his dislike of modern women's behavior leaks out. In fact, a few years ago the Pig caught him off-guard and pointed out that he was a misogynist, the implication being that he lost his rationality and was emotional in his opinions about women.

Spinuzzi listened to this and then assaulted the Pig's attack on his intellectual integrity. He first asked the Pig if he respected the truth instead of the baloney he was being fed by the mass media about life's values. He went a step further, and asked the Pig if he was capable of discerning the truth even if he saw it. If not, he told the Pig, he need not worry, for this was normal in America today.

The Pig was no intellectual match for Spinuzzi, and decided to let him continue. He realized that he might end up looking like a horse's ass, and in the old Italian neighborhood, a horse's ass was a horse's ass for a lifetime. And no one respected a horse's rear end.

Spinuzzi let forth a tirade, which was not his style. He was usually calm, logical and somewhat witty. But the Pig had touched a sensitive spot, and Spinuzzi let loose.

He said, "Pig, I wish you would start thinking with your brains instead of with your *culo*. If you can't see that the woman is the foundation of the family, then go to the *gabinetto* and jerk off.

"Look, these asshole women have too much to say, these days. And they're all fucked up. But the fucked up woman is another issue that's not up for discussion, here."

The feisty Pig aroused himself in order to protect his image. He interjected, "Spinuzzi, aren't the fuckin' men in the United States all fucked up, too?"

Spinuzzi, more coldly than I ever saw, responded, "We're not talking about fuckin' men, but fuckin' women. And when I say, 'fuckin',' I mean both supine and upright."

It's difficult to explain to others, but moments like this made our annual meetings worthwhile. The combination of intellect and emotion is what life is all about. It's kind of like sex, a stimulant. It's cathartic. It's good to dump mental loads, now and then.

Spinuzzi continued, "Now, listen to me. Try to remember ten mature women in the old neighborhood, not teenagers."

Spinuzzi looked around and said, "I'm not saying this just to say it. I want you to think about ten individual mature women in the old neighborhood, and let's not talk for thirty seconds."

Spinuzzi looked at his watch and counted the seconds. Del Monaco, by now, had committed suicide in the last act of *Otello*, and the curtain had descended. What could now be heard was the tenor-soprano duet from the first act of Puccini's, *Madame Butterfly*. It is one of the most beautiful ever written, and the singers, Giuseppe

DiStefano and Victoria De Los Angeles, are almost the perfect match to deliver its vocal beauty.

Spinuzzi then said, "The thirty seconds are up. Now, I'm going to ask you guys a question, and I don't want to hear any hedging. I want an honest, straightforward answer.

Genella said, "What about me, Spinuzzi? I also thought about ten women from my old neighborhood."

Spinuzzi answered, "Why not, *bella* Genella?"

Miserabile said, "I could only think of eight!"

Spinuzzi said, "That's okay. It doesn't matter that much."

Mo said, "Guess what? The first person I thought of was a man." He instinctively was about to look at the Pig but caught himself and continued to face Spinuzzi. "His name was Annibile Astrubile Amabile Ogerino. Why his name came to mind, I haven't the foggiest idea!"

Genella asked, "What do all those names mean?"

Mo answered, "'Annibile means 'Hannibal,' 'Astrubile' means 'from the stars,' and 'Amabile' means 'lovable.' 'Ogerino' is the family name, and I don't know if it has a meaning."

Ignoring Mo, Spinuzzi continued, "Now let's look at what's going on with our women today. It's funny, when I said 'Our women,' I felt that *qualche cosa non va* when I said it. We all used the term 'our women' in an endearing way in the old neighborhood, and the women sensed its meaning and appreciated the commitment behind it. If you use these words today, they will be offended, interpreting the words as words of servitude, instead of love. *Affanculo*, my friends, *affanculo*.

"I want to pick a specific example of what's going on, and then I would like you to compare the reaction of modern women with that of women in the old neighborhood.

"Regarding health matters, up until recent times, men used to live longer than women. It was not uncommon for men to expect to have two wives in their lifetimes, because women died at a much earlier age, largely due to infection after childbirth.

"Before we start feeling too sorry for these women, let's not forget that millions of men, on a regular basis, were wounded or killed on the battlefield, defending their countries and their families. Women and children were frequently spared or taken as slaves. I read somewhere that in all of history, there were only about three hundred years where a war wasn't recorded. And let me tell you, my friends, that's classic bullshit. There were certainly wars during those three hundred years, but either there was nobody that knew how to write to record them or the potential historian was killed by the invaders before he could put his pen to paper.

"Then came modern medicine in the twentieth century. The pharmaceutical industry produced antibiotics that could destroy the bacteria that killed people, along with analgesics—you know, pain killers—that allowed surgeons to operate and remove pockets of infection. These two medical discoveries, antibiotics and painkillers, have dramatically reversed the mortality situation between men and women. Of course, we now have other important drugs, too. Women now live much longer than men. Up to this point, technology has favored women in many sectors of life.

"All you have to do is visit assisted living and nursing homes, and what do you see? Women, women and women. There are a couple of men, but they are in the vast minority. The rest are dead.

"Now that these modern American women are living longer than men, what do these selfish babes want? Chicks' special interest groups are lobbying the government to spend more money on women's health. They don't give a fuck about men.

"Getting back to the ladies in the old Italian neighborhood: If you were to ask them if the government had some big-time extra cash, and had to make a choice whether to spend it on trying to conquer women's or men's diseases, what would be their answer?"

The boys didn't answer immediately. Their brains were bringing back memories of their mothers, sisters, aunts, cousins, lady neighbors and everybody else.

Genella, however, didn't hesitate. "They would vote to spend it on the men."

Spinuzzi said, "Pig, what do you think?"

The Pig answered, "I think they would choose the men."

"Pignachi, your answer?"

"The men."

"Mo, your answer?"

"The men."

"Miserabile, *che ne pensi?*"

"The men."

I chose the men, also, and then I asked Spinuzzi. He also chose the men.

Spinuzzi continued, "Now, what do you think these modern babes would do?"

He seemed to be asking someone and no one at the same time. He was definitely energized.

"Genella, your answer first."

"There's no doubt. Women."

"Pig, your answer?"

"I think they would choose the women."

"Mo?"

"The women."

"Miserabile?"

"The women."

"Pignachi?"

"The men!"

I had the same opinion as the Pig, while Spinuzzi chose the women.

Spinuzzi had the look of victory in his eyes. And it was justified. By using a single example, he vividly demonstrated that there was a big difference in the nature of love in old Italian neighborhood women compared to modern, emancipated women. I was taught by my father when I was a kid that when you're trying to make a point, the use of a good example is much better than thousands of words.

It was obvious that the boys, including myself, were all taken aback by the realization that the old neighborhood ladies, in general, would sacrifice their well-being for their fathers, husbands, brothers, and men in general, while modern ones would not. They had never thought about this issue before.

Genella asked, "What category would the Italian men in the old neighborhood have chosen?"

I said, "Women."

Spinuzzi said, "Women."

Pignachi said, "Women."

Miserabile said, "Women."

Mo said, "Women."

And the Pig said, "Women."

Genella, delighted that by asking this pertinent question she had earned greater respect from the boys, asked a second question. "What category would you boys choose, today?"

All replied, "Women."

"Okay," Genella said. "That's you guys. If you had to ask the modern American man, this very day, what would he answer?"

That was a difficult question that required some thought. The boys needed time to sort it out. One thing for sure: The answer wasn't obvious!

Fortunately, at that point, Pavarotti was singing the role of "Nemorino" in Donizetti's opera, *Elisir D'amore*, a beautiful opera that brings joy to everyone who hears it. It commands attention. It also gave us some breathing room to recharge our mental batteries.

I said, "I think this opera, simple as it is, is one of the most beautiful and complete opera masterpieces of all time. I can't think of any that comes close to it on its level."

The boys said nothing. They were thinking about whether modern American men, whom they generally didn't respect, would place the welfare of their women before their own.

While they thought, Nemorino finally won the heart of his beloved Adina by giving her an elixir of love that contains alcohol, and the opera came to a close.

We suddenly found ourselves in post-opera silence with silence around the table, too. My Uncle Stevenello told me that a friend is a person in whose company you can feel comfortable in silence. Everyone raised their glasses of *grappa* and sipped away, not even looking at each other. What would the boys conclude, and how would it effect their moods? I had the feeling that, if they didn't like or weren't sure of their answers, it could lead to a depressing end to the evening.

I didn't want this, and neither did the boys. But as an old friend once told me, "The truth can be brutal. You've got to handle it or you'll lose in life."

Reacting to my gut instead of my brain, I decided to ask Genella first. I also decided that more uplifting opera music would help in the deliberation.

I called Vinnie over and requested that he play a sparkling part of Rossini's *Barbiere di Seviglia*. I told him to do it quickly. He did, and the music flowed and had its impact on the boys.

The human mind is indeed an interesting thing. It frequently gets stuck and needs a helping hand. What was most unusual about this moment was that everyone appeared to be "stuck," including Genella. The boys had never been confronted by the idea that men would place themselves before women in matters involving life and death. It was inconceivable in the old neighborhood. It was never a point that even qualified for discussion. It was always women first, when they needed help. Yeah, there were a few guys in the old neighborhood who were sissies and maybe would have put themselves before their women. These men talked to women about their runny noses and sleepless nights, because guys wouldn't listen to their laments. They were not considered real men. They were put in a special social category, kind of like limbo, where no one took them seriously. These are the kinds of men that neither wage nor win wars.

Although he had a feeling that the group was not yet comfortable enough to answer the question, Mo seemed fairly certain about his answer. In order to give the boys more time for reflection, he told a story that the evening's conversation had brought to mind, for reasons known only to God.

He began, "About fifteen years ago, I had some business in Italy. I flew to Rome and arrived early in the morning. I went directly from the airport to my favorite hotel, the Hassler. I got there about 10 a.m., checked in and, as I usually do, took a walk to one of my favorite bars.

"Some of you may not know that an Italian bar is nothing like an American bar. It serves sandwiches and pastry, *espresso*, *cappuccino*, juices and everything else. Yes, it does serve booze, but many people don't order it.

"I really look forward to this brief morning interlude, because I enjoy what I taste, and I enjoy the company of real Italians. They know how to enjoy small things: the food they eat, the coffee they drink and the brief conversations with their compatriots. I love New York City, but folks there don't know how to fully enjoy the beauty of the moment, like the Romans do.

"Anyway, after I had my *tramezzino*—a special, tasty Italian sandwich—and an Italian beer, I took a walk and got back to my hotel about 11 a.m. I took a nap, then got up for a meeting that was supposed to last until early evening. Well, the meeting lasted until about nine o'clock that night. This is very unusual; in fact, it is almost unheard of in Rome, although it is quite common in Milan. Milan is the economic machine of Italy. There's an Italian saying, 'The Milanese work and pay taxes so that the Romans can play.' Well, one of the guys at the meeting was one of the last of the great *padroni* of Italy. A *padrone* is a very strong male who owns a company, a vineyard, or whatever, and rules it like a tyrant. Many of them are benevolent types, but they still operate as tyrants.

"Though I would like to say that their word is golden, and that you could depend on a handshake to honor a deal, like they say about the Jewish jewelry dealers in New York City, I have sometimes been disappointed. The *padrone* that I was with that night was one whose word was stronger than a contract, but he rarely gave his word.

"He called me Mo, and I called him Gianni. You must remember that in Italy, in those days, you only called your closest friends and family members by their first names. This name system was based on respect, and guys, I don't want to talk about respect any more, tonight.

"But the son-of-a-bitch was a profound thinker and keen observer of the forces that move human nature. Since he was the guy with the money and the power to decide how to spend it, people he did business with kissed his ass. He loved to bust their balls and make them suffer a bit before he agreed to anything.

"Because I didn't need his business, and he knew it, he respected me more than the others. This behavior is common, which tells me a lot about human nature: The more independent and powerful you are, the more you are respected. Nice guys finish last. I think it was Vince Lombardi who said, 'You show me a good loser and I'll show you a loser.'

"Anyway, I'm getting off the track. He and I went to dinner together at a restaurant near the Piazza Navona. It was about ten at night, and the Romans were still arriving to eat. The Romans eat late, but not nearly as late as the Spaniards, who are still eating at midnight.

"When you go to a restaurant in Italy, you sit down and order immediately. The waiter frequently doesn't bring a menu but hovers over the table and asks you to make your choices then and there. If you ask for a menu, the waiter gets insulted and pissed-off.

"I can't even begin to think about eating until I have my martini. That night, the waiter came over and did what most Italian waiters do. Gianni was watching me, for he knew I had to have my martini before I could think about ordering.

"The waiter gave me the usual Italian 'rush,' which, let me emphasize, is not a 'rush' for the Italians, but a big rush and a pain in the ass for Americans.

"I was tired and said, '*Vorrei un martini Americano,*' and I explained what it is. He understood, and then asked us what we wanted for dinner. I politely told him, in Italian, that I wasn't ready to order dinner, and that I would order after I finished the martini. He couldn't quite understand what I was talking about and, once more, asked us what we wanted for dinner.

"It took a bit of verbal exchange for him to finally understand my position. He walked away without the food order and reluctantly brought me an American martini.

"Gianni was smiling throughout this entire episode. He ordered a bottle of one of my favorite Italian red wines. The martini and the wine arrived and we drank together. Because we were tired, the booze hit us more quickly and with more impact than usual. These are some of the moments in life when the inhibitions of the mind are lowered—so very temporarily.

"We were wondering what life's all about, why there's so much stupid mental pain that shouldn't be and why people aren't as happy as they could be. He had already almost gulped his first glass of wine, a rarity in Italian culture, and was almost through his second.

Gianni was mellow that night, and so was I. He delivered a monologue on what life is all about. It was a real privilege to hear the honest views of those who have lived life to its fullest.

"Gianni had fought in the Italian underground during World War II. The Germans killed his father and a couple of his uncles in order to strike fear in the hearts of the people of the village, so that they wouldn't betray the Germans to the American soldiers. Gianni had a bicycle and became a secret messenger for the Italian Resistance.

"Every Sunday, Gianni went to church on his bicycle and was secretly given an envelope to deliver to the Resistance. He had to pedal by the German soldiers on his way to the hills to deliver the messages. Gianni was a tough son-of-a-bitch. Gianni is now gone. Where he is, who knows? Let's hope it's Heaven."

Mo paused and continued, "Speaking of Gianni and personal strength, I'm now thinking about a few things that I had read and heard about in the past twenty-four hours. A city down on the New Jersey shore has passed a law to stop people from digging deep holes in the sand, because a small kid had fallen in one and was killed, a one-in-a-billion type of event.

"I also read an article where the authorities were concerned that the backpacks that kids carry are too heavy for these poor little things, and they force these kids to buy backpacks with an inflatable cushion on the lower back to help these poor kiddies carry the weight and prevent them from hurting their little fuckin' backs.

"And, just last night, my nephew was over my house. He told me, without batting a fuckin' eyelash, that he was going to a baby shower. I couldn't fuckin' believe it.

"I asked him whether he felt out of place, going to a baby shower where there would be only women. He had a puzzled look on his face and proceeded to tell me that all the husbands and boyfriends were going to baby showers—like it was normal.

"I wanted to tell him that he shouldn't go, but I decided not to. The guy was pussy-whipped and there's nothing you can do with a wimp like that.

"And get this: Last night my wife told me about her nephew and how excited he was to go to his fiancée's Jack-and-Jill party. I didn't want to seem like an idiot, but if you have the right wife, you can sometimes act like one and she will, once in a while, let you get away with it.

"I said, 'Love of my life, what the hell is a Jack-and-Jill party?' She said, 'Honey, this is part of the do-everything-together movement in the United States. Remember your bachelor party before our marriage? Did you know that, like the Jews broadening the Bar Mitzvah to a Bat Mitzvah, bachelorette parties also came in vogue about a decade ago? Now they have the heterosexual Jack-and-Jill parties, which combine the bachelor and bachelorette parties into a single event. It's like what's going on with the baby showers.'

"I tell you, my friends, this ain't good for the men nor the women. They're thinking wrong and paying the price with shaky and broken marriages.

"Do you guys remember? In the old neighborhood, the ladies at the baby showers threatened us with sixty days of sex abstinence, if we showed up at the event. It was for the ladies, only, and the ladies wanted it that way. It was their 'me' time.

"When God created Eve because He thought that it was not good for man to be alone, He didn't intend men to go to baby showers and Jack-and-Jill parties. I can't believe these fuckin' weakling men. More puzzling, I can't believe that these modern women want them there."

Spinuzzi interjected. "I would like to propose a theory: The women want to be with men more and more because they think that being together will prevent divorce. The guys are going along with it because they have the same fears. It's not the right way to live, of course. It's not natural."

Genella looked directly at Miserabile, waiting for him to say something. He didn't say a word.

She then turned her gaze back toward Spinuzzi and asked, "What's wrong with men going to these events? I mean, doesn't it bring the couples closer together? The woman magazines call it 'bonding.' Have you ever thought that maybe the guys like it?"

Spinuzzi answered. "It's just the opposite, *cara* Genella. Though these modern women have much more knowledge about sexual man than women had in the past, they don't have the knowledge of psychological man that the ladies in the old neighborhood had. That's why they're losing their men in droves. The more they fuck around doing the wrong things together, the greater probability that they will lose them."

Genella was not intimidated by Spinuzzi's intellect. In her profession, she, by necessity, was compelled to be an expert in dealing with all types of men.

She said, "You still haven't answered my question about what's actually wrong with these co-ed events."

Spinuzzi leaned back on his chair and put a match to his cigar. He took a few deep puffs, sipped a bit of *grappa* and said, "You know, Genella, it's like the 'respect' thing that we talked about before. You know it's important, but it's difficult to verbalize 'why,' because words are very limited when trying to explain human experience. It is what it is.

"Let me ask you a question, and I want you to answer it honestly. Don't put up any feminist barriers to giving an honest answer. Who would you rather be with, a man who goes to baby showers and Jack-and-Jill parties, or a strong man like Gianni, who has fought life's battles, risked his life for his fellow men, women and children, and also made it in life?"

Genella didn't expect that Spinuzzi would come up with this Kierkegaardian Either-Or analogy. She put a match to her cigarette, sipped her *grappa* and let out a barely audible sigh.

The boys didn't say a word, for there was nothing to say. Spinuzzi had hit it right on the nose.

She sighed again and answered, "I'd, of course, rather be with Gianni."

Spinuzzi said, "Case closed."

I said, "Mo, continue with your story about Gianni. Why did you bring him up, and what are you leading to?"

"To make a long story short," Mo said, "Gianni and I got on the subject of the good life. Though we talked about many things, like the importance of having enough money to be comfortable and to have good health, he got to the core of his personal philosophy.

"He told me that the important thing in life is to not take anything too seriously, except people and things that are very close to you.

"He had a wonderful, general philosophy on how to handle life. I forget the details of the story, but when he had just entered college, he read a play by Ben Jonson called *Volpone*. Now *volpo* means "fox" in Italian: *Volpone* means a big fox.

"*Volpone* was a Zorba, the only difference being that the latter made love to poor women and the former, to rich ones.

"Once more, my memory is failing. I think *Volpone* was actually dying or faking it. While he was on his sick-bed, the rich ladies came to bid him a last farewell. One of them, with a deep cut décolletage and her breasts bulging outwards, asked him something like, '*Volpone, Volpone*, you know how to enjoy life. You also made so many women happy. Before you go bye-bye to the Great Beyond, would you tell poor little me what is your secret to enjoying life?'

"Gianni was a little cynical about people and what was truly behind their words. He told me that he thought that this lady was not at all curious about *Volpone's* secret but was trying to encourage him to invite her into the sack so that she could have her multiple orgasms for the last time in her life. Educated, high-class women usually can only have multiple orgasms with men gifted both physically and mentally, who understand them. The pecker, itself, is not usually enough.

"Well, *Volpone* said something like, 'There are two components to enjoying life. The first is to seek beautiful moments. They do not come unless you make an effort to find and develop them. Then, when you find one, treat it as a great wine. You should sniff its bouquet and make it linger for as long as you can. The second component regards bad moments. When they come, you must speed them up and get rid of them.'

"Gianni went on to say that people seem to like to suffer. He first observed this as a kid, such as when old-timers who were asked to go to someone's house to eat and drink a little and have a good time, and would invariably refuse. But when finally pushed to do so and they did go, they invariably had a good time.

"He thought he had made an independent observation but when he read some of Dostoyevsky's works, he knew that people before him had made this observation. He told me that he learned that this sad human trait is not a product of modern times, but has always been.

"But Gianni was a romantic, and could not accept the fact that people are given the great privilege of being born and having life, and then decide to be miserable instead of enjoying it. It didn't make any sense to him, but reality is reality.

"Then his mind turned to religion and the reason why it exists. He virtually dumped on the intellects who believe that religion exists simply to eliminate the fear of dying by creating Gods and an afterlife. He rejected Voltaire's belief that even if God doesn't exist, mankind would have to create Him. Mankind worships God, though in different forms, under different expressions of religion, because He exists. He believed what Kant believed: That the concept of God is already present in the mind when we are born. He was fascinated by the Sumerians—the culture that provided the foundation of many of the religious beliefs of the great cultures of the Middle East, from the Arabs to the Israelis."

Pignachi looked at Mo with philosophic eyes and said, "This may be well and good for the very few with the strength and resources to live according to Gianni's philosophy, but it's like being Nietchze's Superman. It's extremely difficult, and it applies to less than one percent of mankind."

Miserabile smiled again. "We are talking about the great subject of strength, the strength of our people and the strength of our country: The importance of strength, to my knowledge, has not been discussed much at all in the mass media in recent times." He hesitated and took another sip of the *grappa*. He looked at all of us and said, "What I have to say has been said by others. It's not an optimistic opinion at all."

Then it happened! Once about every four or five years, Miserabile is transformed into another personality. He enters into what seems like a trance and delivers his thoughts and opinions in a way that would have impressed Daniel Webster or Demosthenes. He is both thoughtful and forceful. These moments, evidently, only come to him at our annual dinners. If they came when he's in Congress, he would be in the leadership of his party. Why they didn't come to him or why he refused to use this mental state in Congress, only God knows. Remember what Milton said. "The mind can make a Heaven of Hell or a Hell of Heaven," but he never addressed the issue of what makes the mind choose one or the other.

He started, "I'll start with my conclusion: America is rapidly becoming a weak, insecure nation and will not survive, as we know it, for long. Our men, in particular, are increasingly sitting down when they pee.

"Let me give you a microcosm example that reflects the macrocosm of our nation's consciousness. You all know we Americans are all becoming label freaks. Just go into the stores and you'll see about half of them reading the *maledetti* labels, particularly the warning parts. I recently read two labels that blew my mind. I can't remember the exact words, but one dealt with a pair of athletic shin guards. The label said something like, 'These shin guards can only protect your shins; they do not protect any other part of the body!' Another label dealt with a rock garden set. The label said, 'If you eat rocks you may break your teeth.' As you all know, the list of labels that cater to our insecurity is very long and getting longer. The guys in the old neighborhood, I can tell you, would refuse to buy products with such labels because they insult both their intelligence and masculinity. Frankly speaking, I'm not sure how the ladies would have reacted. They probably would have laughed."

Genella once more took the conversational initiative. "Miserabile, how can we soon lose our strength as a nation, if we are, without doubt, the number one superpower in the world? Everyone says we now stand unchallenged as number one."

Miserabile answered, "You have been indoctrinated, my love, by the politicians and the media. How the hell in God's name can we be called the unchallenged superpower if one night Putin—you know, the guy that runs Russia—could have a nervous breakdown after an argument with his wife about sex, go off his rocker; call his man in charge of thousands of nuclear missiles, and order him to fire them at the United States? Do you know, Genella, that we don't have anything, not a fuckin' thing, to stop those missiles? Those schmucks that ridiculed and blocked President Reagan's anti-missile initiative are responsible for our current situation.

"Well, let's say the missiles are released on Sunday morning. By Sunday night, the United States would be destroyed, a nation of the past. The greatest country in the history of the world could be wiped out in a matter of minutes.

"So is the United States the one and only unchallenged superpower? Bullshit, it is. We are more weak and vulnerable than ever before in our history! The oceans do not protect us anymore."

Genella said, "Well, the newspapers and political experts on television say that the Russians are our friends and we only have to worry about rogue countries with a few missiles. They also say Russia could be destroyed by our missiles, so why would they do it?"

Miserabile exploded. "Those fuckin' so-called media experts should do hard labor for a year to learn what life's all about. It's a fuckin' jungle out there, and the laws of the jungle still reign supreme. They are misleading the public in a big way by telling us goddamn lies. Yeah, Russia may be friendly today, but may be an enemy tomorrow. Who's to say they won't change? Who among us has never lost a friend?

"Also, did you ever hear of those *pazzi* like Nero, Caligula, Genghis Khan, Hitler and Stalin? In the modern setting, leaders with personalities like that could, without hesitation or remorse, press the button of nuclear destruction after, of course, they have their last great supper followed by a superb *pompino*. Cleopatra must have been the greatest *pompinatrice* in recorded history."

"What's a *pompino*?" asked Genella.

"It's oral sex or, like we used to say in the old neighborhood, a blow-job."

Genella segued, "What's a *pompinatrice*?"

"That's the gal that gives the *pompino*. Though there's no tangible evidence to support it, I'm convinced that most of the women who have had the greatest impact on the male leaders of the world were superb *pompinatrici*."

"Amen," said Spinuzzi.

No one else said a word. Genella had a look in her eyes that indicated she was trying to reason out Miserabile's blow-job hypothesis. All the boys noticed that and smiled softly.

Verdi's *Rigoletto* could now be heard in the background. Ah, what a great opera it is. *Rigoletto* is about an Italian Duke who screws every gal in town including the hunchback Rigoletto's daughter. In his middle period, Verdi wrote three great operas in a row: *Il Trovatore*, *Rigoletto* and *La Traviata*, I'm not sure in what order. If the operatic voices are up to the task, each one is truly thrilling. The problem is that the great voices are not around, so modern opera fans may never experience the incomparable beauty of Verdi's operas except through recordings.

Spinuzzi, wanting to encourage Miserabile's rare moment of brilliance and wisdom, said, "Though we do have our differences on certain issues, I agree with what you're saying. I'm reminded of a football game I watched the other night. A guy in the secondary of the defense made a big hit on the tight end, who had just caught the ball.

"The tight end was sprawled on the ground and the guy who made the hit stood over him and evidently said some real nasty words. Then I shit my pants. The referee called a penalty on this guy for 'taunting.' In other words, he was saying nasty things to this poor defenseless guy like, 'I hit you now, mother-fucker, and I'm going to hit you so hard later on that you won't be able to screw your wife for a month.'

"Now those politically correct, self-serving weak shits that control the football league are constantly making new rules in order to avoid upsetting the politically correct media and fans. What they really should do, if they want to do the truly correct thing, is reduce the training programs that increase the physical strength and mental aggressiveness of the players. After all, it's not the taunts that injure the players, but the vicious physical hits they receive, which can put them out of action not only for weeks, but sometimes for an entire season, or even forever.

"I used to play semi-pro football when I was in college. Taunting was part of the game. The strong survived it and were stronger for it. They would either taunt back or they and the other players would team up on the guy and beat the shit out of him for the rest of the game. Football players are, in a sense, gladiators. Can you imagine Julius Caesar saying to the gladiators, 'Beat up and kill each other, but don't taunt?' It's ridiculous."

Mo rejoined the conversation. "Miserabile, what can I say, except to say that what you're saying is *veramente* depressing. Do you remember the 2000 Subway Series between the Mets and the Yankees?

"Roger Clemens threw a pitch at Mike Piazza. Both guys are among the best. Well, Piazza swings and his bat breaks and some of the pieces jet forward to Clemens. Clemens, who has a volatile temper, picks up a piece of the bat and throws it towards Piazza. Now, mind you, the bat piece doesn't hit Piazza, and isn't even close to hitting him.

"The broadcast announcer expressed such extreme shock you would have thought Clemens had stuck a hot poker up Piazza's rear end. All fuckin' night this announcer talked about this horrible act—

throwing a piece of a broken bat back at the ground in the direction of the batter.

"In the old Italian neighborhood this would be considered an act of good competitive spirit and the boys would have enjoyed it. If anyone denounced the act as 'horrible,' the old-time reporters would have agreed with the boys and attacked this guy in their columns. But what happened? Other reporters agreed that Clemens committed an unforgivable act. Would you believe it? I got so irritated I was beside myself. I thought to myself that the American male is becoming weaker and weaker at a rapid pace."

Genella, getting increasingly feisty, said, "Well, you guys seem to be contradicting yourselves. You said that the American male is in the driver's seat, having a good time divorcing his unworthy first wife, often leaving her stranded with children, and marrying a second, younger one, who is more appreciative and more actively sexual."

Spinuzzi, forever the logician, said, "Genella, what you have said does not contradict what the boys are talking about. In fact, one can argue that the reason why there is divorce is because the men are weak and cannot handle their women."

Pignachi said, "We're going off on a tangent, here. Let Miserabile continue, and let's not interrupt him unless we have something really important to say. Weakness in our country, be it male or female weakness, is a real issue."

We could not help but notice that Genella and Miserabile were continuing to hit it off again, more and more as the conversation deepened. Her eyes were riveted on him as he spoke. Intellectual foreplay was taking the place of sexual foreplay. (Spinuzzi, of course, would argue that intellectual foreplay is really sexual foreplay, in disguise.)

I could tell the boys were thinking what I was thinking: Maybe these two are good for each other. They are two highly independent people who really didn't need a partner for their remaining years. But their chemistry appeared good. I looked at Mo to check whether my feelings were on line. He looked back at me, read my eyes and simply shrugged his shoulders in a way that meant, "Maybe; *chi lo sa?*"

But let's not forget Mario. As Genella and Miserabile were exchanging glances, we were periodically looking at Mario. He remained silent, probably because this wasn't his type of conversation. He is a fish out of water unless he's talking about food and his udamanistic philosophy of life. He truly believes that man is born to be happy.

We had already concluded that Mario's chances of hooking up with Genella, either for a now-and-then moment of pleasure or on a more constant basis, were pretty much caput. Genella hardly looked at him during the last hour. But to his credit, Mario had already concluded that there would be no Mario-Genella love affair and had accepted it. And it didn't seem to bother him. He knew how to draw lines in life and protect himself.

He had learned a lesson that we all learned in our old Italian neighborhood—it is important to be able to walk away from a situation. You must prepare yourself for disappointing and painful moments in life. If you don't, you lose. As I mentioned, in the old neighborhood there were quite a few different street corners where different types of people congregated.

One evening, a mad dentist with wild eyes and disheveled hair—we used to call him "Doctor Mussimadman"—was talking about why one of the guys in the neighborhood was excessively depressed after he lost his girlfriend. He said that his great error was that he had become one hundred percent dependent on the relationship; so when it ended, the guy fell apart.

He said he should have set up protective mental barriers, consciously formed a mental attitude that expected this to happen. This way, when it did, he would have been better prepared to walk away, lick his wounds a while, and get on with his life. He advised that one should do this not only in affairs of love but in all walks of life, from the job to family relationships. His constant mantra was, "You got to know where to draw the line in life and be able to walk away."

Mario suddenly got up and left the table. We all realized that Mario had taken Dr. Mussimadman's advice and decided to walk away. We didn't see or hear from him until the end of the evening.

We silently agreed that it was better this way, and we were thankful for Mario's wise move.

I said, "Listen, the hour is late and we can't ramble on too much. Miserabile, just say what comes to your head. After you finish, we'll allow three or four comments and then we can all go bye-bye. But guys and gal: no interruptions. *Capito*?"

Miserabile looked at Genella as if he were going to address her and not the boys, another sign of the power of intellectual foreplay. He began, "I don't want to seem like a real pessimist. Temperamentally, I'm not. But intellectually, the evidence is so compelling that I must confess that I have almost become one.

"To repeat, we're getting weaker and weaker, particularly the men. Let's take a look at what's going on in the American electorate. There are clear-cut patterns that I think are scary.

"Look at some of the following facts: Close to sixty percent of Catholics that go to church voted for Bush. Close to the same number of Catholics who don't go to church voted for Gore. Excluding the Black and Jewish communities, married men and women vote Republican, while single or divorced women vote Democrat. I haven't seen any reliable figures on homosexuals or young college or young working adults, but I would guess that homosexuals are all mainly Democrats.

"In the past twenty years, the Democrats running for President have never won more than forty-three percent of the white male vote. The Hispanic vote is interesting. Currently the vote is definitely Democratic. On the other hand, their history is similar to us Italians. They work hard to save money, and they have close families. The Italians, not only in the old neighborhood but practically everywhere in the United States, used to vote Democrat. As they moved up the economic scale, however, they became more and more Republican, and the more money they make, the more Republican they are.

"A recent survey produced an interesting piece of data: It is difficult to find a Hispanic Democrat whose annual income exceeds fifty-thousand dollars!"

Miserabile was waiting for questions or comments from the gang, but none came. He had, for the moment, forgotten his charge to let it all hang out—without interruption.

He continued, "Now what in my opinion, does it all mean? Is there a big picture to be drawn, or is it all a mystery, defying interpretation? Well, I don't have the answer to such questions, but I do have an opinion."

We all looked at Genella. She was breathing a bit more heavily than normal. I'm sure we were all thinking of what Spinuzzi said. "Intellectual foreplay is a form of sexual foreplay." *Chi lo sa*?

"A great many Americans feel a strong sense of insecurity, particularly—but by no means exclusively—women. Look, as we said before, at what's happening to the family. Women are more alone than ever. Let's look at job security for both men and women. I understand that employment experts are advising their clients that they may have, on the average, five jobs in their lifetimes. That probably would make me an unhappy trooper.

"Then, besides economic security, you have the problems of screwed-up kids, the threat of worldwide nuclear and biological warfare, the first-time experience by young Americans of the fickleness of the stock market, a movement to produce and market human embryos (whether conceived naturally or in a test tube) and the attack on the family by a media which rarely praises motherhood but elevates extra-marital sex to the top of the list of life's values.

Miserabile was still in his trance. "I forgot the old-timer population. I hate that fuckin' term, 'senior citizen,' but I guess we have to live with it. It separates the old from the young in a big way culturally, which is precisely what we don't need.

"The young and middle-aged folks are being deprived of the company and the wisdom of the elderly. The old-timers leave the family community and go to Florida, Arizona or God-knows-where. They have experienced and learned what life's all about. They are a national treasure of wisdom. But modern society shuts them out and won't hear their advice."

I could see Mario by the door smiling and shaking hands with his departing customers. The women took his hand and kissed him on one or two cheeks and the men shook his hand. It was *un vero palcoscenico*, and what is life but a stage—and something more.

I used my privilege as moderator to break the rule of patience.

"Miserabile," I said, "skip over some of the details and give us your conclusions about what is going on in our great country. *Viva America!*" I sounded a bit corny, and *troppo* patriotic, but that's the way I felt at that moment.

I think I hurt Miserabile's feelings by trying to cut him short. But the hour was quite late.

"Well, here's how I see what's going on. There are two guys that clued me in to the importance of feeling secure. One is Carl Jung and the other Salvador Dalí. You remember that Freud stressed sex as the primary motivator of human behavior.

"Jung, one of Freud's contemporaries, felt that man, throughout the ages, has sought a strong foundation of family, state or whatever to lean upon in order to be secure.

"I have seen that the search for personal security is a dominant force in America today."

I noticed that Genella had finished her *grappa* and Vinnie, observing this, poured her another glass. The boys hadn't yet touched theirs. Booze kills mens' peckers, but I'm not so sure what it does to the clitoris. I was afraid to ask Spinuzzi.

Miserabile continued, "Insecurity is running rampant throughout our culture. Divorce, job insecurity, families spread out and not taking care of their own, mobility, the threat of world holocaust—one can go on and on, but it all spells insecurity.

"We all seek security and what better place—at least in the old days—than in the mother's womb. Years ago, Salvador Dalí built a womb room so that patients seeking comfort and security could symbolically walk through the hairy pubic zone, down the vaginal canal, across the cervical canal and into the body of the womb to meet a waiting psychiatrist. That underrated artist had a sense of the importance of security. His womb room made me ponder, in a heavy way, the importance of security.

"Now look what's going on: Religious people and people with families vote Republican. These folks represent traditional American values, you know, marriage, family, job, church. These people are the more secure ones in our culture, for they believe they have the answers to the proper way of living. White, middle-class, working males, and this is only my impression, still appear to me to be the most secure segment of our society, even though, as we talked about tonight, big cracks are appearing in their armor.

"Now let's look at the understandably more insecure part of our population—single women, divorced women, those with job problems. They mostly vote for the Democrats. There is strong evidence that white women are voting the same way as minority groups.

"Now here's the Miserabile Hypothesis: Disruptive forces are rapidly increasing in the United States and the rest of the world, of course. This will create more insecurity and lead to the left of the Democratic Party becoming the ruling party in the United States for a long time to come. Freedom will diminish, and we will become a socialist state like what's happening in Europe.

"I rest my case."

Mo said, "Wait a minute, Miserabile. I agree with a lot of what you've said, but you left out a piece or two of the big picture that support your thinking. I'd like to mention one—the mass media, which feeds the people as never before. Who are these feeders of the people? Ninety percent of the Washington press are Democrats. Most of them don't go to church. So they feed the public a Democrat's point of view. And it's becoming worse. The media moguls who own the newspapers and television companies are Republicans, but they hire Democrats to run the corporate show.

"How the hell do those guys sleep at night?"

"It's easy," said Spinuzzi. "It's money. The more money they make, the easier it is to sleep."

I asked Miserabile, "What do you think of the internet and its impact on politics?"

Miserabile answered, "In the past, I agreed with Ronald Reagan. The guy had vision. He believed that the ability to communicate worldwide, be it via television or the internet, would lead to the toppling of tyranny and the spread of freedom. People could see the benefits of capitalism, where a bricklayer owns a car and a house and eats like a king. He was right. This is happening. I'm not sure, though, what the next phase will be."

"I am!" said Spinuzzi. "The internet, which helped spread freedom, will, paradoxically, lead to a single worldwide tyrant. It is inevitable. It is that or Armageddon. It can't be anything else."

Pignachi knew that Spinuzzi would never make an intense statement like that unless he had thought it out thoroughly.

Pignachi asked, "Why will this come to be? What will lead us all to a single world tyrant?"

Spinuzzi answered, "It's the English."

Pignachi asked, "Are you saying that Great Britain will become the tyrant nation?"

"No," he said, "the English."

Pignachi said, "You're playing games again, Spinuzzi. What do you mean when you say, 'the English?'"

Spinuzzi smiled. He enjoys intellectual play. It makes him feel good.

"My thinking goes as follows," he said. "Number one: A combination of factors such as too much freedom and increased weapons of destruction. People won't be able to handle it psychologically and will desperately look for someone to solve their problems and ease their fears on a global basis.

"Number two: The English. The English language will become the language of the world within the next thirty years, probably less. English will be the global language used on the internet. This phenomenon is well underway.

"Number three: For the first time in the history of mankind, a strong, charismatic personality will be able to communicate with everyone in every country of the world on a daily basis, and in a common language. This charismatic leader will convince people that he will save the earth and bring peace to the world. Remember Bertrand Russell's famous quote about Communism, 'Better Red than dead?' People will buy it and won't consider the trade-off. They will surrender their freedom and an elite group, selected by the new world leader, will control the world. He will, as Aldous Huxley predicted, manipulate the genetic code of all embryos to create an obedient group of earthlings.

"Look, it's already happening now. We are rapidly losing our identities. In the past there was 'James B. Doe.' Then it became 'Jim Doe,' and now it's 'Jim.' Remember, it is the last name that gives an individual his identity, not the first.

"When I watch television programs or call somebody's office, it's the same first name shit. On television, when someone is asked what their name is, they say, 'Jim,' or 'Joan,' or 'Gloria'—never the last name—like they're embarrassed to say it.

"When I call an office and ask for Mr. Doe, the secretary invariably says, 'Jim is not here,' or whatever. She consciously is denying the value of the last name. She's also got this American thing that if you call someone by the first name, you become their equal. That's bullshit, plain and simple."

Genella interjected, "You said, 'he,' regarding the new world tyrant. Could it be a she?"

"Yeah, but she's got to have big tits."

Genella smiled broadly and asked, "Why big tits?"

Spinuzzi also smiled. "It's a matter of myth. Big tits mean lots of milk, which is the fountain of life for the newborn. The mentality of the new human race will be that of newborns."

Mo laughed. "Spinuzzi, have another *grappa* for that one. I can argue that she would have to have a big ass instead of big tits."

Genella asked, "What do you say to that, Mo?"

Mo smiled and replied, "Though we are supposed to be open and discuss what's on our minds, there are limits to what my mentality would permit me to say in the presence of a lady. It's an old Italian neighborhood characteristic that I can't shake, and I cannot, therefore, explain the reason why she'll have a big ass. Maybe we'll talk about it next year."

Genella felt relieved and happy. She was now absolutely sure she would be invited to the annual dinner of 2002. And she was already looking forward to it.

Miserabile got the conversation back on track. "Let me make a few extra comments, then I promise to shut up and listen to you guys.

"Yeah, there's tons of shit going on, and the terds are increasing rapidly, like a huge, mass-production sausage-link machine. And there's little doubt in my mind that people will not be able to understand what's going on without big-time help. But, Spinuzzi, you brought up the future and, the more I think about it, the more I think you may have something, there.

"Though no one is taught this in school and, perhaps, only a handful of people in Washington are aware of it, it is clear, clear and more clear that one of the main lessons of history is that equality and freedom are sworn and eternal enemies. The more equality you want, the more freedom you have to give up. The more freedom you want, the more equality you have to surrender.

"Even my distinguished colleagues in Congress, with the exception of a handful, don't appreciate this powerful reality. Communism was a social experiment in equality. What happened? Leaders of 'equality' arose and quickly suppressed the freedom of the people. Egalitarianism, or attempts to give all people equal rights, cannot succeed simply because people aren't equal. Some people are more intelligent, wiser, stronger and healthier than others.

"Look at television programs on animals. There's the dominant, huge bull elephant, papa muscular *numero uno* gorilla and the big queen bee. Yes, Genella, I agree with both Spinuzzi and Mo that the first world tyrant could be a female. But it won't be her tits or ass that will sway the masses; it'll be her eyes."

Genella asked, "Why the eyes?"

Miserabile answered, "It's obvious, why."

Genella responded, "Not to me. I need more details."

Spinuzzi said, "So do I."

Mo said, "Me, too."

Miserabile said, "I prefer not to talk about it, tonight. It's like Mo and his ass. I can only discuss it in front of the boys."

We all gazed at Genella, and she had a look of determination on her face. I could sense that all the boys suddenly felt sorry for Miserabile. Somehow, someway, she would corner him and bust his chops on this issue and others in the future. Yes, she could be a big-time ballbuster!

Mo said, "Apart from tits, asses and eyes, let's look at our experience in the old Italian neighborhood. Let's take the family: There was no equality there. There was always a strong and undisputed leader. In my experience, half of the family leaders were men, and the other half, women. These hostile feminists could never manage a family like the mothers in the old neighborhood did. One big reason, in my opinion, is they have no desire to get involved in helping their husbands, sons and daughters. They're fuckin' narcissistic in spades. They must be constantly exhausted, thinking about themselves all day long every day of every week."

This opinion, of course, was not acceptable to Genella. She commented, "This is all I have to say on this subject: I think that most women would love to manage or help manage the family, if they had the chance."

Genella was trying to say something that I thought was important. The boys wanted to tell her about the women who controlled the families in the old Italian neighborhood. A man came home from work every Friday night and gave his paycheck to his wife. She gave him his allowance and then managed the entire family budget as well as its activities. Modern women have already rejected this role. But the hour was too late to pursue this, and I had to cut her short. But let's not forget that times frequently change, and maybe there's something to what Genella said. "All things flow," wrote Heraclitus. If you put your foot in a river, take it out, and put it back in, it's no longer the same river.

"Miserabile," I said, "let's hear your conclusions, not so much regarding the world, but about what the big trends are in the United States."

Miserabile paused and once more sipped on his *grappa*. He was open tonight, which, to repeat, is not at all characteristic of him. He made a conscious decision to take one more step and talk about what he was thinking.

"As I said before, I believe that the Democrats on the left will eventually take over American politics. The Republicans represent the old American values of independence, hard work and responsibility. The Democrats represent Spinuzzi's tit remarks: They want the federal government to take care of everyone with problems, whether they're psychological, physical or economic.

"But the problem is that the liberal Democrats love to be controlled, themselves as well as have the government control people. They are against freedom, even though they profess to be the principal champions of it. Pure modern Democrats are entirely different than true modern Republicans. Let me give you a measurable example: The Federal Register is the government publication that contains all the new laws and regulations that control every detail of the behavior of the American people, ranging from how much water should be in your toilet bowl to what type of label should be on your package of food.

"Within the past thirty years, the greatest number of pages printed in the Federal Register was under the presidencies of two liberal Democrats, Carter and Clinton; the fewest, under Nixon and Reagan."

Then Genella offered some teasing insight regarding Miserabile's observations, which she should have done before, when there was more time for discussion.

She said, "Yeah, our big-time Democratic clients like to be with a dominatrix and our Republican ones like to dress up in doll or ladies' clothes and be taken to the potty."

Mamma mia! These were loaded words, and I decided to ignore them. I sensed that Pussey Rapper saw a potential big story in Genella's comments, but he knew that the time was not right. The boys would not permit him to pursue it at this late hour. But I also knew that this potential subject of discussion was another guarantee that Genella would be back next year.

Miserabile continued on his roll. "Let's compare how free we were fifty years ago when we were all jerking off—and Genella, I'm talking about us, not you—to how free we are today. I'm not talking about the issue of big freedom, but multiple infringements that the government, including the courts, has made on our specific acts of everyday life.

"In certain countries like China, Russia, Japan and Germany, at certain times in the past, the government told you what to do regarding the big things—for example, that you cannot vote, that you cannot create opposition to the government, or that you must invade another country and kill its people simply because it extends the territories and powers of the government, and not for reasons of self-defense.

"In the United States, our great country, the government cannot successfully force us to do these big things. It cannot prohibit us from voting. Its citizens would refuse, for example, to invade Mexico or Canada simply to extend our borders. Instead, our government has begun to rob us of our freedom in many aspects of daily life.

"To repeat: Americans must ask themselves whether they have more or less freedom than they did fifty years ago. And if you think about it, there is no question we are much, much less free than we were then. And the great tragedy of it all, and I do really mean great tragedy, is that we are not only accepting this loss of freedom, but embracing it in the name of freedom! Would you fuckin' believe it?"

Genella, almost with adoring eyes—personally, I think she was laying it on a bit, as part of a major move to close in on poor (or should I say "lucky") Miserabile—asked, "Well, I thought the Supreme Court was increasing freedom for everyone in America."

All the boys smiled including the liberal, Pussey Rapper, for they had been down this path before and knew what Miserabile's response would be. In fact, everyone knew everyone else's position regarding the pros and cons of this great institution.

Miserabile said, "Just the opposite. The Supreme Court, and other courts, local, state, and federal governments, have been, on an almost daily basis, robbing us of our freedoms. Just recently, a judged ruled that a mother could not smoke in her house because she would jeopardize the son's health by exposing him to second-hand smoke. The judge ruled that she couldn't smoke in the house, even if the kid was not there. Also, he said the mother couldn't smoke in the car, even while driving alone. What next? You can't give your kids high fat ice cream or take them for a walk in the woods without wearing a helmet?

"Your profession, my dear Genella, for some reason remains one of the last great bastions of freedom. You are self-regulated; you do what you and your customers want to do."

Spinuzzi, who was determined not to interrupt Miserabile, but whose brain was bubbling with thoughts and ideas, could not restrain himself. "There is a logical reason why Genella's great profession has been able to maintain its freedom.

"In Genella's place, a guy can come in and request anything he wants and Genella has the personnel to deliver the goods. Genella also has the option of whether to grant the request or not, and can decide, for instance, whether he must wear a condom or whether he is requesting too severe a physical punishment. Why is this so? Because her profession deals with sex, the thing that drives the world."

Mo signaled to Vinnie, who was standing a few yards away, listening to our conversation. Vinnie came to the table and leaned over to hear what Mo had to say.

Vinnie smiled, said, "*Subito, subito,*" and walked away.

Spinuzzi continued, "What I'm trying to say is that the reason why brothels continue to thrive is because…"

Mo interrupted and beat Spinuzzi to the punchline. "It's Schopenhauer and Freud; it's the sex thing, again—men love it and don't want to get rid of it. Dumping a load, particularly under the right circumstances, is a primary interest of all males. It's like this fanatic anti-smoking movement and the automobile."

I didn't want to destroy Miserabile's rhythm regarding the loss of freedom, but Mo's provocative statement had to be heard.

I said, "Okay, Mo. Tell us about the similarity between sex and the anti-smoking movement in the United States. Did Schopenhauer and Freud write about smoking as well as sex?"

Mo said, "I thought you'd never ask." He laughed and so did we.

"Do you remember Chadrul in the old neighborhood? He was the guy that owned the garage across the street from the public

312

elementary school. Remember I worked for him? I was the clean-up guy, cleaning both the tools that were used and the garage itself.

"The guy's hands and face were always heavy with grease and dirt, and with the passing of time and the accumulation of this crap, kerosene had become less and less effective in removing it from the cracks in his skin.

"In those days, there were only about six or seven cars on each street; just about everyone took trolley cars and buses for transportation to distant places. Otherwise, they walked.

"Chadrul was a hard-working guy and smoked an occasional cigarette during the day only. One very hot summer afternoon, when the air was thick, heavy and still, and Chadrul was working his ass off, sweating like a pig, he said to me, 'Son, these cocksucker cars are the big-time polluters. Everybody wants one, and I'm pretty sure that in the future, practically everyone will have one. And when that happens, the fuckin' earth and people's health will get in pretty bad condition.'"

Mo was becoming a little bit too verbose and I said, "It's late. Would you get to the point?"

"The automobile, one of the biggest polluters in the history of the earth, is causing all kinds of problems, ranging from lung cancer to asthma in children to the warming up of the globe—if there is such a thing.

"But these anti-smoking fuckers never say a word about the powerful detrimental effects of the noxious fumes of the automobile, both on our physical and mental health, because these motherfuckers

313

all own and drive cars, and no one wants to give them up, including myself!"

Mo was not only eloquent but Mo was right. Spinuzzi added the icing to the cake. He said, "Don't forget, my friend, that the automobile industry is one of the great commercial engines that drives the economy. If it sinks, the economy sinks with it. If that happened, politicians would be voted out of office in droves. Jobs would be lost, the housing industry would come to a standstill, and the anti-car people would take a social as well as an economic hit. They would be ostracized.

"It's much easier to create an anti-smoking industry where advocates can make money instead of creating an anti-automobile industry where there is little money to be made and tons to lose. Few would support it."

Genella, apparently frustrated, said, "What does this have to do with the brothel industry?"

Mo laughed a hearty laugh. "I'll be damned, Genella. I certainly let myself go a bit, and I didn't make myself clear. It's a matter of self-interest. Many of those hypocritical do-gooders, in almost every walk of life, act out of their own self-interest. There is little to gain and much to lose by attacking the automobile and brothel industries. *Capito?*"

Genella said, "*Capito.*"

A waiter suddenly arrived at our table with a huge plate of fried zucchini. It really looked good. The problem was that we didn't order it. Besides, we had already had enough to eat.

Pussey Rapper said, "I love this stuff. Don't tell Mario, but I wished he had served this dish at the beginning of the night while we were having our martinis."

Genella commented, "Rocco used to take me to Patsy's, on the West Side. The chef there owns this dish. No one can come close to his fried zucchini. We used to love to eat at Patsy's. There's really no Italian restaurant like it. It was Sinatra's hangout, and one time we sat next to Burt Lancaster. The place is usually packed.

"You're greeted by a class guy, Joe Scognamillo, who has it in his blood to treat his customers as honored guests. Then there's mysterious Frankie. He's the quiet, behind-the-scenes guy who decides whether you get a table or not."

Reluctantly, I called Vinnie over to the table and asked him to take the plate away. It was with deep regret that we watched Vinnie take the fried zucchini to another table, but we just couldn't eat any more.

I said to Miserabile, "We haven't forgotten your thoughts on how we are, step-by-step, losing our freedom. Go on with your comments, my friend."

Miserabile smiled and said, "I thought you'd never ask. There's overwhelming evidence that what we do is being regulated more and more, from the unimportant to the very important. I can't drive my car without my seatbelt fastened without being fined. Kids in elementary school can't point their fingers at other kids and say, 'Bang, bang' without being suspended for violent behavior. People in California cannot smoke even in a strip-tease bar without the threat of a policeman on their backs. Teachers can't spank a brat with a ruler and doctors are not free to treat patients as they believe they should.

"I'll repeat my mantra to you guys: Are we more free now than we were fifty years ago? And I'll answer the question. Of course not."

Spinuzzi asked, "Miserabile, why do you think people aren't upset about this?"

Miserabile responded, "We talked about this before. It's not Freud, Schopenhauer and sex; it's Carl Jung and a national obsession with having almost absolute security. In our era of medical miracles, abundant food, luxury up the ass—like expensive clothes, eating out in restaurants, fancy cars and homes, increasing income—everybody out there is paradoxically becoming more and more insecure. There's insecurity *dappertutto* in our country, from the kids in elementary school to the old-timers awaiting life's last move—going to the nursing homes or directly to the cemetery or crematorium.

"And what really pisses me off is that the people are not only accepting this loss of freedom, but actually welcoming the control of their behavior. This was inconceivable in the old neighborhood. Yes, a little help now and then when someone really needed it, but not a total surrender of one's ability and duty to control one's own destiny as well as one's family's.

"Let me give you two other examples. Both happened a couple of weeks ago at a graduation party of one of my *paesani's* kids.

"There was a guy there with a beautiful convertible. One of the kids at the shindig, about eight or nine years old, fell in love with the convertible. The guy offered to drive the kid around the block. Now, I'm talking about driving the friggin' car, with the kid in it, around a city block. *Capito?*

"Well the guy never wears a seatbelt, because he's an old neighborhood Italian male who never changed. He resents the fact that the law will not permit him to drive his car without seatbelts wrapped around his body. He feels it's an assault on his freedom. But he never discourages the passenger in the seat next to him from using his seatbelt, simply because all hell would break loose if something happened.

"Well, the kid got in the car, but the seatbelt on his side was stuck, so the kid would have had to ride around the block without a seatbelt.

"The mother, noticing this, got borderline hysterical. Almost shrieking, she told the kid that he couldn't go around the block because of the fuckin' broken seatbelt. The kid protested, but to no avail.

"I couldn't help but think that the dumb hysterical mother hadn't the slightest idea of the impact her behavior had on her kid. Modern parents are teaching the kids to be insecure when they should be teaching them to be secure. I said to one of my old friends that our parents would never have prevented us from driving around the block because the fuckin' seatbelts weren't working. First of all, the thought would've never entered their minds, and second of all, even if it did, they wouldn't have protested because it would have violated old neighborhood values of politeness—unless there was a real tangible danger, like being in a car with a nut or a drunk.

317

"And then I was fuckin' floored. My old friend told me he welcomed government regulations like the mandatory use of seatbelts, and agreed with the hysterical mother.

"And, would you believe, that same day I read that the State of New Jersey passed a law that makes car seats for kids be mandatory until they are nine years old? Could you imagine the cost and aggravation to the parents and the kids that this single control-freak law will have? Multiply these types of laws and regulations by the thousands. Like Jesus' loaves of bread, they continue to multiply, not only decreasing freedom but increasing the cost of living and level of mental aggravation. There's a subtle tide of governmental tyranny going on out there, my friends, and the people are either accepting it or, if not, feeling helpless to do anything about it. Where it will end, nobody knows!"

Spinuzzi interjected, "Also, the more laws, the more crimes. Not because people are bad, but because the laws are bad. I'm waiting for someone to do a study to see whether there is a connection between the number of laws and the number of crimes. You will find that our numerous laws are creating a society of criminals."

Miserabile said, "The Founding Fathers of our great country thought of almost every conceivable way to prevent tyranny. The reason why they were so successful is that they understood human nature, both its evil and its good side, and they knew how to handle it while, at the same time, promoting freedom. They were obviously very successful in establishing the principles of a free nation.

"Yes, there are assholes who try to knock our system. We discussed it before: People are knocking at America's door to get in. Few Americans are leaving this country to knock at any other country's door."

Miserabile said, "Though many of the Founding Fathers were great men, in my opinion, Thomas Jefferson stands a little taller than the rest (with the exception of George Washington), because he was obsessed with the importance of individual freedom, and fearful of any type of government which increases its power and diminishes the freedom of the people.

"But today, most people know about him because of the media's coverage of his alleged love affair with a slave named Sally Heming. The media trumpeted the story that she had a child by him, with the implication that, because of this, he wasn't such a great man. What the media didn't tell the American people is that Sally Heming was actually three-quarters white, a mulatto, but there's not much of a story in that.

"And to top things off, a group of about a dozen historians reviewed the evidence of this illicit love affair and, with one exception, concluded that there was little evidence to support the fact that he had sired her child.

"And what did the media do? They ignored it. It was mentioned now and then on page ten of the newspapers, and hardly at all on television."

Genella commented, "I didn't consider this affair something bad. It reminded me of the story of Pocahontas and Captain John Smith. It was romantic."

The boys couldn't believe what Genella said. This woman of the world still had a streak of old-fashioned romanticism in her soul.

Miserabile continued, "The media did not report a far, far more important thing that Jefferson did. He was the man who introduced Italian pasta to the American people."

Genella said, "I don't believe it!"

Miserabile said, "It's true, it's true."

The Pig asked, "If it's true, how come we didn't know about it in the old neighborhood?"

Miserabile answered, "How the hell am I supposed to know why you or anyone else didn't know way back then?"

"Now, we've been talking about the eternal battle between freedom and loss of freedom. The classic examples of a guardian of freedom and someone who welcomed more government control are Thomas Jefferson and Alexander Hamilton—two great patriots who loved America.

And then something strange happened. Miserabile is an accomplished politician, and he knew how to handle a crowd. While he talked, he'd look into the eyes of the people he was addressing, in order to send a message that he was well aware of each individual's existence. And that's important. At this moment, he turned his intense eyes on Pussey Rapper. It was, without a doubt, a challenging look.

Pussey Rapper sent out a clear message that he accepted the challenge. He was ready.

We all noticed it, but we weren't sure that Genella did. Maybe she still had Pocahontas on her mind, or maybe she was pretending not to notice so she wouldn't interfere with the ongoing dialogue. I was sure it was the latter, and time proved me right.

"Pussey Rapper," said Miserabile, "you know very well that Jefferson feared too much control by the Federal Government and was the great champion of states' rights. On the other hand, Hamilton believed that the Federal Government should control a lot of things and that states' rights were of secondary importance.

"They were bitter political and perhaps personal enemies and fought mightily to do what they thought was right. But, Pussey Rapper, the important message is not who won or lost, but that the eternal battle over the power of the central government began almost immediately after the American Revolution, after the Americans got rid of England.

"And today, Hamilton's Federal Government has won the battle and will continue to do so," he said to Pussey Rapper, "with the enormous help of you guys on the left in the media."

Genella was about to say something, but I signaled to her to be quiet.

Pussey Rapper, obviously agitated as well as angry, said, "Are you in your wildest fuckin' imagination telling me that the media is a force against freedom today?"

Miserabile, answered without hesitation, "You bet your ass, I am!"

"Miserabile, we're old friends," Pussey Rapper responded, "and I respect your mind, but tonight you've had too much to drink, and it's clouding your judgment. On the contrary, the media is the great protector of American freedom. It is a self-evident truth. It's so obvious, you don't even have to prove it."

Before Miserabile could answer, Spinuzzi stepped in. "Miserabile has a point. Not only is our Federal Government—in fact, our state and local governments, too—taking away individual freedom, but I fear that our Federal Government is ready to surrender our national sovereignty, as well.

"The Clinton Administration sent positive signals to support a World Court, have our troops take orders from foreign countries, and made statements that the United States should prepare itself to join a world government in the near future.

"You guys and gals in the liberal media never criticized this position, and by not doing so, have gone along with it. You seem to love to surrender. In the meantime, the conservative media cried, 'Never surrender!'

"I'm pretty sure, as I said before, that it has to do with sex."

Pussey Rapper exploded, "What the fuck is this sex thing and the liberal connection that's on your fuckin' brain? Enough of this bullshit!"

I decided to step in and create a diversion. I asked Genella, "Are you following this?"

She answered, "Not really. It's getting a bit too heavy for me at this late hour." She seemed a little tired.

Miserabile, in soft tones, said, "Genella, why not go home? The conversation will get even heavier."

Genella, with sudden newfound energy, perked up. "I'm not going anywhere, you guys. You can't get rid of me, and I don't want to go! *Capito?*"

"*Mamma mia*, this chick has more chutzpah then I thought," I said to myself. I thought about Rocco and how he handled such a complicated woman. I thought about Genella and considered how she could have stayed with a rather boring man for so long.

Miserabile continued, "Could you imagine the guys and ladies in the old neighborhood saying, 'Let's surrender our rights to some fuckin' foreign court,' or 'Let's put our troops under the control of a foreign nation,' or 'Let's keep paying the United Nations the money that keeps them going while they consistently undermine and shit on us?'

"Pussey Rapper, I want you to answer the question, 'Would they surrender their hard-earned sovereignty to some foreign body for some theoretically higher social or egalitarian cause?"

This was a fairly direct question, which Pussey Rapper had to answer. He was obviously pissed-off because we knew what his answer would be and that we would not agree with it.

He said, "They would not surrender any right to any foreign body or institution. But times have changed. There's a good argument that we're gradually moving to a world government."

Miserabile then asked a very good question. "But, Pussey Rapper, does that make it right?"

Pussey Rapper answered, "I'm not so sure whether we can say, at this point in time, whether it is right or wrong. We'll have to wait and see. There is nothing inevitable about the coming of a world government, but it's certainly a real possibility."

Miserabile was persistent and would not let Pussey Rapper off the hook so easily. He said, "Shouldn't the people follow their own self-interest? Shouldn't they protect themselves, their families and their country from their enemies, like we in the United States have done in the past?"

Miserabile was clearly trying to expose what he firmly believed was a lack of strength and masculinity on the part of the liberal community. He was doing a good job.

It was time to wrap up the conversation. I said, "Look, I think what you guys are talking about, in broad political terms, is a national policy of *realpolitik* for the benefit of America versus a policy of the gradual surrendering of our sovereign rights for the benefit of all countries in the world, and world peace."

Genella asked, "What the hell is *realpolitik*?"

I answered, "*Realpolitik* is the political philosophy that says all action taken by the government should be taken in the self-interest of the government.

"Henry Kissinger is the supreme advocate of *realpolitik*. He sees America as first priority, and feels that our actions should focus on the protection of the sovereignty of our country."

Genella said, "Well, that makes a lot of sense to me. Shouldn't we protect ourselves? How can we trust anybody else not to screw us? Miserabile, you guys are really painting a depressing picture of the future of America—our country, for Christ's sake. Spinuzzi believes it's because of the sex thing and you think it's because of a lack of masculinity and strength.

"I don't like what I'm hearing, and this really wonderful evening is now becoming a depressing one."

Miserabile smiled and said, "Well, let me cheer you, *cara* Genella. All is not lost. There's good reason for hope, but if we debate the pros and cons of the way I and the rest of the guys see the future, we'll be here all night.

"I am requesting another five uninterrupted minutes to tell you what I see. If there are any objections, tell me now."

I looked around the table then signaled Miserabile to proceed.

He began. "Let's look at what the great minds thought about the nature of government. I'll choose three of them that represent clear and distinct systems.

"Let's start out with the most overrated philosopher of all time: Plato. The guy must have hated his parents, because he was big-time anti-family. But that's another issue that maybe we can discuss next year.

"Plato believed that the best government was a total dictatorship controlled by a very wise Philosopher King who knows what's best for the people and the country.

"I must confess that it is a very attractive concept. The government or Philosopher King will do what's right for everyone. No political battles, litigation lawyers (Greece, by the way, was loaded with lawyers, which pissed-off the people), battles over taxes, budgets and so forth.

"In theory, this is the perfect system. In reality, there's one major problem that that asshole Plato never resolved—that is, how do we pick the right guy to be the Philosopher King? Pick the wrong guy, and he'll make everyone *miserabile*, like my name. Remember Lord Acton's words, 'Power corrupts, and absolute power corrupts absolutely.'

"For the record, there never has been a Philosopher King and there never will be. Perfection is found in Heaven and not here on Earth.

"Let's take a giant step forward in history, and go to Karl Marx. He said that all the people should be equal in all aspects of life. All people should be equal? This guy was like Plato—a bona fide asshole. He couldn't see the forest for the trees. People are not born equal. Even John Adams, one of the great leaders in the American Revolution, believed that people aren't born equal. Historians say that Thomas Jefferson believed that people are born equal, by which he meant having certain rights guaranteed by the government. Historians are like economists—give them the same set of facts, and they come up with different conclusions.

"Anyway, the Communism of the Soviet Union tested Marx's theory. And what happened? The superior people took over the governments, suppressed and killed the others, and threw the people with beautiful homes out on the street so they could move in, themselves.

"Now let's get to my favorite, Aristotle. This guy's mind has never been equaled, not even close. But he has been ignored by modern philosophers because he is so far above them. They're jealous and can't beat him in his thinking.

"Anyway, his view of a political system was based on the following observations:

"You can't place government power in the hands of a single person, or even a few, because they can't be trusted. Hitler, Stalin and Mao Tse Tung are examples that confirm this hypothesis.

"You can't entrust power to the hands of the masses, because they are restless and they understandably want more. The masses are uncontrollable and cause instability in government; then, to control the masses, a totalitarian government follows. Freedom goes bye-bye. The French Revolution tells the story.

"He believed that the power of government should be placed in the hands of the middle class, for the people there are more or less contented and really want a stable government. They have their jobs, homes, home comforts, cars and everything else. They have much to lose and little to gain from revolutions and unstable governments. It is, therefore, in their own best interests to help the poor so that they will not cause revolution after revolution.

"The Founding Fathers structured the Constitution that fostered this concept, where both the good and bad qualities of man are directed to the common good. And it worked. America stands out in history as a country that, step by step, worked for the good of all. I'm not talking about that pure equality shit, but the opportunity to find one's place in our country by working at it.

"I could go on, but I promised to keep my spiel short."

Spinuzzi could barely resist responding to Miserabile's summary of what a good government should be, but he decided to remain quiet. He later told me that Miserabile made some giant leaps in his reasoning, but that overall it wasn't bad. He decided to return to the subject of the media. He said, "You know, Miserabile, during the Revolution, the media—now we're talking about little newspapers or pamphlets—played an important role in fueling the belief that both individual and national freedom were sacrosanct and not to be tampered with. Freedom, freedom, freedom was what it was all about.

"Now, my friend, I think modern media is working hard to do the opposite, effectively diminishing our freedoms."

Miserabile responded, "In practically all camps in the United States, there are antagonists and protagonists, groups that criticize and battle with each other—Democrats against Republicans, labor unions against corporations, the federal government against the states, environmentalists against oil companies, pro-lifers against abortionists, physicians against HMOs, and so on.

"But the media never attacks or criticizes the media. Now let's look at the media around the time of the American Revolution, and why the First Amendment was a wise and just article of our Constitution."

Genella silently pushed her chair away from the table and pulled up her skirt. She turned her chair to an angle where Miserabile could see her gams, and crossed her legs. They were still in good shape. Though Miserabile pretended not to look, we know he took in an eyeful. It wasn't just the Scorpion that was now in play, but good old-fashioned sex. For reasons that are difficult to explain, Genella's move was quite appropriate for the moment. We all enjoyed it and wondered whether Miserabile had taken his Viagra with him, that night.

Spinuzzi has, with the exception of Mo, more balls than the rest of us. He wasn't about to let Genella get away with her move without a comment.

He said, "Excuse me, Miserabile, but an idea just flashed through my mind. At next year's annual dinner, let's bring a few ladies along. It seems to add to the fire of the evening. I would suggest two or three—no more. On second thought, let's invite just two. Three may be too much to handle."

Miserabile read Spinuzzi well. He leant a light moment to the conversation by actually laughing and saying, "Spinuzzi, that's the first good idea you've had, tonight. I agree. Let's do it!"

The boys laughed and so did Genella. As she laughed, she shifted legs, re-crossing them. When she did this, we really were concerned that Miserabile had forgotten his Viagra. But, who knows: Judging by her sensuality and smart moves, Miserabile could have thrown his

Viagra pills in the toilet bowl and let nature take its course. At his age, it all depends on timing and the right moment, with the right woman. And, let's not forget, the amount of booze imbibed.

And would you believe it! Genella suddenly got up and bent over to pick up her napkin that she ostensibly had dropped on the floor. And she took a long time doing it. We all could see the outline of her beautiful *culo* through her clingy dress. Miserabile could not pretend any more. He looked at her *culo* contour with hormone-tinged eyes.

A few days after the dinner, I spoke to Spinuzzi. He told me that he thought he had seen Genella drop the napkin on purpose. We both agreed that it was a planned move. Who ever drops a napkin after dinner, while drinking *grappa*? On the other hand, she got away with it. Miserabile became more interested than ever!

There was a pause, and I sensed that Miserabile needed help to get back on his monologue regarding the media. One cannot have a hard-on and talk about serious stuff. One way to get Miserabile's mind back on the subject was to deny him his stage for pontificating.

I said, "Okay guys, Miserabile has said his piece. I'm going to go around the table and ask all of you your opinions about the media."

This did the job. Miserabile, looking pissed-off, said, "Hey, wait a minute. I'm not through, yet. When I'm through, then they can talk."

I was right. He was pissed-off.

He then continued, "Listen, let me briefly sum it up: The media ain't what it used to be, and it doesn't deserve the umbrella protection of the First Amendment."

Pussey Rapper could not remain quiet while someone assaulted his profession and its freedom and the media's Holy Grail, the First Amendment. Obviously disturbed, and with more strength than usual in his voice, he said, "Miserabile, here we go again. You've got to be fuckin' kidding! Are you out of your fuckin' mind? You want to tamper with freedom of the press, which is the foundation of America's strength? I know that the media has stuck it up your ass more than once. They've distorted the facts and made you look like shit, but that's the way it is, and that's the way it has always been. No system is perfect.

"I think the booze has gone to your head, and you're now speaking from your ass, instead of your brain. *Vero*, my friend?"

I thought Miserabile would be so offended by these remarks that he would have launched a tirade against Pussey Rapper, but he didn't. Instead, he once again lit his cigar, took another sip of *grappa*, and said, "Pussey Rapper, do you think I'm a goddamn idiot? Do you think I made that statement lightly? Do you think I haven't thought about the importance of the freedom of the press?"

It was obvious that Miserabile had anticipated Pussey Rapper's heated response and respected it.

Pussey Rapper, visibly upset, looked at Miserabile eyeball to eyeball, and unyieldingly said, "If you're saying what I think you're saying, then you're out of your goddamn mind. The First Amendment should never be touched. Never!"

Before Miserabile could answer, Mo shouted across the room, "Hey, Vinnie! *Vieni qui un momento.* I want to ask you something."

Vinnie, who at that time of night probably wanted to go home to his wife and kids, managed to smile and walked over to Mo. Mo whispered in his ear, and Vinnie hurried to the kitchen.

I asked Mo, "What the hell was that about?"

Mo said, "You guys think Mario knows best about what we should eat, *vero*? But I'm still goddamn hungry, and I ordered one last bite to eat. I need a gustatory 'hit' before I leave this place."

"Isn't it funny? I'm hungry, too," said Genella.

The Pig, surprising us all, said, "Genella, you seem to have large appetites."

Genella's smile disappeared, for she wasn't sure what the Pig was up to. Was he about to launch a verbal assault on her?

Miserabile stepped in as the defender of Genella. We had mixed emotions about his rescue attempt, because the purpose of the dinner was to have everyone stand on his own two feet. He asked the Pig, "What do you mean by that?"

The Pig, with a tinge of hostility in his voice, answered, "I'm not talking to you, Miserabile. I'm talking to Genella."

Hostility or not, the Pig was right. It was not Miserabile's role to answer for or defend Genella.

Miserabile's angry reaction was instantaneous. He was about to retort, but Pignachi saw it coming and made a move to block it.

He quickly asked, "Mo, what the heck did you order? I'm not a constitutional scholar, but I think we all have a right to know."

Mo laughed a big one and decided so surrender his secret. "I ordered enough for everyone, but don't fuckin' eat it just to please me. I don't expect anyone to have an appetite at this late hour. A little ziti with corn oil, garlic and salt."

Pussey Rapper was still upset, his adrenalin effect in full bloom. The foundation of his occupational bread and butter, the First Amendment, was being challenged.

He, like a commander barking an order, said, "Miserabile, give us your reasons for challenging the First Amendment. Give us your reasons why you want government to control the newspapers. Give us…"

"Wait a minute," exclaimed Miserabile. "I never said, 'I want the government to control the news,' but I have great fears, and so should you. You must admit that it's tough for you to be open-minded when someone is challenging your business, isn't it?"

This remark took a little bit of the wind out of Pussey Rapper's sails. Not a lot, but definitely enough to calm him down. After all, it was the truth.

Spinuzzi turned toward Miserabile and said, "I'm not so sure I agree with you about Pussey Rapper's objectivity. There are two schools of thought regarding how we judge certain situations. For example, is a patient with tuberculosis more objective about his disease than his doctor, who doesn't have it, or is he less objective because he has the disease and can't see the forest for the trees?"

Mo was annoyed. "Spinuzzi, stick your shitty analogy up your ass. It's faulty. Miserabile is correct. Remember that one of your heroes, St. Thomas Aquinas, wrote that all analogies are faulty.

Anyway, Miserabile, get going and finish up your thoughts. Let him finish without interruption."

Spinuzzi let it go and Miserabile continued.

"You guys know that the vast majority of our voters are not constitutional scholars and are not concerned about the First Amendment. And most of them don't know that their opinions about everything from fat in the diet to the need to raise taxes are based on what they read, see and hear. They are puppets of the information system. The media denies them the truth under the pretext of telling the truth.

"Let's discuss the issue of truth in reporting.

"Take the example of the press corps in Washington. As we said before, most of them don't go to church and about ninety percent are registered Democrats. How in God's name can you expect them to be objective and represent both the Republican and Democrat points of view with fairness? No fuckin' way. These guys distort the news to favor the Democrats. It's human nature. I would do the same thing. I would certainly push the thing that I believe in and not the things that I disagree with.

"Pussy Rapper, count the time that the media uses the term, 'Conservative Republican' versus 'Liberal Democrat.' You hardly ever hear or see the latter term in print. Those media Democrats know that the public is highly suspicious of many failed liberal policies and are trying to hide it and switch the blame to Conservative Republicans.

"How can you sit in your chair, Pussey Rapper, and defend the First Amendment when the truth about national policy is being massively altered on a daily basis by the media, with a strong bias to the left? The American people are busy in life and assume that what they hear is true.

"Plus, as I said before, the cocksuckers don't criticize each other, because they're all in cahoots with each other. They share the same bed and are having great success, fooling the American people.

"They are an arrogant lot. They believe they know what's best for America and instead of feeding the public the truth, they feed them distortions of the truth to sway Americans to think their way."

Spinuzzi stepped in and asked, "Do you want new laws to prevent the media from indoctrinating instead of reporting?"

Miserabile answered, "No way! No way!"

Pussey Rapper asked, "Then what the hell is your point?"

"I'm getting to two issues: The truth, and the values by which we live. Regarding the truth, you cannot expect the media—particularly the modern media—to tell the truth, but I don't believe we should pass any laws to regulate what the media wants to say, except in rare cases such as those involving national security. Yes, the conservative media are much more honest than the liberal folks. Conservatives attack conservatives, often times forcefully if there is disagreement, but liberals rarely attack liberals, and when they do, the attacks are very mild.

"Now, let's get to the economic motive that people working in mass media have. You must admit that the mass media is now a big business. Many media companies are now public and on the stock market, and the primary purpose of these businesses is to make money. Sure there are good guys and gals in the media industry who try to report important stories that the public doesn't give a shit about. But if viewership and sales go down because of their attempts, they are told to change their ways; if they don't, then out the door they go.

"So they sell sex, drugs, narcissism, violence—anything but traditional family values. When they talk about family values, it is usually, for example, about homosexual couples or heroic single dads raising their children without the mother around. And the coverage is almost always positive.

"You don't see mass media coverage of the beauty of traditional motherhood, or of the importance of a married man who takes care of his family. Oh, yes, there's lots of coverage of the woman who is the breadwinner of the family, though.

"Getting to religion, I'll bet you only one out of five media reports are favorable toward religion. You rarely hear of the millions of good deeds done by those with religious callings around the world.

"I can go on and on, but you know what I'm talking about. And do you know why? It's because the media is loaded with full-time working mothers and weak, narcissistic males who do not live in traditional family settings and do not have traditional family values. They're like the press corps in Washington. They bias their coverage against traditional values."

The Pig said, "Miserabile, you're kind of contradicting yourself. Are you saying that the media covers all the shit that goes on in life, like the sex lives of Hollywood starlets, in order to make more money, or are you saying it's because they're on a crusade to push their values instead of traditional ones? You're also implying, though you haven't said it explicitly, that the people like this shit and that the media only feed people what they want, and make money by selling *merda*.

"What's wrong with that? It's good old-fashioned capitalism. It drives the economy."

Miserabile snapped back, "So does war. Should we, therefore, have more wars?"

He paused then went on. "You're correct that lots of people want to hear and see stuff about vice instead of virtue. Why? Because a scorpion is a scorpion!"

He continued, "In conclusion, the media is a powerful money-making machine that makes more money by marketing more shit, which has had and continues to have a powerful impact on traditional values, and which has created a new *cacca* value system that is characterized by everything that we've talked about tonight—and more."

Pussey Rapper saw what Miserabile had in mind and asked, "Miserabile, are you saying that shit media moments should be taken away from people?"

Miserabile said, "Yes, a lot of them," and Pussey Rapper almost shit his pants. The rest of us around the table thought that Miserabile had made a good point. If the First Amendment or, that is, the current interpretation of the First Amendment, permits the powerful media machine to bring out the bad in us at the expense of the good on a national level, then something should be done about it.

In the manner of prosecutor in a courtroom, Pussey Rapper asked, "And, my friend, how do you propose that this should be done?"

Miserabile, in a depressed tone, answered, "I don't know. I really don't know. There was a bright guy at Yale, by the name of Bickel, who once said something—I think it was regarding the Pentagon Papers and the media—about how we sometimes have to err in order to maintain freedom in media. It's like the pork in Congress. Though people think it's wrong, it keeps the Congressional machinery going. Stop pork money and Congress will come to a standstill. You have to make deals in order to get the right things done. But we've gone too far. If we don't do something soon, America's value system will be in chaos and that, Pussey Rapper, is not where we want to be."

Mo suddenly began to giggle a little. This was a most inappropriate reaction to a very serious conversation.

"What the hell are you giggling about?" asked the Pig.

"I'm sorry guys," Mo said, "but I had a flashback to the old neighborhood while you guys were talking about values. Why it came to mind—who the hell knows?

"Do you remember the guy we used to call Nuts and Bolts' Brother? He was always trying to buy porn. The guy must have jerked off every day. Years later I was talking to a guy who knew Nuts and Bolts' Brother very well. He said he used to wonder where he got his name, because there was no Nuts and Bolts guy in the old neighborhood. Where the hell did he get his name, if his brother didn't exist?"

Earlier in the evening, this story would have provoked laughter, but the hour was late. It was greeted with total silence.

But the silence had more to do with the fact that we were waiting for Pussey Rapper to attack Miserabile than with the whereabouts of Nuts and Bolts' Brother's brother. Miserabile had questioned the interpretation of the First Amendment by judicial scholars, and the powerful negative impact the courts have had on traditional values. Pussey Rapper was bound to respond.

At moments like this, wise old Spinuzzi would offer some type of resolution. Oftentimes he sounded like a High Priest at the Delphic Oracle speaking in foreign tongues, but sometimes he really comes through. Tonight he both took the bull by the horns.

He said, "My friends, remember that there are few answers in life, but we do know that it is not uncommon that when things look gloomy, the unexpected occurs and things get better.

"Pussey Rapper, the truth is the truth. Our Founding Fathers did not put the First Amendment in the Constitution based on our modern media phenomenon. Media has, in my opinion, more power and subtle influence than all the religious movements of all time. There is little doubt that the attraction the public has to the media shit is similar to dietary supplements. It's like cocaine. The more people are exposed to it, the more they want it. It's depressing to see how the media constantly delivers negative messages, stressing that people are helpless and need the government to solve their problems.

"But here's the good news. Despite the media barrage of the Liberal Left, voters still vote for Republican presidents, governors and congressmen. Not that it is necessarily important to vote Republican; the issue is that Americans still are not totally controlled by the media."

Everyone was puffing away, and billows of smoke hovered over the table. Observing this, Spinuzzi cajoled, "Hey, you guys, you're now being exposed to secondary smoke. Is any one of you shitting in your pants?"

Genella leaned forward and cut to the quick. "*Me ne frega* and fuck it."

"Amen," added Mo.

Miserabile did not appreciate this language emanating from the mouth of his potential honeybun. I'm sure he was thinking that her language reflected another side of her personality that he hadn't yet seen and would have trouble accepting.

He took a particularly bold position and admonished her. "Genella, ladies in the old neighborhood didn't use such language in public."

Genella, her Irish up, was about to rebut, but wisdom and extraordinary willpower led her to remain silent.

Spinuzzi continued. "Look, there are reasonable grounds to be optimistic about the media and its impact on American thinking. Don't get me wrong. If it doesn't happen, I wouldn't be surprised. I think the way to counter shit media that people love is to create non-shit media that people also love. This, my friends, is one of the most profound statements of the century! *D'accordo?*"

It was obvious that the boys agreed with Spinuzzi's proposition.

He continued, "Now, it makes sense to fight fire with fire. *Vero*? It makes sense to counter negative media with positive media. *Vero?*"

Genella enthusiastically answered, "*Vero!*"

"As we all know," he continued, "big media is not only very liberal, but strongly anti-conservative. Big media is buying up or having business ventures with other media, big and small. It is therefore reasonable to conclude that what and how Americans think will be determined by a giant liberal media establishment. *D'accordo?*

"Well, I'm not so sure of that. We are entering an era where all kinds of new print, radio and television media organizations are springing up almost every day. The internet itself represents huge multiple media fronts.

"My hope—and I must confess that I'm not that confident—is that common-sense, charismatic media groups will dominate these new communication outlets, preaching the message of liberty instead of control, and making tons of money by doing so."

Spinuzzi stopped and said no more. He looked at Genella, and for reasons unknown, she turned him on. He thought to himself, "If I could, I would; but I can't."

Father Pignachi's Peroration and The Farewell

There was a pause in the conversation and everyone seemed a little down. After all, the night's conversation regarding modern America and the people in it was not very encouraging. Yes, there were light moments and even moments of profound beauty, but they were already distant memories. Pessimism was the paint that covered the modern American portrait. Spinuzzi's somewhat optimistic media comments were not enthusiastically embraced by the group.

It was evident that Genella was particularly disturbed. At a dinner many years ago we concluded that women are often more vicious than men. We also concluded that if all the emperors and kings were, instead, empresses and queens, there would have been a hundred times more wars and a hundred times fewer people on earth today. Paradoxically, we also concluded that women have a much greater capacity for love and self-sacrifice. To this day, we cannot explain our paradoxical feelings. Tonight, the love side of Genella's personality was dominant and she didn't like what we were saying.

The conclusions of the evening, though not yet concluded, were fairly obvious. There is little hope for mankind. Technology is giving us the seeds for a global holocaust, and man will plant these accursed seeds. America is all screwed up and the Scorpion is real and won't go away.

Just when everyone was beginning to succumb to the venomous sucking Scorpion, the depressing silence was suddenly interrupted, and it was a very good thing. As Heraclitus once said, "The mixture which is not shaken decomposes."

A red-faced Pignachi stood up, expanded his chest, and exclaimed, "*Basta,* and I mean *basta con queste sciocchezze*! All that I've heard tonight is unbalanced thinking. You're thinking with your brains only, instead of with your hearts, and the heart has reason that the brain can never know."

Pignachi paused, his near-rage subsiding, and turned to Spinuzzi. "Spinuzzi, who said that brain-versus-heart quote? Pascal?"

Spinuzzi thought a moment and answered, "You've got me on that one, Pignachi."

"*Communque*: Whoever it was," Pignachi continued, "it is the foundation of hope for the future. Look, you guys have been talking about the history and dynamics of bad things. One reason is that books, radio, and television only talk about the bad things in life, and this has conditioned your minds. No one writes about the goodness of life and the good that people do. I am still waiting for such a book to be written. Where is this person who will write such a book?"

Spinuzzi, before he could stop himself from doing so, asked, "Pignachi, have you ever tried to figure out why no one has written this book?"

This question really pissed off Pignachi. His anger returned, and he said, "What the hell difference does that make, whether someone writes or doesn't write a book about something, if that something exists and can be seen and felt by everyone? Spinuzzi, if you help someone solve a real problem and nobody writes about it or puts it on television, does that render your good deed insignificant or nonexistent? I would say that almost one hundred percent of good deeds are never recognized, let alone recorded."

Spinuzzi, partly because he agreed with Pignachi's position and partly because he wanted to assuage him a little, said, "I agree, Pignachi, I agree. There was a Roman poet by the name of Juvenal who lived in central Italy and was a champion of the poor and the oppressed. He was great at satire, and attacked government corruption, immoral behavior and crime. He said that news about good deeds is short-lived. People simply don't dwell on good news. They are much more interested in bad news and prone to accept the truth of such news with little evidence to support it. And the bad news lingers on."

It was obvious by the expression on Pignachi's face that he appreciated Spinuzzi's comments.

Genella, feeling the significance of this moment, smiled and asked, "Is this the Scorpion thing you guys were talking about?"

The boys smiled and, in unison, nodded their heads in the affirmative. The Scorpion was undoubtedly becoming, like the beginning of the universe, a puzzling reality and beginning to win the war against sex.

Vinnie arrived at the table and saw that all the *grappa* glasses were empty. He picked up the bottle of *grappa* and was ready to fill them again. I motioned to him to stop. I told him we had had enough to drink and that he should bring us more hot *espresso*. Mo objected and said that it would not be out of order to have a last *grappa* for the road.

Vinnie poured the *grappa* and I made a secret Sign of the Cross, hoping that everyone would make it home safely that night. In fact, at the end of the evening I suggested that those who had driven to La Strega should take a taxi to wherever they were staying and pick up their cars the next day. They refused. I then made another Sign of the Cross, figuring that two were better than one when asking the Boss for a favor.

Pignachi continued. "I want to tell you what's both on my mind and in my heart. Sure, these are the most radically changing times in all of history. Sure, because of this, tradition is being challenged, and there's lots of confusion and instability out there because it's difficult to determine what is right or wrong. Sure, materialism is running wild and, as we all know, materialism is not the foundation for stability, love and a strong people.

"Maybe it was mentioned once or twice, tonight, but I don't remember hearing the word, 'love,' which is the most important part of being a human being. What is life without love?"

We could all see that Spinuzzi wanted to answer Pignachi's question philosophically, but he held back.

Then Pignachi pulled a surprise on Spinuzzi. He questioned him. He asked, "Spinuzzi, you're half Jewish and you know the culture well. I'm speaking from the pulpit of a Catholic priest, and some of you might think that I'm speaking from a limited position.

. "What is the Jewish position on the importance of love?"

We all became a bit uneasy, because we knew that Spinuzzi always seemed reluctant to speak about his Jewishness. But we were pleasantly surprised. In a relaxed tone of voice, he said, "Jews are full of love for each other. That's in their history."

Then Mo, surprising us all by the seriousness of the timbre of his voice, said, "How about love for non-Jews? Are they full of love for gentiles?"

Spinuzzi knew that Mo was a kind man and not a bigot. He also knew that Mo asked the question because he simply wasn't sure of the answer—and it bothered him.

Spinuzzi replied, "*Una buona domanda, mio amico*, a very good question, indeed. Are you ready for my answer?"

Mo smiled and said, "Spinuzzi, my friend, I may not be ready for your answer, but I look forward to hearing it."

Spinuzzi continued. "Let me turn to our favorite philosopher, Aristotle. He's the guy that invented the syllogism which is the best way that I know, outside of intuition, to arrive at the truth.

"We all know that Jews are great, if not the greatest, contributors to charity in the United States. Most of these charities do not deal with Jewish concerns, but with those of people in general, ranging from the oppressed to those afflicted with disease.

"Now, here's the syllogism:

"Good people contribute to charities

"Jews contribute to charities

"Therefore, Jews are good people.

"*Va bene?*"

Mo smiled and replied, "*Va bene*, but let's discuss this in more depth at our dinner next year." In a gesture of good will, Mo raised his glass of *grappa* and toasted, "*L'Chaim!*"

Genella made another *sbaglio*, or misjudgment, because what she said could be interpreted by the very sensitive as an anti-Semitic remark. She said, "Why are we talking only about Jews? Are they so special? Aren't the Arabs good people, too?"

Silence prevailed. This question was Spinuzzi's responsibility to answer. The boys wouldn't touch it.

Spinuzzi looked at her kindly. He said, "Don't tell Father Pignachi, but civilization came from the great Arab cultures, and they were frequently more tolerant of foreign religions than the Christians, including Catholics."

I then said, "Pignachi, we've gotten off the beaten track. Let's wrap up the night by hearing your closing remarks."

Pignachi began. "Sure, there will always be wars, and sure, weapons are increasing in their destructive capacity, and sure, the future is uncertain. What's new? The future has and always will be uncertain.

"But what do we gain by being pessimistic? We gain nothing. Pessimism is the mentality of losers.

"We have nothing to lose and much to be gained by being optimistic and hopeful. The world is full of people who do good deeds. We must find a way to make these acts more visible to mankind, as a basis for developing the will and strength to prevent wars.

"Miserabile mentioned the lack of great leaders today, but they must, and they will, arrive. There's now a real need and a big vacuum. Nature abhors a vacuum, and some leader will come forth and fill this vacuum.

"Look, Churchill was nothing until a need arose for a man of his character. Without Hitler, Churchill would now be a forgotten man, hardly mentioned in the pages of history.

"We're not talking about an obvious Hitler now. We're talking about something we can't see or quantify but can feel is creeping throughout our society. It's plain and simple materialism. We've got too much, and it's infecting us and affecting our values. I think people more or less sense this, but need a leader to help them do something about it.

"Miserabile, even those great leaders, Jefferson and Hamilton, who were sworn enemies, came together in a time of national need. Hamilton supported Jefferson—not only his enemy, but also the leader of the opposition party—for president rather than the candidate from his own party, Aaron Burr, whom he did not trust. This is one reason why the pistol duel between Burr and Hamilton occurred, and Hamilton lost his life. By the way, Hamilton refused to pull the trigger. Try and figure that one out!"

Genella struck again. "Father Pignachi, if you were our leader, what would you do with our kids in elementary school?"

I heard Spinuzzi whisper to himself, "Where the hell did that question come from?"

Pignachi smiled a big one and said, "I'd make it mandatory that all kids must watch John Wayne's cowboy movies and Johnny Weismuller's Tarzan movies at least five days a week."

In a quick aside, Spinuzzi mentioned to me how he wanted to tell Pignachi that a war, plague or big meteor from the sky would be the only thing to bring out the good in people, as well as bring them together. "Tragedy is what makes nations great," he suggested.

He also wanted to tell Pignachi that some hysterical mother would object to the violence in these cowboy and jungle films and take the case to court, where liberal judges would rule in her favor. Though Pignachi didn't realize it, his vision of what should be done would require a very strong charismatic leader with a powerful mandate from the people.

But this was Pignachi's moment, and Spinuzzi thought that Pignachi probably would agree with him on most issues, if not all of them.

Pignachi knew that he had to keep his sermon short—and it was a sermon—in order for it to have an impact. Truth is more often found in brevity.

He said, "Love is everywhere, guys. I'm not like a wishy-washy evangelist speaking with his hormones and not his brains. I'm speaking simply from what I have observed in life. I see it every day. A mother's acts of love for her child are *qualche cosa meravigliosa*. There's nothing more beautiful in the world, and it happens a billion times a day. A policeman risking his life to save someone else's life, soldiers risking their lives in war to keep their families from harm's way, rescuers on dangerous missions to save lives in danger, religious and other charities ministering to the poor and needy.

"And how about the man or woman who's in trouble. I've seen families and friends come to the aid of each other more times than I can count."

And then, to our delight, Pignachi reverted to his old Italian neighborhood language. He stood up and, with the index finger of his left hand pointing toward Heaven, he said, "And it is time to flush the goddamn pessimistic assholes down the goddamn toilet!"

Pignachi concluded, "When do we ever hear from the mass media about the importance of love, kindness, good mothers and, yes, good fathers? When do you ever hear from the media that the Catholic Church is devoted to and cares for those afflicted with AIDS? Instead, the media highlights the Church's opposition to homosexuality as if Mother Church doesn't love those poor souls with AIDS and doesn't help them. Damn it! The Church spends enormous amounts of money and time tending to the care of AIDS patients.

"There is a vacuum of truth regarding people's goodness that will be filled soon, I promise you!"

Pignachi sat down. There was a relatively long moment of silence because no one felt like attacking the message of love.

Genella got up, walked over to Pignachi and kissed him on the forehead.

I decided that to proceed would be anti-climactic. The intellectual gas tank was empty. The dinner of 2001 was over, and it was time to say goodbye.

I said, "Guys, the party's over and it's time to go. Let me just say that it was one of our better nights. We managed to get through an evening of hot and heavy debate, and we're all still friends.

"Before I forget, I would like to tell Genella—and I'm speaking for all of us, Genella—that your presence and contributions to this evening's events were welcome. You brought a lady's touch to the table, which both lightened and enlightened the evening."

I decided not to ask her back for next year's dinner, because I wasn't sure how the boys would react. It would have to be a unanimous decision.

I went on, "We didn't cover lots of subjects, like stem cell research and the threat of lawsuits which rob Americans of their freedom and their strength. We didn't talk about the aging population and euthanasia and the weakness of the United States in preparing for and pre-empting all kinds of attacks, which we all know will arrive."

And will wonders never cease? Pignachi eyed the bottle of *grappa*. A big grin appeared on his kisser, and he said, "There's still plenty of *grappa*. Let's each have a little bit. You know, one for the road."

Vinnie heard these words and arrived immediately. He poured each of us a little *grappa* and almost imperceptibly took the bottle away with him. It was his subtle way of saying, "I'm tired and I want to go home. *Basta!*"

Pignachi said, "Spinuzzi would say '*L'Chaim*,' or 'To Life.' I would add, 'Here's to Love.'"

It was beautifully said, and we all finished off the *grappa* in a single gulp.

There was a pause, and little left to say. We all then pushed our seats away from the table. Pleasantries were exchanged—*un abbraccio*, the Italian hug and kiss on the cheeks, followed—with one exception. Genella grabbed Miserabile and planted a healthy kiss on his lips. Normally, Miserabile would try to avoid something as intimate as this, particularly in public, but he didn't this time. His hair was exceptionally long, almost reaching his shoulders. Samson and Delilah suddenly jumped to mind. I had no doubt that the next time that I saw him his hair would be short.

As we were leaving, Mario appeared and said goodbye to all of us in a gracious way. He handled Genella just like he did the rest of us—with genuine but careful warmth.

The guy was a pro and we all appreciated it. He had the hots for Genella, but she had chosen Miserabile. He knew that, and also knew where to draw the line in life, and he did. And, to be truthful, at that time of night, the guy was probably dead tired and didn't give a shit about puntang.

Everyone said *Ciao* to each other, and began to part ways. Genella grabbed Miserabile's hand and they walked away together before the rest of us had made our parting moves.

Spinuzzi smiled broadly and said, "Guys, it's that sex thing, again."

Mo said, "Spinuzzi, I don't agree. I think it's the Scorpion."

And the curtain fell on the year 2001 on the day of September 7.

Or did it?

Attack on America

We bade farewell to La Strega and Mario on September 7, 2001. Mo and Pussey Rapper's executive summary was due on September 16. Then, on September 11, the attack on America occurred. Because of this, the executive summary was never written and other events transpired.

The day that the giant airplanes destroyed the Twin Towers and severely damaged the Pentagon, a mighty impact on the American way of life began, one which it is yet too early to assess. Within the time span of a single day, we jumped from a mindset of materialism and weakness to one of temporary national unity and strength. The event was ugly, but the short-term response was a thing of beauty.

On September 12, I got a conference call from Mo and Pussey Rapper. They told me that they couldn't write the executive summary because of the attack. They said that the executive summary dealt with our conclusions about our nation's values up until September 11. They believed that the attack may have already changed them. On the other hand, the changes might be short-lived, which would not surprise future historians. Regarding the long-term effect, who has the infallible crystal ball?

In any event, they insisted that we all get together for another dinner to assess what had happened, what was happening, and how it might affect our values.

I told them I would call everyone to set up a date at Mario's. They told me that they thought it wasn't a good idea to return to La Strega, unless we didn't invite Genella. If she came, the sex thing would undoubtedly arise, and the seriousness of the evening would be tarred. Mario's a proud guy, and he might give Genella a second try; and Miserabile is a jealous fellow and would not permit it. This combination spelled trouble.

I agreed, but insisted that it would still be out of order to exclude her. If, for some reason, we didn't want her next year, we could make that decision later on. Besides, Miserabile might lose his cool if we shut her out, which was not a risk worth taking.

I said it would be no big deal to find another appropriate restaurant in New York City. We could decide where to dine at the last minute because the restaurants had become empty since the attack. People were scared and staying home.

I called all the guys and saved Genella for last. She seemed excited and said that the attack had made her think about our dinner conversation, and she had some things she wanted to talk about.

When I told her we wouldn't be returning to Mario's place, she seemed sincerely relieved. I told her that I would choose a restaurant at a later date, but she came up with an interesting surprise. She offered to have the dinner at her home, and, if the boys felt comfortable about it, she'd put them up for the night. She said the boys didn't have to worry, "After all, Rocco lived here."

Mamma mia! Rocco lived there! No wonder he always looked tired.

The idea intrigued me, and I decided to call Mo first, since he's the most conservative. When I told Mo about Genella's offer, he burst into hearty laughter.

"Why not?" he said. "I'll do it on one condition. No ladies of the night can be present. This is not a party, but an evening of serious discussion."

"What about Pignachi?" I asked. "How will he handle it?"

Once again, Mo laughed. "He's so goddamn innocent that he probably won't know that Genella's house is what it is. He'll probably think that's where she and Rocco used to live and that her business establishment is elsewhere."

I laughed and said, "You're probably right on both counts, my friend."

I called all the guys about Genella's proposition and no one objected. In fact, they all were looking forward to an unusual evening.

I called Genella back to inform her that the boys had accepted her invitation. I asked her if she had a cook. She said, "I used to do all the cooking for Rocco."

We discussed the dinner and decided to order out. I wanted her to relax on that night. We decided to be a little crazy and have take-out Italian food from Patsy's and also Chinese food from Chin-Chin, an unusual combination, indeed. I said that we must have Patsy's fried zucchini and *pollo scarpariello*, and she recommended Chin-Chin's jellyfish and pork wontons. We would decide on the vegetables and dessert later on.

Getting back to the dinner: Most of us had never been to Chin-Chin, and we asked Genella about it. She said it was one of the few Chinese restaurants in New York City where the food was not only top-rate, but also consistent from night to night.

Her eyes smiled as she spoke about the enthusiastic warm reception given by Sal, and how Jimmy circulated around the tables, making the clientele feel welcome. She also described how tall Errol is constantly surveying the restaurant's activity, with no one aware of why he's doing so.

I told Genella that we'd need someone to serve the food. She said it was no problem, that she would ask a couple of her ladies to be waitresses for the evening. I said that would not be appropriate.

We thought for a while, and then I came up with the idea of having Vinnie for the night; he could bring a waiter or two along with him. She thought that was a great idea, but said that she would have a gal or two hidden away somewhere, in case there were problems.

I didn't like that idea, but I went along with it because she seemed to want it so much. She later told me that some of her ladies love to play the role of dinner hostess because it brings back traditional female values. Not that they want to play this role forever, only now and then. I thought to myself, "You can't have it both ways."

To tell the truth, despite the fact that we were curious and had accepted the invitation, the boys all felt that there was a little something *che non va* with the idea of meeting in a whorehouse to discuss a very serious and historic event. It was a bizarre scenario indeed. But it would be a once-in-a-lifetime experience, and, honestly speaking, we looked forward to it. It was more than the puntang thing. Or was it? Don't forget, men can never rid themselves of Schopenhauer, Freud, et al., not even in their dreams!

Genella wanted to set the time for eight o'clock, but I told her that the boys were getting old and it would be best to start cocktails at six o'clock, and let the food follow at about seven-thirty. She laughed and agreed. She understood that as old age approaches, both men and women have more fixed behavior patterns, particularly when it involves the limited energy levels available to both the mind and the body. Late nights are rarely welcomed. The summertime of boundless energetic youth is long gone.

The night of the gathering arrived, and everyone was on time. Vinnie was there in a tuxedo with one waiter to help out.

Genella, wearing a black dress that both was classy and sensual, showing her anterior and posterior wares, escorted all of us into the large, narrow living room of her brownstone. Personally speaking, brownstones always give me a feeling of claustrophobia. But as a kid I learned *"Ciascuno al suo gusto."*

Long, heavy curtains covered the windows and an artificial log burned in the fireplace. Everything that we sat on was bulky and puffy. Lighted candles were everywhere, and there was a pleasant smell of incense in the air.

Vinnie knew we all drank martinis and, under Genella's orders, I'm sure, brought us humungous ones! She was obviously trying to get us high, quickly! Why? She was obviously a bit nervous and was anxious for us to relax, put aside our apprehension over being in a whorehouse—probably a first time event for most of the boys—and discuss the attack on America.

The boys understood and appreciated Genella's move. They, too, were a bit nervous. Genella joined the boys in the martini drinking.

We made small talk as we drank. After about half an hour, we were somewhat relaxed, and it was time for another martini. In reality the first martini was equivalent to two, and the second would equal four. But when Vinnie arrived with the next round, no one objected. The tone of the evening was set. The attack on America may have set the tone for the twenty-first century, and the boys were anxious to talk about it.

Vinnie's waiter appeared with two huge plates of Patsy's deep fried zucchini. Deep fried zucchini should be eaten almost immediately after it's cooked. If not, it becomes soggy and loses its taste. From the time they were cooked at Patsy's to the time they arrived on our plates, it would have been about half an hour. But these were the best, in terms of both taste and texture. When the Pig commented on this culinary miracle, Genella smiled and said, "Mr. Scognamillo did me a special favor. When he heard about this special gathering, he sent one of his chef's men over here to cook the zucchini. I have a deep fryer in the kitchen that I used a lot for Rocco. He loved his *fritto misto*."

Genella put her finger on her lips to advise us that a secret was forthcoming. She looked around and whispered, "Joe Scognamillo was so impressed with Vinnie that he offered him a job. And guess what? Vinnie accepted! Maybe we should go to Patsy's for the 2002 annual dinner."

We all noticed she said, "we" instead of "you." But that was okay. Unless something unforeseen happened that night, we expected her to be there.

We finished off both plates of zucchini, and Vinnie brought one more.

While we were sipping the second martini, ballsy Mo asked, "Genella, did Rocco live here?"

Genella said, "Yes."

Mo asked, "Who else lives here?"

Genella said, "A few tenants."

Mo asked, "Who are these tenants?"

Miserabile said, "That's none of your fuckin' business."

Pignachi asked, "Vinnie, are there more zucchini?"

Vinnie said, "Sorry, Father, the cook has gone back to Patsy's."

Spinuzzi asked, "What's next?"

Vinnie, with the broadest smile that his facial muscles would allow, was standing behind Genella. The waiter stood beside him holding a tray on which sat two large serving dishes with silver covers.

I asked Vinnie, "*Perche sorridi?*"

He answered, "*La medusa è arrivata.*"

Genella asked, "Vinnie, what's a *medusa?*"

Vinnie, still broadly smiling, said, "Jellyfish, Miss Genella, jellyfish from Chin-Chin."

Genella visibly paled. Though she had recommended the jellyfish for dinner, it had been an act of bravado to prove something to the boys. Looking at her, I realized that the martinis had made her lose her nerve. For reasons only known to God, women have problems with jellyfish, mice, snakes, and cockroaches.

Vinnie, the pro that he is, banished the smile from his face and said, "*Signora*, it tastes like a good pasta. My wife loves it."

He was lying, of course. His wife would never eat jellyfish or be able to sleep with a mouse in the bedroom or boldly confront a snake in the garden.

Vinnie then served the *medusa*. He was about to return to the kitchen when Spinuzzi asked, "Vinnie, are there any chopsticks?"

Vinnie answered, "You know, I didn't even think of them. *Scusatemi*, but there are only forks tonight."

Spinuzzi said, "I can't remember ever eating Chinese food with a fork. Anyway, there's always a first time in life."

The boys dug into their plates and ate with gusto. It was damn good. Genella did manage to put a little into her digestive system, but she gave up after a couple of swallows.

I decided to proceed with the subject of the evening. I began, "Lady and gentlemen, not too long ago at La Strega we discussed what's going on in modern America. We covered a lot of territory, and some of our major conclusions were that Americans are too materialistic, too self-centered and too weak, both as individuals and as a nation. With the exception of Pignachi, and maybe Genella, we were all somewhat pessimistic. Spinuzzi suggested that we would need some type of major crisis to reverse the trend.

"No one disagreed because we all know that significant national crises, particularly war, often bring the people together. But none of us ever dreamed that there really would be a national crisis on the home soil of our great country in the near future. Then the attack happened and Americans have responded, at least up to now, in an impressively patriotic way. Flags are flying and Americans support President Bush's objective to rid the world of terrorists and terrorism.

"Mo and Pussey Rapper decided not to write the executive summary of our last evening's conversation because the magnitude of the attack may have a major impact on American values in the long term.

"But who the hell knows? Maybe we have been living in materialistic shitsville too long to expect a sustained effort to become strong, based on the old neighborhood values that we sincerely believe in, despite our differences.

"Spinuzzi, since you believed that a catastrophe would be needed to bring Americans back to their senses, I think you should start off and give us your opinion."

It was obvious that Spinuzzi was not ready to accept the challenge yet. He looked in Genella's direction and said, "Listen, I still have Victorian values. I believe that ladies should go first; we should hear what Genella has to say. *Vero?*"

Though Genella did not look at all uneasy, Miserabile surely did. He said, "I think because Genella is new at this game, she should hear what we have to say first and then give her opinion."

There was a moment of unsettling silence. We were honestly pissed-off at Miserabile with this puntang-based remark. Genella put her hand on Miserabile's forearm and, without looking at him, said, "I think I have something to say now, and then maybe again, later on, after I hear what the boys have to say."

She is a wise woman. She knew that the boys would begin to shun Miserabile as a victim of puntang if he continued to defend and protect her. Maybe she was really falling in love with the guy. Though I wouldn't be surprised if it happened, I don't know of any member of Congress who has ever had a madam for a wife.

One of Genella's favorite clients lost a friend in the Twin Towers collapse. She told us about the client, a nice guy who came to her pad about once a month. He wasn't married, and he liked to come early and leave early.

She continued, "He didn't require much, or anything specific. He used to talk to the girls and bring gifts for everyone, a case of wine or a carton of spices.

"Bottom line, he seemed to be a lonely guy periodically seeking a relaxing moment with a woman. He didn't talk much about his personal life, but one day he came early in the afternoon and shocked the shit out of us all. He said he wanted some coke and marijuana.

"The girls really liked the guy and were a little bit worried about whether he could handle this drug load. He wasn't a druggie. But that's what our profession is all about, helping men relax."

Spinuzzi interrupted, "That's not true, Genella. That's not what your profession is all about."

Spinuzzi had done it again, another disruptive remark. We all knew, judging from the tone of his voice, that it wasn't a complimentary one. But it was, without doubt, a provocative one.

Genella asked, "Spinuzzi, what do you mean by that?"

Spinuzzi answered, "No offense, Genella, but you gals are in business like everyone else in any other kind of business. You're in it to make money!"

Genella suddenly became serious, and I mean deadly serious. She then took her first big step in becoming a partner with the boys as a respected logical thinker. She asked, "Spinuzzi, do medical doctors ever feel sorry for or share the pain of their patients?"

Spinuzzi immediately knew what Genella was up to, and, in a funny kind of way, he was happy that she would challenge his position and even prove him wrong. In fact, he pre-empted her, by saying, "Yes, they often do or they wouldn't be human. And your next question will probably be whether physicians accept a fee as payment not only for their medical services, but also for sharing the pain of their patients."

Genella triumphantly replied, "That's exactly right!"

Spinuzzi unabashedly answered, "You're right, Genella, and I stand corrected."

Spinuzzi has a quality that most of us envy. He has no problem admitting that he is wrong. The bugger learns from his mistakes.

Genella went on. "Anyway, this guy ranted and raved and cried about the death of his friend in the Twin Towers tragedy and the amount of hate in the world. He simply could not handle the awfulness of the tragedy, the death of his friend and the hate behind it."

Miserabile said, "Hate will always be with us. Why was he so surprised to see hate rear his ugly head?"

Spinuzzi said, "You mean 'her' head, don't you?"

Nobody commented. It was another Spinuzzi remark that was interesting but did not fit the moment. He then followed with one that did.

"Genella," he said, "did he ask for some sexual relief?"

Genella smiled and answered, "No. The gals gave him a rub down and soon, despite the stimulating effect of the coke, the smoke helped him fall into a deep sleep. And, yes, Spinuzzi, he did pay for his visit. In fact, he gave a large tip to the gals. Is there anything wrong with that?"

And will wonders never cease! Pignachi, with his complicated simplicity, answered the question!

He said, "No, nothing at all. Kindness should be repaid with kindness."

Pussey Rapper said, "Getting back to the subject of hate, Miserabile hit it right on the nose. Hate simply won't go away.

"You'd think that after the attack, American hate, except for Osama bin Laden and his terrorist buddies, would take a back seat, for awhile, right? Wrong. It depends on who the haters are.

"The hatemongers from both the left and the right, those fuckin' idiots, came out with remarks that were unbelievable. Interestingly enough, the reasons they gave to justify their hate were different.

"The jerk-off extreme left liberals said that America is an evil imperialistic nation that has provoked an understandable and just counter-reaction by the Muslim terrorists. They called our great country a fascist one which cruelly mistreats the people of the Middle East and unfairly favors Israel. For this reason, they say, it is America's fault, not that of the killer terrorists, that the Twin Towers and the Pentagon were bombed.

"The tight-assed, extreme conservative right, the bastion of fire-and-brimstone religion, said that the attack was God punishing us for all our sexual sins, from abortion to homosexuality.

"In the old neighborhood, these *gavoni* would have been beaten up and punched out after they opened their big fuckin' mouths in public. The old neighborhood people instinctively knew that a house divided would not survive. They knew what loyalty was."

Spinuzzi asked, "Pussey Rapper, would you beat up a woman?"

Pussey Rapper answered, "That's a good question, Spinuzzi. If she fomented hate and preached that the Muslims were justified in killing our people in the Twin Towers, you bet your ass I would. Let me qualify that statement: I would do so if I knew I couldn't be sued."

Everyone smiled at Pussey Rapper's surprising opinion.

Spinuzzi asked, "Genella, do you agree?"

Genella answered, "I'd join in and add a few licks, yes. They should all be put in jail and fed only bread and water until they repent."

I was about to ask the rest of the group the same question, when Pignachi stood up.

He said, "You may think that I, as a man of the cloth, should not be saying what I'm going to say. But we have had a problem in America with understanding what 'hate' is. We sometimes confuse it with justified anger. But even considering this, there is indeed such a thing as justified hate, which is a natural and good quality of mankind. After all, God didn't give us this mental characteristic for nothing!"

I must admit that we were all taken aback by this kind-hearted Catholic priest saying that hate is sometimes okay. We all picked up our martini glasses, looked at each other and took a healthy swig.

He continued, "I don't want to belabor the point, but let me give you a simple example: If your loved one were killed in the Twin Towers or at the Pentagon, it would be both natural and good for you to hate the terrorists behind this Satanic act. And it would also be good and natural to seek revenge and go to war against the people who were behind the act. The Bible clearly supports this position. In fact—forgive me but the martini is clouding my memory—I think it was St. Augustine who said there was *jus ad bello*, which was his argument supporting the idea of just wars.

"You see, we must not confuse the hate in the extreme, bad elements of the liberal left and the conservative right with the good and understandable hate of those who lost loved ones in the attack and of those who sympathize with the victims. Without justified and moral hate that fights back, we would all have succumbed to the evil hate that Pussey Rapper touched upon. A country cannot be free unless it is prepared to fight wars to defend its freedom. It is as simple as that."

Genella asked, "Father Pignachi, are you saying that we catch those terrorists and kill them?"

He answered, "Genella, I think in the old neighborhood and in many old neighborhoods, including those in the Arab world, revenge was acceptable. It's all a question of where one draws the line."

I decided to pursue the point of justified anger that had been raised by Pignachi. Rather than put him on the spot and ask him further questions—for he, like the rest of us, had had a hell of a lot to drink already—I turned to Miserabile.

"Miserabile," I asked, "do you agree with Pignachi's observation that we have confused justified anger with hate?"

Miserabile paused, sipped his *grappa*, and answered, "Big time!"

"And the reason?" I asked.

He answered, "The Civil Rights movement."

"The Civil Rights movement?" asked the Pig.

"Yes, the Civil Rights movement," answered Miserabile.

Politicians are a funny breed. They have three objectives: To win an election, to satisfy the needs of the people who voted for them, and to try to get done what they really believe in, whether their constituents agree or not. Great men can balance these objectives to the benefit of all of America; lesser men manipulate them for personal gain only. On any scale of one to ten, there are few tens in any category of life, including politics.

Miserabile continued, "What I mean by the Civil Rights movement is a general phenomenon that has touched all segments of American life. The government tells you what you can or cannot do and, but by doing so, has encouraged a culture of both hate and anger. I agree with Pignachi. When people talk about hate, most of the time it's really strong, justified anger. Hate takes a long time to go away; anger subsides quickly.

"Let me give you a couple of examples: About ten years ago, a friend of mine that had a small business wanted to fire a black woman because she was incompetent. He is a good-hearted liberal who had already hired a number of black and Hispanic employees, and he was happy with the results.

"However, because she was black and not white, he called his lawyers to see whether there would be a legal problem if he fired her. The lawyer said that she could go to some Civil Rights government agency and complain against discrimination. He also said that, according to the law, she didn't have to prove that she was discriminated against. All she had to do was make the accusation. The burden of proof was on the company, which is a time-consuming and costly process. To get the point across to you guys—and also to you, Genella—this chick could go to a Civil Rights Commission and say, "My boss pisses on me every time I'm late for work," and the Commission would not require her to prove it. Instead, they would require that the boss prove he didn't piss on her, and how *nel nome di Dio* do you prove that? Anyway, because of the mentality of the time, there was a good probability that the government would rule in her favor.

"My friend has balls and decided to fire her and see what happened. She arrogantly told him she was going to get a government lawyer, at no cost to her, and sue the company for discrimination. He spoke to his lawyer and decided to back off because of the enormous costs and personal aggravation involved.

"She stayed on the job, continued to come in late to stick it up her boss's ass, and her performance got really bad. She was an arrogant son-of-a-bitch.

"The other employees in the office were, understandably, really pissed-off. Then business got bad and my friend had to lay some people off. She should have been the first to go, but he didn't want any more problems, particularly when times were hard and he couldn't afford to pay lawyers.

"He let three people go. The rest of the employees now not only intensely hated the black woman, but also began to hate my friend. In the old neighborhood, we would have asked *Il Mostro* to solve the problem. And he would have!

"Now multiply this type of thing millions of times—because of bad black leaders, bad laws and bad judges—and this adds up to lots of unnecessary anger and hate which, like an amoeba, grows and multiplies and feeds on itself.

"Let me give you another example of a hate-producing side-effect of the Civil Rights movement: divorce.

"Now, feminist leaders did a great job in initiating an equal rights movement. One thing they wanted was to make divorce easy. They didn't foresee that, as a result of their efforts, life for divorced women would be much more difficult than it is for men.

"In the old days, as part of the divorce settlement, the man had to pay his wife a ton of money. If they had kids, he would have to pay up the ass. The women were the dear favorites in the eyes of the courts.

"Now, because of new laws that are supposed to make women equal, the divorced man doesn't have to pay as much, and many women have to work to support themselves and their kids. The liberation movement has lessened the obligation of the divorced husband to support the women and the kids.

"This creates a hell of a lot of anger and hate. Time and time again, I've seen bona fide hatred between a divorced husband and wife, mainly because of the money issue. Also, I've noticed that when the wife finally does receive sufficient money from the husband, the anger quickly subsides. But not all the time, which means that there was real hate involved.

"That adds up to a lot of hate that spreads through the families of the divorced couple, including the kids, pitting one family against the other, like in Romeo and Juliet.

"I'll give you one more example that doesn't seem big, but is. There are a lot of small events that don't seem to be anger producers, but really are. And when you add them all up, it's big-time anger.

"This deals with laws that try to protect the civil rights of folks with disabilities. Now, who the hell can argue against the intent of laws to help disabled people? But that's not the issue. It's the nature of the law itself and its application that's important.

"Recently, there was a disabled golfer, confined to a wheelchair, who wanted to play in a major professional golf tournament; I've forgotten which one. Now the rules of the golf organization did not permit a disabled person to play in a professional tournament. There are many legitimate and solid reasons why, but let me give you one analogy that makes the position clearer: The baseball, football and basketball organizations wouldn't permit a guy in a wheelchair to play the game with the regular players. That would not only detract from the sport, but also make it more theater than sport. It would be laughable.

"Now, this disabled guy takes the case to the Supreme Court, and the Court rules in the guy's favor. It's hard to believe, but the Court, in its decision, became a little bit wacky. Sometimes you wonder whether these guys ever had a real job and had to fight to hold it.

"Lots of people became quite pissed-off. This anger spills over to all disabled people, which is not a good thing. It's like the situation my friend had with his black female employee.

"One can go on and on. It's never-ending. The American hate machine will continue to grow, unless we do something about it soon."

Genella asked, "What can we do about it?"

Miserabile paused and then answered, "We have to learn where to draw the limits on government activism and know when to say, "*Basta.*" It has to start with the people understanding that we have gone too far, and then we need leaders to make it happen. In my opinion, the attack could be the spark to make great leaders arise and bring us back to our senses, like it was in the old neighborhood."

Mo looked serious, because he strongly believes that the world has entered a new era with an uncertain future. He began, "We should change the calendar and eliminate everything from January First through September Tenth. The twenty-first century started on September Eleventh. It was that big a day.

"Anyway, do you guys remember when we were at La Strega and someone asked what the women and men in the old neighborhood would do about whether the government should spend more money either on men's or women's health? Well, I am thinking how they would answer in these days.

"In the old neighborhood, the women were mostly all 'givers' and not 'takers.' The 'taker' woman was a *costumata*. The husbands had to make enough money—and it was rarely much—to support the family, and the women managed the family both emotionally and economically. They were peaceful folks unless—and this is important to note—they were attacked by the slings and arrows of life. They were territorial, indeed.

"Let me rattle off some of the things they would have thought in the old neighborhood about the attack:

"If you don't kill those that try to kill you, you lose.

"If you don't take revenge, you're a loser.

"We came to this country in search of freedom and the opportunity to earn a living; we will fight anyone to maintain this privilege.

"Stop them—the terrorists—before they get us. Use any means. If the innocent are killed, that's a price we have to accept and not let it get in our way.

"Do you guys remember my *La Pettone*? She was the gal with big tits who was one of the first women in the old neighborhood to wear tight sweaters. Guys used to jerk off fantasizing about her.

"Anyway, she's still alive, and she lost one of her sons in the Twin Towers tragedy. *Mamma mia, che tragedia!*

"Her brother, Larry, is a good friend of mine. We were talking about the tragedy, and I asked him how it affected his mother.

"He said that the one thing that she spoke about was cold-blooded revenge. She said that we should find the leaders, put them in the cockpit of an airplane, tie them to their seats and suture their eyelids open so that they couldn't close them. Then she said we should put the plane on automatic pilot and aim it at a mountain, going slow so that they suffer more before it crashes."

Genella smiled and said, "Mo, you're right. When old neighborhood women lost their loved ones, they wanted to see blood. Their protective mother instinct was a powerful thing.

"But, Mo, what about the men?"

Mo replied, "They would have reacted almost the same way, with one exception: The gals would not go out, themselves, and perform the acts of revenge. The men would do it."

Genella laughed, nodded her head in the affirmative and asked, "What about the liberated women of today? Would they ask the men to do it rather than do it themselves?"

Mo, without hesitation, answered, "Without doubt!"

Genella asked, "Why do you think so?"

Mo answered, "Ah, Genella. *Chi lo sa*? Who the hell knows? It's the Scorpion! I just can't see thousands of women paratrooping into Afghanistan to search for and combat bin Laden and his henchmen in the fuckin' caves. They know that if they were captured, bin Laden and his men would be fuckin' them. It's that fuckin' sex thing, again!"

He continued, "I'm not convinced that we have now suddenly become a strong nation. That remains to be seen.

"Don't forget: before the attack and during good economic times, some very good minds wrote about the importance of patriotism and how it was fading away from the American landscape. The mass media completely ignored these warnings and concentrated on material things and national gossip. The economy stole the stage during the Clinton years. Remember, the theme of the Clinton years regarding how to get elected was simple. It was, 'It's the economy, stupid,' not patriotism or family values.

"Unfortunately, that's the way human nature is. It's the Scorpion again!"

Mo is a solid realist and his message was depressing. I decided to ask the most practical man at our table to respond to Mo's somewhat pessimistic outlook.

I asked, "Miserabile, what's your take on that?"

Miserabile sat back in his chair and said, "You know, guys, we haven't heard much from the Pig, tonight. I'd like to hear from him before I pontificate. Pig, let's hear it."

Pig answered, "It's funny you ask. I do have some thoughts, and it has to do with America and religion. Basically, I'm talking about Judaic-Christian religion, and not the others around the world.

"Yes, I know that there are now more Muslims than Episcopalians in the United States, and that our religious scenery is changing rapidly. But I don't know the Muslim culture well, and I am not qualified to offer a well thought-out opinion on this great religion. The same holds true for Buddhism, Hinduism, Taoism and all of the other major 'isms' of the world."

Spinuzzi interrupted the Pig's dissertation and did it again! He said, "Do you guys know that Saladin is one of my favorite of all historic figures?"

Genella asked, "Who's Saladin?"

Spinuzzi answered, "Saladin was perhaps the greatest and wisest ruler in the Moslem world. He lived in the Middle Ages and was a great Moslem warrior. He was not only revered by the Moslem world, but also very highly respected by Christians for his honesty and bravery.

"He was Sultan of Egypt and was highly civilized, helping his people instead of taking advantage of them. He built schools, canals and mosques. He tried to make sure that his people ate well. In a sense, he came close to Plato's concept of the Philosopher King.

Then Spinuzzi stopped and silence reigned. We were all a little bit lost.

The Pig said, "Spinuzzi, I missed your point. What's your message?"

Spinuzzi answered, "Pardon me for my ambiguity, Pig. Today, we are sorely in need of constructive, wise leaders not only at home, but in the Middle East, too. I'm hoping that another Saladin will come forth in that part of the world. The times call for it.

"I think it was Thomas Carlyle who wrote that the history of the world is, in large part, shaped by the great men who moved life's events. Look at the young drunk, Alexander the Great. This Macedonian conquered much of the civilized world simply because his persona was loaded with greatness.

"With about 30,000 troops, he blocked the invasion of Greece by Darius (I forget which one) of Persia, who led 600,000 troops. If that isn't greatness then nothing is. It changed the course of history, making possible the rise of Western Civilization and eventually the United States.

"Pig, I'm sorry I interrupted you. I promise to keep my mouth shut—for a while."

Everyone smiled, because they knew this promise would be impossible for Spinuzzi to keep.

The Pig continued, "Well, here's what I think: Terrorism, both big-time and small-time, is here to stay, at least for our lifetimes. People in America will be living in, more or less, constant fear, growing anger, and periodic hate. Because, before September 11th, we were all living in an age of unprecedented materialism and psychological instability, we were all consciously or unconsciously yearning to return to religion. I truly believe that was our mindset. Materialism is never enough to satisfy our needs.

"Now I don't want to get too wishy-washy like a fuzzy intellectual, but believe it or not, while we were talking I was thinking of two of my most favorite poets, Housman and Yeats. Their poems often dealt with the subject of religion.

"May I recite some poetry by memory, or would that be too corny and out of order, tonight?"

I said, "Go ahead, my friend. Anything that will help make a point is what this evening's all about."

"The first poem, 'The Second Coming,' is by Yeats. It deals symbolically with the second coming of Christ. Though it was written almost a hundred years ago, it addresses the confusion and fear in our times, as well as the fear of what type of religion people will embrace as a result of this.

"The poem opens up:

'Turning and turning in the widening gyre

'The falcon cannot hear the falconer;

'Things fall apart; the center cannot hold;

'Mere anarchy is loosed upon the world...'

"And it concludes with:

'And what rough beast, its hour come round at last,

'Slouches towards Bethlehem to be born?'

"That 'rough beast' is a potential new religion which can either be a constructive or a destructive one.

"Now, Housman's poem, 'Easter Hymn,' is also about Jesus Christ. The message of the first part is directed to Christ. If Christ was really not divine and therefore can't help with the problems of the world, then, Housman writes, 'Sleep well and see no morning, son of man.'

"The second part basically says that if you are the Divine Christ, then do something about it. I'll never forget these lines, unless I get Alzheimer's. They go as follows:

'But if, the grave rent and the stone rolled by,

'At the right hand of majesty on high

'You sit, and sitting so remember yet

'Your tears, your agony and bloody sweat,

'Your cross and passion and the life you gave,

'Bow hither out of heaven and see and save.'

"And I think the American people may well be in the mood for someone to 'bow out of heaven' and save the world from a potential catastrophe. It's what that 'heaven' is that scares the shit out of me."

Genella, transfixed and obviously tranquilized, said, "Pig, that was beautiful. I love poetry."

"*La Pietanza è arrivata!*" Vinnie surprised us with the strength of his voice. The heavy conversation came to an abrupt halt. We all just smiled and welcomed the arrival of a moment of pleasure. We waited for Vinnie to lead us through the main course.

Vinnie announced, "We have the *pollo scapariello* from Patsy's and the pork fried wontons from Chin-Chin.

"Also, we have a variety of vegetable dishes, including *un insalata*. But I want you all to taste my wife's string beans."

Spinuzzi laughed. "*Caro* Vinnie, how did your wife's string beans enter into this evening's dinner?"

Vinnie's smile was warm and broad. "Nobody but my wife knows how to cook string beans the way I like them. You boil the string beans until they soften. Then you throw them into a frying pan with lots of olive oil and garlic—and I mean lots. Then you use a pepper grinder and put lots and lots of pepper on the string beans while they're cooking in the frying pan. And a lot of salt. It's important to put enough on them. We do not fear salt at our home. Then you let *i fagiolini* sit for about ten minutes before serving.

"But *i fagiolini* are even better the next day. You can let them marinate overnight and eat them at room temperature the next day. *Paradiso, i miei amici, paradiso.* Or you can reheat them, as I did tonight."

Spinuzzi laughed again. "Is it me, or is something crazy going on? At La Strega, we had turnips with *straccetti*, and tonight we're having pork wontons with *pollo scarpariello*. And to make it more interesting, we have Vinnie's wife's string beans to look forward to."

"*Mangiamo è beviamo*," said Pussey Rapper. It was good eating. The pork in the wontons was succulent and tasty, and the chicken was crisp on the outside and moist and soft on the inside.

And the string beans were a knock-out!

While we were eating, I asked Miserabile, "What do you think about the Pig's take on the coming return of religion—perhaps the wrong kind?"

Miserabile paid Pig a compliment.

"Pig, you're a sensitive person with poetic insight and intuition that I don't have. I know what you're saying, and it may or may not be true. You may be right that something powerful is indeed coming. But I do strongly believe that leaders will arrive on the world stage, because of the attack.

"Look at Mayor Giuliani and President Bush. There's no doubt that Giuliani was a strong leader with strong convictions before the attack. After the attack, however, he demonstrated super qualities of leadership and crisis management. We weren't sure who Bush really was before the attack. To date, he has emerged as a superb leader and also a superb crisis manager."

Mo said, "Miserabile, I agree with you that a crisis either makes or breaks a leader. Look at what the hostages in Iran did to that talented guy, Jimmy Carter.

"But I don't agree that you need a crisis to become a great leader. Clinton had a huge opportunity to help solve the problems of Social

Security, Medicare and even that of terrorism. But he did diddly-twat. The guy simply had no vision, no balls."

Miserabile answered, "You have a point, Mo, you have a point. But I repeat, you can never know about this guy."

I decided to turn to Spinuzzi for his insight.

Leaning forward over the table, Spinuzzi said, "Believe it or not, guys, besides being confident, the hallmark of our new leader will be to effectively tell the *truth* to the American people. The scene is set, and the demand there. We are entering an era of truth telling. Leaders must now deliver the truth rather than spin and Fantasy Island bullshit.

"I used to get chest pain when I heard all those assholes in Washington telling people about the budget surplus, like it was going to last forever!

"Everyone in his right mind, including many of those trumpeting the so-called New Economy that was fueling the budget surplus, knew that surpluses come and surpluses go. There's no way of predicting, and you can't count on them, particularly in the long run. But the politicians believed people couldn't handle the truth. Sure there was a handful of those guys that really believed the New Economy would last forever. This world is full of dreamers!

"As we discussed many times in the past, if you give one hundred economists the same economic data, you will receive one hundred different opinions. Economics is not a science, it's a guessing game, and you don't plan the future of the United States on unpredictable events! It's Las Vegas in spades!

"Also, the glorious period of surpluses was due in large part to the Clinton Administration cutting the military budget big-time.

"To repeat, I don't remember even one major political figure that told the truth about the fact that you cannot count on surpluses. The Americans were all fooled by the cats in Washington and all those pompous mediocre media pundits. How do these guys sleep at night?

"With certain exceptions in Washington, and they were few, the liberal media joined the Washington cats and convinced everyone that government, with these eternal surpluses, could handle all problems in our country. Some were even talking about having Medicare cover the healthcare costs of care of animals! The eternal surplus was a big lie, and the American people are beginning to appreciate this and are looking for the truth, and the truth shall keep us fuckin' free."

Mo said, "I think that a new leader will come soon and educate the American people that we must change our attitudes about killing people, about killing the enemies of our country. A great leader must change our system so that we can kill terrorists on the spot or execute them within thirty days. The Pope may not agree—and I do love this Pope—but remember, he is only infallible on certain issues regarding Catholic dogma."

Strangely enough, no one seemed disturbed by Mo's position. Maybe it wasn't so strange. About one hundred percent of the gang in the old neighborhood would have gone along with this. They would, like Macchiavelli, have had no time for Civil Rights issues when the country is in danger.

I then said, "Well, this position brings up the entire issue of civil rights and civil liberties, and where to draw the line."

Mo answered, "You're right, and it's time to move the line to the right!"

Pussey Rapper, somewhat disturbed, asked, "What, exactly do you mean, 'Move the line to the Right?'"

Pussey Rapper's question was not just a mere question. By the tone of his voice, Mo knew that Pussey Rapper was pissed-off and actually reprimanding him.

Mo was in a relaxed and somewhat mellow mood that night, and he decided not to enter into a heated debate with Pussey Rapper. Mo's intellect and temperament are on the conservative right side, and Pussey Rapper's are on the liberal left, and never the twain shall meet—except during a tragic national crisis.

Mo calmly said, "Pussey Rapper, when an armed group of terrorists attacks your embassies, your boats, your Marine barracks, your Twin Towers, your Pentagon, and tries to attack the White House, it surrenders its civil rights, because it threatens the very country we live in; it threatens our very existence. It's not like minority employees doing a sit-in because they believe a corporation is discriminating against them and they can make a lot of money if they win in court. It's self defense.

"If someone is caught putting anthrax in an envelope, the fucker should be shot on the spot. No fucking courts, no due process of law; just shoot him in the balls, wait a while a while until he realizes he's lost his masculinity, and finish him off with a bullet between the eyes.

Torture and kill the mother-fuckers like the Arabs do to their criminals."

Spinuzzi asked, "Mo, where would you shoot first, if the terrorist were a woman?"

Mo laughed and shot back, "Fuck you, Spinuzzi."

A very brief, mild dialogue followed between the two, which sent a message to the gang that all of us were getting old and mellow. In the past, the temperature of this type of discussion would generally be sky high, and no resolution would be made.

Pussey Rapper, like Mo, was not in a truly combative mood. He said, "Mo, my old buddy of many years, are you saying that an unchecked American Gestapo, the police, military or whatever, should be permitted to make judgments on life and death—without restraints? You know how some of these guys are: They'll abuse the shit out of their power and many innocent people will suffer or even be killed. There are lots of skinheads out there."

Before Mo could respond, Spinuzzi said, "Why do you refer to the baddies as 'guys?' Women are now in the police and military ranks, and there's good reason to believe that women are crueler than men."

Genella, somewhat perplexed, asked, "Spinuzzi, do you really believe that crap?"

Spinuzzi, though he really believed in 'this crap,' decided not to answer, and it was a wise move. It would have created a heated debate that would overpower the current discussion on civil rights, civil liberties, and who should die and who should live.

I decided to push Mo and Pussey Rapper to wrap up their arguments. "Mo, Pussey Rapper has a good point that you can't ignore, *vero*?"

Mo smiled and replied, "What do you think I am, a skinhead? All I'm saying is that we have to get rid of these assassins, and we can't do it with our current civil liberties-oriented, liberal judicial system. It will rob us of our ability to solve the problem, and our country will lose the battle. Is this what we want? Remember, everything in life has its price. If you want freedom, you have to pay the price!

"Yes, innocent people will suffer, but isn't that true of all wars? We're at war, you know, and until the war's over, we must handle the problem in a military and not a civil-judiciary way."

Pussey Rapper answered, "But we have to draw the line somewhere. Don't you agree?"

Mo answered, "Of course, of course. Life is all a matter of where you draw the lines. We've all agreed on this, in the past."

Pussey Rapper said, "Well, where do we draw these elusive lines?"

Mo answered, "We have to play it by ear. After all, we're in America and we have to trust in ourselves, and believe that we're able to distinguish between acceptable and unacceptable retaliation. We are not Stalinist communists, you know. There's no fuckin' Siberia in North Dakota."

Miserabile said, "That's where great leaders come in. America will need them to help us decide where to draw the line. It's interesting to note that elements of both the conservative and liberal wings of Congress are concerned about the threat to our civil liberties. That doesn't happen too often, my friends."

I felt that this conversation had gone quite well and far enough, and it was time to call it a night. But before I could do so, Pignachi made a comment.

He said, "We cannot do this without God's guidance and the light of reason. I think people intuitively know this. Because of the attack, there are more people coming to my church than ever before. Donations are up and so are spirits. People are turning back to God in droves. I believe that the 'beast slouching toward Bethlehem' is a kind and generous one."

"Amen," said the Pig.

"Amen," added Genella.

And we all took our last drink of the night.

Light conversation followed for a short time. During this period, I shut out most of the conversation and thought about what really happened at La Strega and the night at Genella's. To tell you the truth, I was pleasantly surprised. Old Italian neighborhood values came through with shining colors!

Despite the differences in temperament and philosophical points of view, the boys demonstrate two basic characteristics: optimism and strength.

In the old Italian neighborhood, the men and women were always optimistic about not only living itself, but life in America, the land of opportunity. They had the strength to go forward and seize the opportunity.

As my attention turned back to Genella and the boys, I thought of a missed opportunity. Wouldn't it be wonderful to have filmed these two evenings, a la *Candid Camera*, to make them available for all Americans to see.

Perhaps I'll do it at next year's dinner.

Epilogue

You may be curious to know what transpired at Genella's place after the serious conversation had come to an end.

Pignachi, somewhat restless, sat back in his chair and said, "*Basta* with the conversation. All that I'm interested in at this point in time is dessert. Genella, what do you have for dessert, and where the hell is it?"

Suddenly, a booming voice came out of nowhere and said, "It's funny you should ask, Father Pignachi; the dessert has arrived, and it is rum cake."

And would you believe it? There was Vinnie, standing between two attractive young ladies in their late twenties or early thirties, each holding a tray with a big rum cake sitting on it.

Vinnie was smiling, big-time. The girls were dressed somewhat conservatively, with the exception that their skirts were about a foot long, and their bare legs were there to behold. And they had nice legs.

I asked the smiling Vinnie, "Vinnie, my friend, where did you find such lovely ladies?"

Vinnie said, "They live here. They had just come home, and they were going to their rooms, when I told them what was going on.

"They told me that they love dinner parties, and really love serving food and making people happy."

Genella decided to step in and introduce the gals. She walked over to them and said, "This is Bianca, and this is Serafina. They're from out of town, and are staying here and renting one of my rooms until they find an apartment."

Everyone knew that this was a white lie. But my father always told me that white lies, like pork in governmental appropriations, are essential to make the wheels of life function smoothly.

Bianca and Serafina sat down and joined us, bringing light moments to the dinner table right up until evening's end.

I knew what most of the guys were thinking. At our age, colored by old neighborhood values, when we see ladies in their twenties and early thirties, we don't think of sex. We think of them as our own potential daughters or nieces, who must be protected and cared for. With certain exceptions—and there are always exceptions—they simply don't arouse our libidinal hormones. We have to become, like the Hellenic Greeks, a little older to become attracted to ladies of that age.

It's when they hit their early forties that our minds begin to turn to sexual fantasies and the bedroom.

Why is it this way? Who the hell knows? It is either "Sex" or "the Scorpion."

But then, as Heraclitus said, "All things change." The gals began to play, in a subtle way, teasing games. Laughter abounded. They became touchy-touchy and suddenly both of them looked over forty!

I then thought that if Osama bin Laden could spend a couple of weeks with Bianca and Serafina, his energies might flow in the right directions! Pascal once said that little things and events can change history. We shall see.

I asked Vinnie to bring us both the *espresso* and *grappa* together, instead of one at a time. The conversation became livelier, and the light, happy moments were welcomed, indeed.

And I could tell we all sensed that the world might be going in the opposite direction of these light moments. We all finished our *espresso* and knew that the night had come to an end.

Bianca and Serafina kissed everyone goodnight and went to bed. We all watched them leave the room and climb the steps, and I can tell you that the old neighborhood values were surging through everyone's mind. They were all thinking, "What the hell are nice gals like those doing in a place like this!" I can also tell you that they were thinking other contradictory old neighborhood things. It is indeed a wonderful world, if one has a sense of humor!

The boys were now tired, and it was time to hit the sack. Genella appeared quite tired, herself. I thought perhaps she had had a busy week, working both the daytime and midnight shifts and supervising her girls and clients up until the crack of dawn while preparing our get-together. Who the hell knows? With aging comes unexpected periods of fatigue. Medicine has yet to figure out the reason or reasons why. Nobody likes it, but that's the way life is. Getting old is not such a pleasant thing; just read Montaigne's essays!

To tell the truth, none of us had ever slept in a whorehouse, and we were ambivalent about it. Sex was not yet a dead issue in the lives of these guys, myself included!

Then came the expected. Pignachi said, "Listen, Genella: I have a five o'clock mass tomorrow morning, commemorating the deaths of firemen and policemen in our community who lost their lives trying to save the lives of people trapped in the Twin Towers.

"I had a driver bring me here tonight, and he is waiting for me outside to take me home.

"Genella, *grazie tanto per tutto*, and I look forward to meeting you once again. You are a kind woman, and God loves you."

Tears came to Genella's eyes. The boys knew that there were many messages behind those tears, but they decided not to pursue them. This was a private moment that belonged to Genella, and that was that.

Genella took Pignachi by the hand and escorted him to the door. They spoke to each other in whispered voices. Both smiled. Genella kissed him on both cheeks and Pignachi left.

When she returned to the table, tears were still in her eyes. We were at a loss for words, but, as usual, Spinuzzi broke the silence, this time in the right kind of way.

"You know," he said, "priests are very good at telling white lies. I'll bet you all that there is no five o'clock mass tomorrow, and that Pignachi was scared shitless to sleep in Genella's pad. Also, America is now loaded with low-life squealers, and maybe either one of those gals, Vinnie, or his assistant would leak it to the press."

Everyone smiled a little, realizing that Spinuzzi was not serious about the possibility of squealers being in Genella's home.

Pussey Rapper added, "Vinnie is not a squealer; that I can tell you."

No one even thought to argue. It was time to climb the steps to the bedrooms of the unknown.

Genella escorted us to our respective rooms. Each room had an adjoining bath. She told us that breakfast would be served, starting at nine in the morning. What she didn't know was that nine in the morning for these aging boys was almost lunchtime. But they didn't say a word. Genella was a gracious hostess, and they respected that.

Incredible as it may seem, tears still lingered in her eyes. Something was going through her mind that only she and God could understand. She, by the way, looked absolutely beautiful. Women are, indeed, different than men. They often look more beautiful when they suffer!

As with Pignachi, she kissed all of us on both our cheeks before we passed through our doors. The only difference, and it was a significant one, was that Pignachi had passed through the purity door that led to the street, while we passed through the doors of the bedrooms of a whorehouse, trapped for the night. There's something about a door…!

The boys, as usual, woke up shortly after the crack of dawn. They didn't bother to shower and shave. They were in a hurry to leave. Though they all left, more or less, during a one-hour period, none saw each other. Maybe God wanted it that way.

A few months later, we had an afternoon telephone conference call regarding the importance of stem cell research and the controversial moral issues surrounding it. The Pig was in a particularly jovial mood, and he wanted to talk about what we did and what we thought about after we each went to our rooms that night in Genella's lovely pad of the ladies of the night. Since the guys weren't drinking at that time of day, they refused to discuss such personal matters.

Later on, however, I had one-on-one talks with each of the boys, regarding this very subject matter. Here are some of the things that happened:

- All of the boys were curious, and each searched his room for sexual paraphernalia or whatever.

- Pussey Rapper opened his closet door and found four to five large size ballerina outfits, as well as ballerina shoes. They were men's sizes. Also, there were wigs of black and blonde hair. Upon finding the outfits, Pussey Rapper chuckled and said to himself, "This is probably the room for right conservative Republican clients."

- Mo found boots, chains and masks in his closet. He also chuckled, and he said to himself, "This must be the room for left liberal Democrat clients."

- Each of the boys went to bed with eyes wide open, thinking of—and maybe wishing for—the possibility that Serafina or Bianca might come knocking at his door.

The knocks never came.

About the Author

Stephen L. DeFelice, M.D. is the founder and chairman of FIM, The Foundation for Innovation in Medicine, a non-profit educational organization whose mission is to help speed up medical discovery in order to reduce unnecessary suffering and premature death. He believes that the potential weapons of modern technology can dramatically reduce or eliminate many diseases. He is an author of a number of books on medicine and health, and this is his first novel.

His interest in medical discovery began in 1965 when he conducted the first United States clinical study with carnitine, a naturally occurring substance, which is now approved by FDA and has saved the lives or reduced the suffering of children with rare diseases.

As a young medical researcher, Dr. DeFelice was heavily involved in directing clinical studies on psychotropic drugs for anxiety, depression and a variety of major psychotic conditions such as schizophrenia and manic depression. Regarding the latter, he was involved in the development of lithium.

At that time we were in the so-called Age of Anxiety and beginning to enter the Age of Depression. With the technologic revolution came personal and familial instability, and the use of psychotropic drugs increased dramatically to help people cope. Parallel to this came an explosion of conditions such as divorce, hyperkinetic children, bulimia, anorexia nervosa and numerous types of phobias. Support groups suddenly appeared for almost any type of situation ranging from divorce to the loss of a pet. This all led to family and personal turbulence resulting in the most rapid change of a society's values in the history of mankind - and it continues!

Dr. DeFelice was reared in an old Italian neighborhood where stability and strong family bonds were common. There were no restaurants in the neighborhood and families ate at home every night. There were five cars on a city block of about fifty row homes. Women did not smoke, drink or drive cars and most of the men went to bed very early exhausted from days of hard labor. But there was much love and consideration for others. Italian immigrant parents, enthralled by the opportunities in America, worked hard and saved money to send their children to college - and a number of them made it. Few, if any, took medications for mental problems. Drugs were nowhere to be seen and alcoholics a rarity. These were verboten and closely monitored by family and neighbors.

Dr. DeFelice is fully aware that we cannot return to the lifestyle and values of the old Italian neighborhood but believes there is much to be learned from this tradition that can be helpful to many of the readers in these trying times. For example, respect for others was on the top of the list of values but, according to Dr. DeFelice, seems to be disappearing at a rapid rate playing a significant role in the unhappiness in our country.

In "Old Italian Neighborhood Values," Dr. DeFelice draws from his personal experiences to give readers a revealing look at how traditional values are changing in modern America.

To him, coping with life is as important as conquering disease, and he hopes that this book will help you in some way.

To directly order "Old Italian Neighborhood Values," visit the website www.olditalianvalues.com.

What the Reviewers Say

"In the tradition of Plato's "Symposium," Dante's "Il Convivio," and more recently, Frank Lentricchia's "Music of the Inferno," DeFelice's dinner conversations provide a sense of spiritual renewal through a remembrance of things past. We get to eavesdrop on the dinner conversation of six men all from a Philadelphia Little Italy and the former lover of one of their dead buddies (the only woman happens to run a classy house of ill repute). It all takes place on September 7, 2001, the night of La Luna Stregata (the witch's moon) in a New York restaurant appropriately named La Strega.

From the opening martini cocktails, through the peasant antipasto, the pasta, pietanza, dolce, espresso, and finally grappa, we move deeper into life, from casual observations about kids, families, divorce and their relationship to calcium and highways of today, to heated arguments about sex, politics, God, the liberal media, and many other controversial subjects. "Old Italian Neighborhood Values" is required reading for anyone who has grown up in a Little Italy; those who didn't will wish they had. In a time when people are leaving little Italys left and right, DeFelice's imagination has given us all a way back home."

> *Professor Fred Gardaphe, Director of Italian American Studies*
> *Stony Brook University*

"It's a revealing look at what the group believes are some values of wisdom and behavior that could be helpful to you, your family and friends. Dr. DeFelice knows that we can't bring back the old neighborhood, but we can certainly bring back those values we held so closely."

> *Patrick Wood, Greenbay News-Chronicle*

"DeFelice is giving readers more than a healthy dose of ethical advice, but a novel packed with robust characters, which brings the ethos to life. Now, more than ever…tradition can heal an irresponsible society."

> *Michelle H. LePoidevin, Westfield Leader and The Times*

"This bittersweet novel takes a hard look at how American values have changed in the past 50 years through the eyes of this group of colorful paesans from 'the old neighborhood.'"

> *Italian Tribune*

"Forget about all the stereotypes that portray Italian-Americans in a negative light. This book is a lesson in how American life can be improved by a return to those values our parents and grandparents forged back in the old neighborhood. It provides valuable lessons for all of us."

> *Paul DePace, Primo Magazine*

What The Readers Say

"A reminiscent read! I am 1/2 Italian and 1/2 German and raised around family from Italy. I really enjoyed this book because it reunited me in a sense with my Italian family. Even if you're not Italian, it's a wild ride and a fun peak into a very cultural exchange about traditional values as well as the modern lifestyle and how it has affected our values. It hits every topic imaginable -- family, kids, sex, 9/11."

Susan Allen - MarketSense

"What Dr. DeFelice presents is - more than a book - an invitation to a dinner party. Through the conversation Dr. DeFelice touches - with light fingers but in unexpected depth - most of the important issues the Nation (USA) and the world are facing to-day. In summary, a pleasant and easy reading full of profound thoughts and 'food for thinking.'"

Bruno Modanesi - Milan, Italy

"I thoroughly enjoyed your book. The conversation touches on many aspects of our evolving society and most importantly, the author does not shy away from tackling all aspects of change, both those that are a net loss to society as well as those that improve us on the whole. Bravissimo!"

Frank Sasinowski, Esq.

"I am 100 pages into Spinuzzi! I love it! P.S. Do you have Genella's phone number?"

Tony Archambault

"I have found your book fascinating and thought provoking, and am enjoying it very much."

Keith Morris - England

"It expressed values - like respect and saving money - which my grandparents had but that weren't passed on to my generation."

Jennifer Rentz

"It was hard to put down! I resonate with the part about one of the boys negotiating a bargain with God to help a loved one get out of trouble - I still do it!"

Louis Lasagna, M.D.

"What is a mild mannered Jewish guy doing in an old Italian neighborhood... Loving every minute of it! Dr. DeFelice's novel may be about Italian-Americans but it resonates in a far more universal way. It takes us back to the values of caring family, friends and neighborhoods."

Allen R. Kipnes, Esq.

"This book really brought back pleasant memories of dinnertime with my family...a hard-headed brother and three sisters talking over each other...and Mom and Dad trying to mediate. All this to the accompaniment of Caruso. Dr. DeFelice brings it all to life."

Frank Catanzano, Sr.

Printed in the United States
6923